Healing Touch and Saving Word

Healing Touch and
SAVING WORD

sacraments of healing, instruments of grace

Linda M. Malia

PICKWICK *Publications* · Eugene, Oregon

Pickwick Publications
An imprint of Wipf and Stock Publishers
199 W. 8th Avenue, Suite 3
Eugene, OR 97401

www.wipfandstock.com

ISBN: 978-1-62032-007-5

Cataloging-in-publication data:

Malia, Linda M.
    Healing touch and saving word : sacraments of healing, instruments of grace / Linda M. Malia with a Foreword by R. William Franklin.

    xx + 256 p. ; 23 cm—Includes bibliographical references.

    ISBN 13: 978-1-62032-007-5

    1. Anointing of the sick. 2. Extreme unction. 3. Healing—Religious aspects—Episcopal Church 4. Sacraments—Anglican Communion. 5. Episcopal Church—Liturgy—History. I. Franklin, R. W., 1947–

BX2035.6 A553 M100 2013

Dedicated to my husband, Bill, my muse and my inspiration,
with love to my mother and my family,
and with special thanks to
The Rt. Rev. R. William Franklin,
The Rev. David Reed, Wycliffe College, Toronto
Dr. Michael Stoeber, Regis College, Toronto,
The Rev. Dr. John R Kevern
The Rev. Dr. Arie Johannes (Han) van den Blink
The Very Reverend Dr. William H. Petersen
The Rev. Dr. Robert D. Hughes III, University of the South at Sewanee
The Rev. Dr. Ruth Meyers
The Rev. Dr. Jennifer Philips
Phoebe Pettingell,
The Rev. Russell A. Newbert,
and The Rev. Dr. Leonel Mitchell,
and to my friend and mentor, the Rev. John Richards,
with heartfelt gratitude for your guidance and support.

In baptism the person was commissioned to offer praise in the assembly and to fulfill the mission given to the Church by Christ. It becomes the purpose of anointing to help the sick persons to continue to function as people baptized.

—James Empereur, *Prophetic Anointing*

Contents

Foreword

A Book for Our Time

The Rt. Rev. R. William Franklin
Bishop of Western New York

LINDA MALIA IS A priest of the Diocese of Western New York who serves historic parishes of South Buffalo. She approaches this book as an author who has pastoral experience, the personal experience of dealing with long-term illness, and the scholarly background to connect the inter-linked questions of healing in the Church, the sacraments and the liturgy, and human suffering, all linked in her noteworthy volume to the long-standing Christian tradition. She not only has had the formation to understand this topic wrought by life knowledge and the pastoral exercise of ministry, but she has gained a doctorate in Christian spirituality from the Toronto School of Theology as well as a master of arts in theology and ethics from the Colgate Rochester Divinity School, all of which provide a very solid theoretical foundation.

Many dioceses of the Episcopal Church are struggling with answers to questions that our own Diocese of Western New York is asking: What is the legitimate role of a healing ministry in a parish? How do we draw the line between acceptable forms of healing ministry and those that are not acceptable?

What is the sacramental nature of healing, and in particular, what is the relationship of healing to the Holy Eucharist? What are the proper roles of the laity and of ordained ministers in exercising the ministry of healing? Who in a diocese should be authorized to be a minister of healing?

In *Healing Touch and Saving Word*, Linda Malia provides a much-needed theological and practical response to these questions. This volume is based on the author's deep study of the Anglican tradition, and of the entire catholic heritage of the Church of Christ. She shows how Anglican rites of healing have evolved from the sixteenth-century forms. She examines carefully our currently authorized liturgical sources, such as the 1979 *Book of Common Prayer*, *The Book of Occasional Services*, and *Enriching Our Worship 2*; and she raises challenging questions about the ongoing and needed work of reviewing and reenvisioning our liturgical rites of healing used in the Episcopal Church.

What is so heartening to me about *Healing Touch* is that it is not at all based on fads and unauthorized new departures. It stands upon what the *Book of Common Prayer* actually says about healing and the theological analysis of those words.

And what is unique about this book is that theological analysis is constantly applied to practical liturgical contexts and pastoral settings.

The theology of the corporate, ecclesial, sacramental dimension that binds all the theory and praxis of the volume into one whole is neatly summed up by one quote that Malia has found from theologian Richard Lambourne, "[In the church's healing] a new relationship is established between the sufferer, the minister, and the other participant observers of the act and Christ the author of the act, by which they all receive Grace. They are all healed as they enter into a new wholeness of a new *koinonia*, and the evil of the sickness, like the evil of the Cross, has been made in Christ the grounds of the fellowship's salvation." These are powerful words, and such a theology needs to be widely known.

All of this is communicated by Malia with the simple and elegant language of a theologian and priest who is also a short story writer and columnist. As such *Healing Touch and Saving Word* is a book I heartily recommend to our bishops, and their Commissions on the Ministry, to seminary students, particularly those preparing for the General Ordination Examination, and for all of those who want to know more about how we experience God's saving Grace in the sacrament of healing.

February 20, 2012

Preface

IN THE ANOINTING OF the sick and in the laying on of hands, says Richard Lambourne, "those who gather around the man [or woman] do not gather only to do something to them, for by the sacramental act they corporately become Christ as they put on Christ. A new relationship is established between the sufferer, the minister, and the other participant observers of the act and Christ the author of the act, by which they all receive Grace. They are all healed as they enter into a new wholeness of a new *koinonia*, and the evil of the sickness, like the evil of the Cross, has been made in Christ the grounds of the fellowship's salvation."[1]

This is a remarkably succinct and profound summarization of the theology at the heart of our Anglican sacramental rites of healing. In only a generation or so, the sacramental rite of unction—once rarely employed by Anglicans other than in the capacity of last rites—has become a regular part of the lives of most Episcopalians. It is the rare parish nowadays that does not celebrate sacramental healing on a regular basis, either in the course of Sunday worship or during weekday services. Many parishes today have parish healing teams or healing ministries composed of both laity and clergy who participate in their parish's services of healing and visit the sick and the homebound.

It would appear that we have come a long way in a short time. However, the way in which our sacramental rites of healing are perceived by most Episcopalians, and the scope of the theology given expression by our liturgical celebrations, does not yet begin to match the depth of vision expressed by Lambourne back in 1963. Throughout the course of my research and my discussions with fellow Episcopalians, what I came to realize is that while we Episcopalians today are less likely to associate unction with last rites, we continue, by and large, to fail to fully appreciate the potential of this important sacramental rite to assist the faithful

---

1. Lambourne. *Community, Church and Healing*, 134.

at every age, at every stage of life, and in every circumstance, to reassess and renew that commitment to the gospel and its mission for which we are baptized.

"Christianity," observes the 1964 report by the Episcopal Church's Joint Commission on the Ministry of Healing, "is a healing religion. Christ is a healing Saviour. He heals all brokenness: broken relationships as well as broken spirits, broken hearts as well as broken bodies. In the deepest sense, He came to heal the world."[2] The 1964 report goes on to say: "Everyone who has experienced the healing power of the risen Christ and whose heart is set on fire by the Holy Ghost is already in His ministry, whether he recognizes it or not. There is a sense in which one does not 'enter' the ministry, but rather finds himself already in it."[3] It is not a question, in other words, of whether or not we have a part to play in this apostolic ministry, but instead how each of us is to share in it through "the cultivation and exercise of talent, gift, and skill, within the framework of the mending ministry of God."[4]

Say the words "ministry of healing," and what most likely springs to mind is a sacramental liturgy with the laying on of hands and anointing, or the hospital chaplain making his or her rounds, Communion kit in hand. While these are powerful expressions of the church's healing ministry, in fact there are a variety of other ways in which this holy ministry finds expression in the everyday life of the church. It is, in fact, one ministry with many ministers. There is much to be done, and many ways in which every parish community can be a powerful expression of this important work. Some of these means of expression require special skills and training, while others require only a willing heart and a little time and effort. These include ministries to the sick and dying, as well as ministries of practical assistance, ministries of hospitality, ministries of spiritual and emotional support and guidance, ministries of prayer and of proclamation, ministries of reconciliation, ministries of visitation, and ministries of encouragement. The church's ministry of healing may find expression in a visit to a shut-in by the Parish Nurse, in the prayers of the faithful week after week, or in the self-giving of the volunteer who offers his or her time on behalf of another with a ride to the doctor or a

2. Episcopal Church, Joint Commission on the Ministry of Healing, *Report of the Joint Commission on the Ministry of Healing*, 3.

3. Ibid.

4. Ibid., 7.

hand with the household chores. Each sacramental action, each practical expression of love and caring, is in its way a prayer in the name of Jesus Christ through Christ's Body which carries out this salvific work in his Name. "It must . . . be recognized by the Church" reads the 1964 report, "that both priest and people must be caught up in this life-giving, life-mending experience."[5]

It is my intention to show how our rites of healing are examples of the provision our sacramental tradition makes in order to nurture our faith and to enable our growth into the likeness of Christ to continue at each new turning point in our lives, and to show, moreover, that our sacramental rites are meant to engage us in a mutuality of ministry.

Beginning with The Visitation of the Sick in the first *Book of Common Prayer* of 1549, continuing up through the American Prayer Book of 1928, and concluding, finally, with The Ministry to the Sick from the 1979 *Book of Common Prayer*,[6] A Public Service of Healing from *The Book of Occasional Services*,[7] and last, A Public Service of Healing from *Enriching Our Worship 2: Ministry with the Sick or Dying and Burial of a Child*,[8] I will examine the ways in which the Episcopal Church's liturgical rites of healing reflect a changing theology of health and ministry. Much of the information I will be drawing upon has been obtained first-hand from the very individuals who helped to create the Episcopal Church's newest sacramental liturgies of healing.

It is my hope that this study will help to create a greater awareness of the role our rites of healing serve (as part of the church's greater ministry of healing) in equipping the worshipping community for ministry and mission. My analysis will be guided by various questions pertaining to the status and nature of sacraments, such as: *Do our current rites of healing adequately express a theology of the ministry of all the baptized? Do they enable us to maintain our identity as the people of God, and to claim our vocation as ministers of the church throughout our various and changing life-situations, in spite of the limitations or obstacles placed upon or before us by sickness or old age? Why or why not?*

---

5. Ibid., 8.

6. Episcopal Church, *The Book of Common Prayer and Administration of the Sacraments and Other Rites and Ceremonies of the Church Together with the Psalter or Psalms of David according to the Use of the Episcopal Church.*

7. Episcopal Church, *The Book of Occasional Services.*

8. Episcopal Church, *Enriching Our Worship 2.*

In order to combine theory with practical experience, I continue to participate on a regular basis in the celebration of these rites of healing, both as they now stand, and also with the incorporation of some of my proposed suggestions. In addition, in the course of my explorations, I sat down one on one with many of the laity and clergy from my diocese in order to hear what they had to say.

The time has come for we Episcopalians to begin to look at our sacramental rites of healing in a new light, not simply as spiritual medicine for our broken and ailing bodies or psyches, but as true gospel medicine, by which, as Lambourne observes, "sickness and sin are made to be salvation events."[9] In addition to the best insights and practices of our own Anglican faith tradition, I have drawn upon the works of many well-known and highly respected Roman Catholic theologians, such as Karl Rahner, whose renewed vision of the nature of sacraments, as Robert Hughes has observed, was "clearly anticipated by [William Porcher] Dubose and other Anglican theologians."[10]

I am well aware of the fact that there exist, in respect to our Roman Catholic and Anglican sacramental traditions, important and yet unresolved points of disagreement in regard to such matters as validity and liciety.[11] I believe, however, that the sacramental theology expressed in this study is consistent with contemporary Anglican sacramental theology. As Donald Baillie observed back in 1957, "it has become plain in recent years that the antithesis of Catholic and Protestant is far from clear and cannot be identified with any denominational boundaries but cuts right across these boundaries . . . And in many of the Churches of the Reformation tradition there has been something of a beginning of rediscovery of the sacraments, or at least a yearning for such a rediscovery and feeling after it."[12]

In regard to methodology, I will begin with a brief overview of the theology of sacraments, particularly in light of our changing theology of health and ecclesiology. I will then proceed to an analysis and critique of certain previous Anglican rites of healing according to these models of analysis. Following this I will explore possible creative revisions to our three current liturgical rites of healing in light of the analysis of previous

9. Lambourne, *Community, Church and Healing,* 134.

10. Hughes, "Sacraments and Ordination."

11. Liciety: Conforming to the requirements and regulations of [canon] law.

12. Baillie, *The Theology of the Sacraments and Other Papers,* 39.

chapters, examining the dynamics of ritual performance, language, and symbolism in proposing ways of creatively 're-imagining' our healing rites.

It is my intention to show how our healing liturgies—and indeed, all of our sacraments/sacramental rites—by their very nature possess both a *personal* dimension (because the mystery of Christ is a personal mystery) as well as a *corporate*[13] dimension (because we are all baptized into Christ and share "Christ's mission to all people."[14]) I will be particularly concerned with the question of how effectively the Episcopal Church's past and present sacramental rites of healing support the gradual, cumulative and ongoing spiritual conversion, renewal and growth of both individual and worshipping community in such a way as to form a ministering/sacramental community whose mission it is to serve God through participation in Christ's redeeming work of healing.

13. Relating to a unified body of individuals.
14. *The Book of Common Prayer*, 854.

Acknowledgments

Grateful acknowledgment is made to the following publishers and individuals for permission to quote their published (and unpublished) works:

The Rev. Dr. Ruth Meyers, the Rev. Dr. Jennifer Philips, and Phoebe Pettingell, the Rev. Russell A. Newbert, and the Rev. Dr. Leonel Mitchell for their assistance and their valuable personal insights on the subject of liturgy and sacraments.

The Rev. Larry D. Ellis for permission to quote excerpt from "When, Why and How Do We Change the Words of Choral Music, Hymns and Liturgy to Use Inclusive and Expansive Language?" in *Worship and Church Music*, copyright © 2000 by The Rev. Larry D. Ellis.

The Rev. Dr. James Empereur, SJ, for permission to quote excerpts from *Prophetic Anointing: God's Call to the Sick, the Elderly, and the Dying* © The Rev. James Empereur.

The Rev. Dr. Robert D. Hughes III, for permission to quote excerpts from "Sacraments and Ordination, Incorporating Points from Tad Guzie's *Book of Sacramental Basics* (New York: Paulist Press, 1981)," course material for Senior Ecclesiology, School of Theology, University of the South, Sewanee, Tennessee, Fall 2001, by permission of the author.

The Rev. Michael W. Merriman for permission to quote excerpts from *The Baptismal Mystery and the Catechumenate*.

The Rev. Dr. David Neelands, Dean, Faculty of Divinity of Trinity College, Toronto, for permission to quote excerpts from "Studies in Anglican Theology" (TRT 3566F), Trinity College, Toronto, September 16, 1999.

The Rev. Dr. Robert W. Prichard for permission to quote excerpts from "Lecture 1B "Sickness, Healing, and Forgiveness," Virginia Theological Seminary. Course lecture for LTG 6, Introduction to Anglican Worship. Spring 2005.

The Family of the Rev. John Richards for permission to quote excerpts from *But Deliver Us From Evil: An Introduction to the Demonic Dimension in Pastoral Care.*

The Rev. Thomas Richstatter, OFM, for permission to quote excerpt from General and Introductory Materials: Part 3 Theological Issues Chapter d31 Sacrament."

Dr. Michael F. Skelley for permission to quote excerpt from *The Liturgy of the World: Karl Rahner's Theology of Worship.*

Dr. Charles Wohlers for permission to cite portions of earlier Visitation Offices (1549, 1552, 1662, 1789, 1928) from the Book of Common Prayer found on *The Book of Common Prayer* website, part of the Anglican Resource Collection, with thanks to the Society of Archbishop Justus.

Episcopal News Service, Domestic and Foreign Missionary Society for permission to quote excerpts from "From Canterbury: glimpses of the eternal design" by the Rt. Rev. Frank T. Griswold, copyright © 1988 by Episcopal Life Magazine, and for "Praying as we believe—and living as we pray" by the Rt. Rev. Frank T. Griswold, copyright © 2000 by Episcopal Life Magazine.

The General Board of Examining Chaplains of the Episcopal Church. Background Material for permission to quote materials from "Set. 2. Liturgy and Church Music." The General Board of Examining Chaplains of the Episcopal Church.

Church Publishing for permission to cite material from the following sources: A Public Service of Healing from *The Book of Occasional Services*; A Public Service of Healing from *Enriching Our Worship 2*; quotes from *An Episcopal Dictionary of the Church.*

Acknowledgments

Excerpts from: *Faithful Living, Faithful Dying: Anglican Reflections on End of Life Care*, by Cynthia Cohen; *How Shall We Pray? Expanding Our language about God*, by Ruth Meyers; *Understanding the Faith of the Church*, by Richard Norris; *Praying Shapes Believing*, by Leonel Mitchell; *Occasions of Grace*, by Byron Stuhlman

The Anglican Church of Canada—Diocese of Toronto for permission to cite "Ministry of Healing" and "Licensing of Laity for Anointing with Oil," from Liturgical Standards and Resources Book.

Church House Publishing for permission to quote excerpts from *A Time to Heal: A Report for the House of Bishops on the Healing Ministry*.

International Commission on English in the Liturgy Corporation for permission to quote excerpts from *Pastoral Care of the Sick: Rites of Anointing and Viaticum* © 1982. All rights reserved.

World Council of Churches for permission to quote excerpts from "Not an Option: Ministry with and for People with Disabilities" by Nyambura J. Njoroge and "The Place of People with Disabilities in the Mission and Calling of the Church" by Samuel Kabue from *Ministerial Formation*.

The Anglican Theological Review for permission to quote excerpts from "What Do We Bless, and Why?," by Charles Hefling, copyright © 2003 by *The Anglican Theological Review*.

Continuum International Publishing Group for permission to cite quotations from *A Guide to the Sacraments* by John Macquarrie.

CrossCurrents Magazine for permission to cite portions of "The Common Word: Recovering Liturgical Speech—Prayer" by Catherine Madsen, copyright © 1983 by *CrossCurrents Magazine*.

The Crossroad Publishing Company, Inc., Publisher of Crossroad and Herder & Herder Books for permission to cite portions of *Health and Medicine in the Anglican Tradition: Conscience, Community, and Compromise* by David H. Smith, copyright © 1986 by The Crossroad Publishing Company and *How to Understand the Liturgy*, by Jean Lebon.

Darton, Longman & Todd for permission to cite portions of *Community, Church and Healing: A Study of Some of the Corporate Aspects of the Church's Ministry to the Sick* R. A. Lambourne, copyright © 1963 by Darton, Longman & Todd.

Excerpts from *Commentary on the American Prayer Book* copyright © 1980 by Marion J. Hatchett; *Prayer Is Good Medicine* copyright © 1996 by Larry Dossey, MD; *Reinventing Medicine: Beyond Mind-Body to a New Era of Healing* © 1999 by Larry Dossey, MD; and *Healing Words* copyright © 1993 by Larry Dossey, MD, reprinted by permission of HarperCollins Publishers.

Libreria Editrice Vaticana for permission to cite excerpts from Constitution on The Sacred Liturgy/*Sacrosanctum Concilium* and Dogmatic Constitution on the Church/*Lumen Gentium*.

Liguori Books for permission to cite excerpts from *Doors to the Sacred: A Historical Introduction to Sacraments in the Catholic Church* by Joseph Martos.

Liturgical Press permission to cite material from *Praying the Sacraments* by Peter E. Fink and *Elements of Rite: A Handbook of Liturgical Style,* by Aiden Kavanagh; *Alternative Futures for Worship.* Vol. 4, *Reconciliation* ed. by Bernard J. Lee and Peter E. Fink; and *Alternative Futures for Worship.* Vol. 7, *Anointing of the Sick* by Bernard J. Lee and Peter E. Fink.

Excerpts from *The Oxford Illustrated History of Christianity* by John Mc-Manners, reproduced by permission of Oxford University Press (www.oup.com).

Rowman & Littlefield Publishing Group for permission to quote excerpts from *Opening the Prayer Book: New Church's Teaching Series; vol. 7* by Jeffrey D. Lee, copyright ©1999 by Cowley Publications, and *Pastoral and Occasional Liturgies: A Ceremonial Guide by* Leonel Mitchell, ©1998 by Cowley Publications.

Sewanee Theological Review for permission to quote excerpts from "A Riotous Mixture of Phrases: Ian Ramsey's Assertion of the Impropriety

Acknowledgments

of Religious Language, the Need for This in Liturgical Texts, and How One Contemporary Rite Fails to Be Odd Enough," by J. Barrington Bates.

SPCK Publishing & Sheldon Press for permission to quote excerpts from *The Oil of Gladness: Anointing in the Christian Tradition*, Martin Dudley and Geoffrey Rowell, copyright © 1993 by SPCK; *The Christian Healing Ministry* by Morris Maddocks, copyright © 1981 by SPCK; *Twenty Questions about Healing* by Morris Maddock, copyright © 1988 by SPCK; *The Study of Anglicanism*, Stephen Sykes and John E. Booty, editors; and *Liturgy, Pastoral and Parochial* by Michael Perham, copyright © 1988 by SPCK.

Twenty-Third Publications for permission to quote excerpts from *Sacraments and Sacramentality* by Bernard Cooke, copyright © by Twenty-Third Publications.

United States Conference of Catholic Bishops for permission to cite excerpts from *Built of Living Stones: Art, Architecture, and Worship*.

University of California Press for permission to quote excerpt from *Deeply into the Bone: Re-inventing Rites of Passage* by Ronald Grimes, copyright © 2000 by the Regents of the University of California, University of California Press.

Wipf and Stock Publishers for permission to quote excerpts from *A Roman Catholic Theology of Pastoral Care* by Regis Duffy, copyright © 2010 2010 Wipf & Stock Publishers.

1

Defining Sacraments

Sacraments and The Book of Common Prayer

THERE IS ALWAYS THE temptation, when writing on the subject of sacraments, to immediately launch into a detailed sacraments-through-the-ages type of analysis. While this study will, of necessity, touch briefly on the evolution of our sacraments and sacramental rites, I will not attempt to embark on an exhaustive study of their origins, not simply for want of space, but because so many others have done it already, and done it well, as the many fine books lining my shelves, such as Marion Hatchett's *Commentary on the American Prayer Book*[1] or Charles Price and Louis Weil's *Liturgy for Living*[2] can attest. Since this is not an historical study so much as a critical examination of the Episcopal Church's liturgies of healing and what they reveal about our ever-evolving theology of church, ministry and health, I have chosen to concentrate in particular on the corporate and transformational nature of sacraments and what they mean for us as Christians.

Having said this, I am reminded of an encounter not so long ago in which I was asked, by someone from a non-Anglican faith tradition, "What do Episcopalians believe? Where can I find a summary of your faith?" My answer was to hand him a copy of *The Book of Common Prayer*. A stranger to the Anglican faith wishing to learn about its theology need look no further than the Prayer Book. To Anglicans, *The Book of Common Prayer* is

1. Hatchett, *Commentary on the American Prayer Book.*
2. Price and Weil, *Liturgy for Living*, rev. ed.

1

more than simply a book of rites and ceremonies: it is a treasure of the Anglican faith, through which our theology is expressed and driven. In the words of Leonel Mitchell, "Not only do we use *The Book of Common Prayer* for the conduct of our public services: it is the guide for our private prayer and the source of most of our theology."[3] Within the Prayer Book's covers is contained the width and breadth of the Episcopal Church's worship, from the Daily Offices to its sacramental rites.[4] It is rooted in Scripture—which accounts for some 80 percent of its content—and rich in centuries of Christian tradition. The poetry of its language resonates, as Barbara Brown Taylor observes, "with historical accents that reach all the way back to first-century Palestine."[5] Its chief architect, Thomas Cranmer, envisioned it as a means by which all the faithful might be edified in "heart, spirit and mind" by participation in a pattern of daily prayer and sacramental worship, at the heart of which is the Eucharist, by which the people of God are "knit together," made one body in Christ and with one another.

What Anglicans believe is interpreted through the form of the Church's ritual prayer—her liturgies—and the faithful, in turn, are formed through their participation. In the words of the Most Reverend Frank T. Griswold, twenty-fifth Presiding Bishop of the Episcopal Church, "For Anglicans, our various prayer books provide for the ordering of time in such a way that we meet Christ in the unfolding of our lives both personally and corporately."[6] The Anglican faith finds outward expression in the rites and ceremonies[7] found in *The Book of Common Prayer, The Book of Occasional Services*,[8]

---

3. Mitchell, Introduction, *Praying Shapes Believing*, 1.

4. The Episcopal Church (sometimes referred to by the abbreviation ECUSA, or The Episcopal Church in the United States of America), is a member of the Anglican Communion, the associated churches throughout the world in communion with the See of Canterbury, which is to say, the Church of England. "Member churches exercise jurisdictional independence but share a common heritage concerning Anglican identity and commitment to scripture, tradition, and reason as sources of authority. Churches in the Anglican Communion continue to reflect the balance of Catholic and Protestant principles that characterized the *via media* of the Elizabethan settlement." Don S. Armentrout and Robert Boak Slocum, "Anglican Communion." In *An Episcopal Dictionary of the Church*, 16.

5. Taylor, *The Preaching Life*, 65.

6. Griswold, "From Canterbury: Glimpses of the Eternal Design."

7. "In liturgical use the word 'rites' usually refers to the texts of services and the word 'ceremonies' to the actions." Hatchett, *Commentary on the American Prayer Book*, 16.

8. *The Book of Occasional Services*, Preface: "*The Book of Occasional Services* is a collection of liturgical resources related to occasions which do not occur with sufficient

and other authorized supplemental liturgies. Again, in the words of the previous Presiding Bishop: "As such the Prayer Book shapes and forms our consciousness over time through its recurring rhythms of praise, petition and penitence grounded in the continual recalling of 'God's saving deeds' as proclaimed in scripture and made present in our lives in sign, symbol and the sacraments."[9]

Sacrament: Mystery, Sign, and Symbol

For Episcopalians everywhere, whether brought up on the 1928 or 1979 Prayer Book, the definition of a sacrament, found in the Church's Catechism, is "an outward and visible sign of inward and spiritual grace, given by Christ as sure and certain means by which we receive that grace."[10] This familiar and concise explanation as it stands is adequate enough. However, as the introductory section titled "Concerning the Catechism" advises the reader, this very succinct definition "is not meant to be a complete statement of belief and practice" but to serve as "a point of departure."[11] Accordingly, it is my hope that this examination of our rites of healing and of our understanding of the theology of sacraments will serve to fill out and illuminate this catechetical statement, therein enabling us to perceive sacraments in a more dynamic and relational way.

As those from nonliturgical Christian faith traditions are often quick to point out, the term *sacrament* is foreign to the New Testament. Certainly Jesus never spoke of sacraments, and while it would be accurate to say that our present day sacraments have their origin in the life and ministry of Jesus, we have no proof that our Lord himself created any formal sacramental liturgies, nor is there any direct evidence to indicate that he intended to institute a sacramental system such as that with which we are familiar. Does this mean that sacraments are mere human inventions?

The answer is a complex one, and at its heart lies, first and foremost, the mystery of salvation. But what do we mean by mystery? In its everyday usage the word *mystery* has the sense of something essentially unknowable,

---

frequency to warrant their inclusion in the *Book of Common Prayer*," 5.

9. Griswold, "Praying as We Believe," 28.

10. "An Outline of the Faith, commonly called the Catechism," in *The Book of Common Prayer*, 857. Hereafter, all references to "An Outline of the Faith" will appear in the text as "Catechism," followed by the appropriate page number(s).

11. *The Book of Common Prayer*, 844.

inexplicable, or unfathomable; something whose meaning is hidden. In a theological sense, however, while retaining this basic connotation, the term *mystery* takes on a greater complexity of meaning. To illustrate, for St. Paul the term *mystery* is often used in reference to God's thoughts and designs for creation, once hidden but now revealed through the gospel, as in Colossians 2:2: "the knowledge of God's *mystery*, of Christ, in whom are hid all the treasures of wisdom and knowledge."[12] At other times, such as in Ephesians 5:32, *mystery* refers to something whose truth is to be grasped in an allegorical or typological way (i.e., marriage is a mystery whose meaning is to be understood in the light of Christ's union with his church).

The Greek word *mysterion*—the source of our own word *mystery*—has the sense of something that is both hidden and revealed. The mystery cults, with which the early church often found itself in competition, were in essence secret societies. Many of them found their way into the West, in the wake of the conquests of Alexander the Great, from Persia, Egypt, Asia Minor, and so on, while other mystery cults, like those of Dionysius and Demeter, arose from their native soil of Greece. The Greek verb *myo*—"to close or shut"—from which the word *mysterion* is derived, has both the sense of the *revealing* of that which was hidden and of the *revelation* itself. Through a secret initiation ceremony, one entered into the mystery, and suddenly, what had previously been hidden was now dramatically revealed. In the case of the mystery cults, this secret invariably centered on the particular cult's founding myth.[13] In the semidarkness in which most initiation rituals took place, initiates underwent a mystical experience, generally related to the death and rebirth of the deity in question. It was more than simply an emotional experience. For worshipers it provided a direct and personal encounter with the sacred.

The Latin word *sacramentum*, from which our word *sacrament* is derived, is a translation of the Greek *mysterion*. So, in Latin a *sacrament* is a mystery, a secret. At the same time, in keeping with the original sense of the

---

12. All biblical citations are from the Revised Standard Version unless otherwise noted.

13. While the word *myth* comes from a Greek word meaning "fable" or "tale," in the technical sense in which it is employed by biblical scholars and anthropologists, *myth* refers to a culture's sacred history, a founding narrative that expresses a society's shared understanding of that from which it derives its ultimate meaning. In other words, myths are "the deepest expressions of truth that a culture or people can speak, and these truths cannot be simply restated in everyday street language without losing something from their meaning" (*Education for Ministry, Year One*, 22).

word from which it derives, it can mean something secret which is *revealed*: the *sacramentum* is the secret which is revealed to the initiate in the course of his or her initiation.

Mystery, by its very nature, gives expression to a dimension of reality not transmissible through ordinary channels, one that relates not merely information but also insight. Access to this mystery calls for a special means of communication, a language capable of expressing not just rational thought but nondiscursive sorts of information (i.e., those concepts, notions, intuitions, innermost feelings, and so on, for which ordinary language is insufficient). In short, it requires *symbols*.

While the terms *sign* and *symbol* are frequently employed both in secular and religious discourse, the interpretation of the significance and intensity of the relationship of either to the reality to which it refers may vary from one context to another, or from one tradition to another. In order to understand sacraments within this particular framework—a Christian framework, and one within the Anglo-Catholic tradition—one must first understand how they are thought to act as signs and symbols by certain sacramental theologians. What do we mean by signs and symbols with respect to sacraments, and how does the one differ from the other?

The old familiar definition of a sacrament provides us with a starting point: "*outward and visible signs*." Sacraments possess level upon level of meaning. The first level of meaning is that of the *sign*. Both human beings and animals employ and respond to signs. Signs tend to be simple and direct in meaning, and generally bear a designative or representative relationship to that to which they refer. They *signify*, or draw attention to something other than themselves. For example, the sign posted on the wall, which announces "This Way to the Buffet," is not the immediate object of our concern. It is of secondary importance: we are interested in the buffet itself, which would continue to exist even if the sign should fall down from the wall. Some signs, like the smoke that alerts us to the presence of a fire, or the clap of thunder that warns us of an approaching storm, are *natural* signs; others, like flags, traffic lights or door bells are *conventional* signs, that is to say, their meaning is assigned to them or agreed upon.

While they are related to something other than themselves, signs do not represent that other thing in its entirety. Rather, a sign directs our attention to something else that may or may not be immediately evident, such as the railroad-crossing signal that warns of the approach of a yet-unseen oncoming railway train, or the physical symptoms that indicate the onset of a cold.

Signs may refer to some other object or situation by virtue of a *causal link*, in the same sort of way that a blush may serve as a sign of shame or embarrassment on the part of the individual, or a crumbling porch may serve as a sign of the presence of termites. To give another example of a causal link, an elevated temperature may serve as a sign by drawing our attention to the presence of an infectious process. Whether natural or artificial, however, what these signs themselves share in common is the fact that they are *interpreted* as such by someone. The fact that a fever does indeed indicate the presence of an infection is not contingent on our interpreting it as such. However, the fact that we have chosen to do so—to draw a connection between *x* and *y*—allows it to serve for us as a sign. To this degree, signs stand for something else in some capacity or respect without necessarily *being* that object.

This is the first—and necessary—level of a sacrament. However, mere signs are inadequate for the purpose of communicating spiritual realities—which are *mysterious*—because of the essential one-dimensional nature of signs. A special medium is required, one that, while employing the physical, discernible elements of the sign, is capable of expressing those non-perceptible, non-tangible realities whose complexity cannot be reduced to a simple meaning. This special medium is the *symbol*. The word 'symbol' comes from the Greek *symbolein*, which means, roughly, "to put together," or "to bring together," in the sense of uniting two halves of the one object. In antiquity a *symbol* was a piece of pottery that was broken in half and then divided between two parties, who might at some point in the future need to verify a message sent by one to the other. When this occurred the messenger would produce one half of the pottery, which was fitted to the other half like a piece of a jigsaw puzzle, and the authenticity of the message was thus confirmed. Other examples of the unifying nature of symbols can be found in other sources, such as the Bible. Consider this excerpt from the book of Tobit:

> Then Tobias answered his father Tobit, "I will do everything that you have commanded me, father; but how can I obtain the money from [Gabael son of Gabrias], since he does not know me and I do not know him? What evidence am I to give him so that he will recognize and trust me, and give me the money?" Then Tobit answered his son Tobias, "He gave me his bond and I gave him my

bond. I divided his in two; we each took one part, and I put one with the money."[14]

While there is no universally agreed upon definition of *symbol*, most authorities concur on this point: that symbols differ from signs in various ways, but in most particular because of the richness of meaning that they embody. This surplus of meaning enables symbols to convey more than is immediately apparent, and to serve as vehicles for communicating those ideas, sensations, experiences, feelings, impressions, and concepts whose significance cannot be adequately captured by normal means of expression. Moreover, unlike a simple sign, the symbol bears an intrinsic relationship to that which it signifies. In the words of Paul Moyaert, writing on the subject of sacred symbols: "What is indicated by a symbol also affects the symbol. The signifying power of what symbols indicate penetrates into the symbol. In a symbolic relationship, the related terms flow into each other without completely overlapping or simply coinciding with each other. A symbol not only refers to something; it is also an *embodiment* of that to which it refers. One can more fully describe this interwovenness by saying both that the symbol is a component of what it symbolizes and that it partially contains what it expresses."[15]

So it is clear that while all symbols are also signs, not all signs are symbols. On one level symbols have the function of a sign—they put us in mind of something else—but on another, more complex level their relationship to that which they signify is, as theologians would say, not subordinate but intrinsic. That is, while they continue to possess an essential sign function, without which they could not serve as symbols, unlike simple signs, which function literally in order to alert us to the existence of some other thing with which they are associated, symbols also convey the *idea* or *concept* of something. That is why we say that for human beings symbols are transparent in nature, because they reveal to us another underlying reality.

Furthermore, signs tend to affect us simply, while symbols affect us on a more profound, more personal level. This is because symbols not only direct our attention beyond the things themselves, but also call forth the memories that we associate with these things, as well as the ideas, concepts, feelings, and the like, that arise as we relate the one with the other. The complex nature of the sorts of realities expressed by symbols is such that they

14. Tob 5:1–3 (NRSV).

15. Moyaert, "The Sense of Symbols as the Core of Religion: A Philosophical Approach to a Theological Debate." In *Transcendence in Philosophy and Religion*, 58.

generally evoke from us some sort of an emotional response. An American flag, for instance, at one level, fulfills its purpose by serving as an official insignia of the United States. That is its sign value. However, for a veteran of the armed forces, especially one who has served in combat, the flag's symbolic value is not merely functional, but deeply personal and moving. These familiar symbols such as flags, thus endued with special meaning, invite our *participation* in them to no small degree through the way in which we are able to personally connect with them through memory. By relating them to our own personal experience, from which they derive much of their power for us, we reconstruct their significance by combining them with other references in a way that gives them a greater depth of meaning. They "not only stand for objects," observe Price and Weil, "but can evoke feelings, call forth memories long buried, and combine references in a way that makes the world new."[16]

Every symbol begins with a sign that possesses certain constitutive elements that we recognize and that have some inherent degree of meaning for us. We, in turn, relate this particular sign to the realities of our own subjective experience, and as we do so it evokes for us those complex experiences and sensations that everyday forms of expression can only begin to convey: it becomes *symbol*. It does what mere signs cannot. How, for instance, can one adequately describe in mere words the depth of feeling conveyed by a particular piece of music, or the superabundance of meaning summed up for a particular individual by a simple gold wedding band whose luster for them remains undiminished through years of loving relationship? Symbolic language allows us to say, Such and such an object (or concept or experience, e.g.) is *like* this, but not *confined* to this. By means of symbols the horizon of our personal experience is broadened beyond the limitations of ordinary literal interpretation. Through symbolization our experiences of the world are contextualized and are able to take on for us deeply personal meaning. Signs, it is often said, affect us simply, while symbols affect us on a more personal level, because what they lead us to perceive is not the things themselves so much as the memories and associations which they call forth, and the concepts which arise out of the association of the one with the other. Symbols evoke a more personal response from us because they engage not simply our intellect, but our imagination and our emotions.

---

16. Price and Weil, *Liturgy for Living*, 23.

Returning to the aforementioned definition of sacraments given in the Catechism, we find sacraments described as "outward and visible signs of inward and spiritual grace." While symbols in their function as signs may take the outward form of familiar, everyday physical things—bread, wine, national flags, buildings, and so on—in their symbolic function these physical objects serve as means of expression for "inward and spiritual" realities. As we have noted, all symbols are also signs, though not all signs are symbols. Moreover, a symbol is not simply something that signifies something else that is (or has been, or will be). Unlike a sign, which directs our attention to the existence of something else, a symbol, in the words of the American philosopher Susanne Langer, is a "vehicle of meaning."[17] In theological terms, the symbol allows the other reality to be "actualized." By providing it with a means of expression, a symbol actually makes it *possible* for the other reality to be present. It is more than just a representation of the other: it is the very means by which the other is able to express its essential nature and thereby realize—'make real'– itself. Just as we ourselves, for instance, seek to realize our selves through personal expression—in our outward appearance, through our words, by way of our actions, and so on—there are many realities that *require* symbolic expression in order to actualize what they truly are.

Little wonder that it is symbolism we draw upon when attempting to convey the mystery of faith. As John Polkinghorne observes, "Attempts to articulate the knowledge of God will require language to be stretched by analogy. In consequence theology must avail itself of the openness of reference provided by symbol. Such a recognition is the essence of a rational theology, not its negation. Recourse to symbol is in no way incompatible with the assertion of truth; indeed, some deep truths can only be expressed symbolically.[18]

As embodied creatures, human beings are constantly creating and employing symbols. From the first cave dweller who left the mark of his handprint on the cave wall, and perhaps even before, human beings have long been endeavoring to make sense of themselves and of the world around them through creating and employing symbols. Even as we sleep, our dreams are busily producing symbols to help us analyze our waking experiences.

17. Langer, *Philosophy in a New Key.*
18. Polkinghorne, *The Faith of a Physicist*, 40.

While Scripture assures us that we are made in the image of God, we are likewise creatures of flesh and blood, with all the blessings and limitations this implies. Unlike the angels, we are not purely spiritual beings, and accordingly, our knowledge of the world is mediated to us first and foremost through our senses, through the created realities of people, things, and events. Nonetheless, while rooted in the temporal and material world, as embodied spiritual beings we also possess what Karl Rahner calls a fundamental openness to the transcendent. That is, while we seek to make sense of ourselves and of the world around us by way of our rational faculties and the information we process through our senses, we also seem to be created with an inherent awareness of, and an orientation to, the divine. Essential to the notion of what it means to be human, it would seem, is a fundamental openness to God's self-revelation. Accordingly, our complex creaturely and spiritual nature, for its fulfillment, requires the use of sacramental symbols in order for us to make sense of our existence in a way that does justice to that complexity.

The essayist Andre Debus declared, "*A sacrament is physical, and within it is God's love.*"[19] Debus spoke eloquently of his need for sacraments, and the importance of their outward, visible—and tangible- aspect: "'I need sacraments I can receive through my senses. I need God manifested as Christ, who ate and drank . . . and suffered and laughed. So I can dance with Him as the leaf dances in the breeze under the sun.'"[20] We seek, says John Schanz, "to express our inner feelings and desires, especially deep-seated feelings such as love, in an external bodily way by signs, gestures, and words that reveal and express our inmost self."[21] For this reason, observe Radner and Sumner, we employ symbols, for symbols "carry a plenitude of meaning that is invoked rather than explicitly stated. The knowledge created by symbol is not merely speculative, but is participatory and self-involving. The symbol invites us to situate ourselves within a universe of meaning and value, which it opens up, and, insofar as it is self-involving, has a transformative effect on the person."[22]

More than sign, as *symbol*, sacrament draws spirit into matter. True to its definition of that which "unites" or "brings together," a symbol does what a mere sign cannot: it enables spiritual and material realities to engage one

19. Quoted in *Preaching to the Hungers of the Heart*, 73–74.

20. Ibid.

21. Schanz, *Introduction to the Sacraments*, 12.

22. Radner and Sumner. *The Rule of Faith*, 98.

another. This involves another level of meaning beyond the sacrament in its function as sign, an interior level that is established in faith, and by which the participant becomes part of the process. This level is two-dimensional: it incorporates the *faith* of the believer—for faith, like love, requires someone to confess it—and the *believer*. That is, at this level there is the believer and there is that in which the believer believes. I *believe*. *What* do I believe? That through Christ, who is present in the sacraments, God is revealed.

In summary, a sacrament has three levels. First, there is the level of the *sign*, which draws our attention to something other than itself. We have observed that there are different sorts of signs. Some are what we refer to as 'conventional' signs: their meaning is established or imposed upon them by society or by general agreement. The red stoplight, a national flag, or the "SALE" sign in the shop window fall into this category. The meaning conveyed by conventional signs is usually clear and concrete. There are natural signs as well, whose meaning we learn to interpret from experience, such as the smoke that indicates the presence of fire, or the changing color of the leaves signaling the onset of cold weather.

Then there is the second level of the sacrament, that of the *symbol*. Symbols have their origin in signs—that is, they are tangible and perceptible—but they embody a surplus of meaning much greater and richer than that of the original sign. Symbols engage our senses, our emotions, our reasoning processes, our memories. Accordingly, because of this richness and complexity of meaning they are able to embody, symbols may—and usually do—possess more than one meaning. Symbols have the power to convey concepts and feelings in a way that mere words cannot.

Finally, there is the third level of the sacrament, its ultimate meaning, in which one encounters not just the meaning of the inner reality to which sign and symbol point, but the reality itself. This is the level of *participation*, the level that one might term mystical. Sacraments are not simply symbols, but *efficacious* symbols. In the words of the *Catechism of the Catholic Church*, "Celebrated worthily in faith, the sacraments confer the grace that they signify. They are efficacious because in them Christ himself is at work: it is he who baptizes, he who acts in his sacraments in order to communicate the grace that each sacrament signifies."[23]

23. Catholic Church,*Catechism of the Catholic Church*. Online: http://www.vatican.va/archive/ENG0015/__P38.htm/.

It might be helpful, at this point, to consider the various levels contained in a sacrament according to Thomas Aquinas'[24] famous threefold analysis:

1. The *sacramentum tantum*, the "matter" and "form" of the sacrament. This is the tangible, perceptible aspect: the sacramental rite's external level, not just the material employed, but also the words and gestures of which the sacrament is composed. A sacramental rite utilizes certain objects—such as the water of baptism or the bread and wine of the Eucharist—as well as certain actions and words. Within the context of the sacramental liturgy, all these serve to make up the 'outward and visible' aspect of the sacrament. This is the first level of a sacrament, the *sign* alone.

2. The *res et sacramentum*, literally, the "reality and sign": *the inward reality* signified by the outward sign, sometimes referred to as the first "effect" of the sacrament, or the "character" of the sacrament (imparted to the believer by virtue of the sacrament which has been enacted *ex opere operato*[25]), which is identified with the presence of Christ. "The first level," notes Tibor Horvath, "points to the second level—that of the invisible created power, the grace, which further signifies and points beyond itself and is therefore called the *res et sacramentum*."[26]

   While theologians have for centuries debated the nature of this indelible character imparted to the believer[27]—a topic that time and space do not permit us to discuss further—it is helpful to think of the *res et sacramentum* as what George Worgul describes as "incorporation into or deepening participation within the ecclesial fellowship [which] is the vehicle by which God's self-communication

---

24. Thomas Aquinas: (1225–1274) b. Roccasecca, Italy. Catholic priest in the Dominican Order, philosopher, theologian, and Doctor of the Church. Known as the Angelic Doctor.

25. Lit., "from the work of the work itself": by virtue of the validly performed rite, which is enacted according to the mind and intent of the Church (with the implicit understanding, of course, that the sacramental action is the action of Christ).

26. Horvath. *Thinking about Faith*, 73.

27. As Robert Hughes observes, it is this middle level that proves most problematic for many Protestants. However, it may be helpful to note that many of the perceived difficulties have arisen from a misreading of Catholic sacramental theology. Robert D. Hughes, "Retrieving and Reconstructing," *Sewanee Theological Review*, 45:1 (2001), 51–71 (sub-edited issue).

is accomplished within sacramental celebrations."[28] Many leading contemporary Roman Catholic theologians—notably Karl Rahner—define this second level in regard to the special relationship created of the believer to the Church. As Schanz notes, "the mysteries of *Christ*, his *incarnation*, the *Church*, and the *faithful* must be linked together. The mystery of Christ is prolonged in the Church, his personal sacrament on earth, which in turn communicates the mystery of Jesus to the faithful through the great sacramental act."[29] Herbert Vorgrimler notes that "an individual sacrament always actualizes the fundamental sacrament that is Church [that is, allows the Church to become what it truly is by expressing itself in the sacraments] and incorporates those celebrating the sacrament [both ordained and *laos*[30]], in a way unique to each sacrament, into that fundamental sacrament [Jesus Christ]."[31]

3. The *res tantum* (or *res sacramenti*): the reality of the sacrament itself, the "inward and spiritual grace." This is the third level of the sacrament, an inner level, one that we might term *mystical*, in which the sacrament not only expresses and signifies a reality beyond itself—grace, its spiritual dimension, its ultimate meaning—but effectively *communicates* it to the believer who is properly disposed, or, in the words of the Council of Trent, "places no obstacle in the way." To quote John Macquarrie: "A sacrament fulfills its intention when it effects its reality into the life of the believer."[32] It is at this third level that the believer is able not only to perceive the mystery communicated through the symbols employing the stuff of everyday life—water, bread, wine, oil, and so on—but to be engaged by it and to *participate* in it. Thus sacraments become personal encounters with the divine, and through our participation in them we are transformed.

If one wished to put it more simply, it might be helpful to think of sacraments in this way:

1. The first level would be the *literal* or *external* level of the sacrament. This is concerned with what St. Augustine would call the "elements"

---

28. Worgul, *From Magic to Metaphor*, 162.

29. Schanz, *The Sacraments of Life and Worship*, 60.

30. *Laos*: the laity, i.e., not members of the clergy. From the Greek *laikos* ("of the people").

31. Vorgrimler, *Sacramental Theology*, 92.

32. Macquarrie, *A Guide to the Sacraments*, 47.

of the sacrament: the matter (the *res sensibiles*, or "sensible sign"[33]) and the form (the accompanying words) employed within the context of the liturgical rite. This is the perceptible level of the sacrament: certain gestures, certain words, certain things used in the context of the ritual. It is necessary to recognize the importance of the first level of the sacrament—its outward, external level—as a medium by which the second level is expressed. By means of this external dimension of the ritual we have access to the second level.

2. The next level is the level of the *reality* and the *sign*, "connected intimately to the first," says Peter Fink, in which "religious symbolism expresses human relationship to the Sacred."[34] This could be called the level of *meaning*, at which the rite proclaims and articulates the deeper reality of the ritual. Without this second level the ritual is liable to degenerate into mere superstition: magical words and gestures. One ends up with special ritual formulas and props, but no real sense of the true underlying meaning. For this reason, it is important that the rite should clearly articulate how that which the sacrament signifies *relates* to the Christian faith. To illustrate, let us consider the sacrament of the Eucharist. At the first level we have its outward aspect: a communal meal. There is a table to be set, food and drink to be prepared and shared. This is something to which we can all immediately relate on an outward level. At the next level it is revealed that these familiar items and actions express something deeper, more profound, which is related to the life, death, and resurrection of our Lord. Without these first two very important levels we have no access to the third and final level.

3. At this final level we arrive at *the ultimate meaning* of the sacrament in which that which has been proclaimed and expressed becomes real for the believer. The believer is no longer a mere bystander but in some way has become incorporated into this deeper reality. This third level is the level of *participation*, without which the sacrament is reduced

---

33. *Matter*, as we have noted, may refer to the physical substance as well as the ritual words and actions. The matter of the sacrament, in the words of A. M. Roguet, may involve "an act, a gesture, some kind of human demeanor." Says Roguet: "Matter is a sign, as yet vague and indeterminate, and form comes to round off its significance." A. M. Roguet, *Christ Acts through the Sacraments*, 20–21.

34. Fink, *Worship: Praying the Sacraments*, 33. Fink and others have found Paul Ricoeur's reflections on the symbol and its various levels of "multimeaning expressions" extremely helpful in understanding the role of symbols in Christian worship.

to a formal profession of faith ("This symbolizes what I believe"), or degenerates into legalism ("I must do this because the church requires me to do so"), or intellectualism ("I do this because I agree with its exemplary message," or perhaps, "I do this because it expresses an important truth").[35] Like the wife who tells her husband (or the husband who tells his wife) "I *know* you love me, but I need to *hear* it," spiritual realities, such as love, need some tangible way in which to be expressed and thereby actualized. At this level, mere understanding is transcended as the reality of the sacrament is personally encountered by the believer, and the distance between what is believed and the object of one's belief, gives way to participation.

Arriving at an Understanding of Sacraments

Before proceeding further, it is important to articulate the understanding of sacraments upon which this study of our sacramental rites of healing is founded. I think it would be accurate to say that it corresponds with the traditional definition of sacraments contained in the Episcopal Church's Catechism, but serves, I hope, to flesh out this definition in a way that gives emphasis to:

- *The importance of their essential liturgical setting. Sacraments cannot be truly understood outside of this essential context.*

- *The fact that it is indeed the church—the whole body of Christ—which celebrates the sacraments.*

- *The understanding that the grace conveyed by the sacraments is not some impersonal metaphysical reality bestowed upon the recipient like spiritual medicine, but the very love of God, God's efficacious self-communication in Christ to the believer.*

- *That while the sacraments are "doors to the sacred" (as religious scholar Mircea Eliade has termed them[36]) not everything that leads to the sacred is necessarily a sacrament or even sacramental.[37]*

35. Tavard, Course lecture for TRT 3566F, "Spirituality and Symbolism," Regis College, Toronto, March 15, 1999.

36. Eliade, *The Sacred and the Profane.*

37. There is a danger in stretching the definition of *sacrament* so far that it becomes virtually meaningless. To give an example, I have heard well-meaning clergy declare that preaching must surely be a sacrament in its own right because of its ability to energize

- *That sacraments are not merely external signs of God's promises, but transforming encounters with God through Christ by the power of the Holy Spirit, which draw us into the life of the Trinity and into a deeper commitment to living a Christian life.*

- *That the effect of the grace of the sacraments is not confined to the moment of celebration: the fullness of the sacraments is lived out throughout the successive stages of our lives.*

- *That as well as serving as vehicles of spiritual nurture and growth, sacraments, in the words of Regis Duffy, support the "ongoing conversion and renewal" of Christians, permitting them* "a wider vision and deeper commitment to the gospel and its mission."[38]

Sacrament and Ritual

There is no question but that Anglican theology is liturgically driven. In the words of David H. Smith, "[the Anglican] community is established in ritual and worship. Indeed, some observers claim that Anglicanism is held together more by a common attitude toward ritual than by anything else."[39] A brief but serviceable definition of ritual, according to Joseph Stoutzenberger, is "symbolic action."[40] Through ritual, human beings instinctively seek to give symbolic expression to those realities, values, beliefs, mysteries, and the like, central to their lives.

The need to express one's beliefs in the form of ritual is fundamental, but certainly not unique to, Anglicans and Roman Catholics. We seek through ritual to give meaningful expression to the central events of our lives. By means of ritual we mark, celebrate, and interpret these significant events in their lived context. The meaning that such moments and circumstances

---

and inspire the faithful. While the awareness and understanding conveyed through preaching is integral to the sacramental event, this well-intentioned but rather casual application of the term *sacrament* fails to do justice to the complexity and depth of the underlying theology of sacraments. It is, perhaps, an indication as well of the Episcopal Church's need for an updated, enriched Catechism, which, while remaining faithful to the tradition out of which our sacramental theology derives, could be complemented and enhanced by the use of accompanying footnotes, explanations, and other supplementary materials.

38. Duffy, *A Roman Catholic Theology of Pastoral Care*, 86.

39. Smith, *Health and Medicine in the Anglican Tradition*, 12.

40. Stoutzenberger, *Celebrating Sacraments*, 34.

acquire for us in the recounting, reliving and sharing of them in some way makes their effects accessible to us in the present moment, and in so doing allows us to interpret our present experience through the insights they afford us. As Bernard Cooke explains, ritual celebrations "are important contributors to our hermeneutic[41] of experience. They make us more aware of the significance of the key experiences of our lives, and this significance throws light on the meaning of the rest of our lives."[42] Furthermore, ritual helps to create community by uniting participants in a shared past, joining them together in the present by a common celebration and a shared understanding of the meaning of such events, as well as drawing participants together in a collective future by entrusting the members of the community with the responsibility of passing on such shared understandings. In this way ritual helps to ensure a continuity of order by serving as a medium by which communities are able to transmit their traditions and values.

We share an intrinsic need with humans everywhere and at all times to give symbolic expression in word, object, and ritual action to that which we most value. This expression takes the form of our worship. In fact, the very word *worship* derives from the Anglo-Saxon *worth-ship*. As the word suggests, observe Price and Weil, worship is "assigning worth to that which is thought to be worthy and giving expression to that estimate of value."[43]

Worship, says Weil, is the means through which human beings "express the ultimate place of God in their lives."[44] Rituals—those shared and repeated symbolic words and gestures by which a community or a people seeks to express, celebrate, and unite itself with those significant events and values from which it draws its identity—take the form, in our Anglican worship, of liturgy. Nowadays we have an understandable tendency to think of liturgy solely in terms of religious ceremony. However, the original Greek word *leitourgia*, from which we derive our own word *liturgy*, was not initially religious in nature. Roughly translated as "the work of the people" (from *laos,* "people") and *ergon,* "work"), the original sense of the term *liturgy* was more that of some sort of community service or duty, a public work or even an entertainment, undertaken *for* the people *by* a private citizen at his own expense.

---

41. Hermeneutic: pertaining to interpretation or explanation.
42. Cooke, *Sacraments and Sacramentality,* 39.
43. Price and Weil, *Liturgy for Living,* 8.
44. Weil, *Sacraments and Liturgy,* 1.

In time, the word *liturgy*, which had been employed by the Greek translators of the Old Testament (the Septuagint) chiefly in reference to the services of the temple in Jerusalem, found its way into the New Testament (in preference to the more common Greek term for religious services, *orgia*, the source of our English word *orgy*). While the term *liturgy* at first retained its older connotation, it gradually began to refer more and more to the liturgy of Christ, "our great high priest,"[45] whose ultimate public work or ministry/liturgy—the offering up of himself once and for all for our salvation—has secured for us what no other ministry could: redemption from sin and death.[46]

The letters of St. Paul expand on this idea of Christ as the true high priest. What this means for us as Christians, Price and Weil note, is that "Christ's life and death is in fact the one liturgy; and Christians whose lives are 'in Christ,' formed and shaped in his likeness, constitute a liturgy also. It would even be better to say that they constitute a working out and a making present 'in all times and in all places' of the one liturgy."[47] Christ's life and death, and his total obedience to God, have, as the author of the letter to the Hebrews declares, obtained for us a ministry (or in Greek, *liturgy*) of which all other worship is but a copy and a shadow. "By him, and with him, and in him, in the unity of the Holy Spirit" through our participation with and in Christ as his body, the church, the assembly of faith partakes in this one liturgy: Christ's liturgy.

However, one must never forget that at some level every sacramental rite is a genuinely human event. In other words, "the secret of Jesus' real presence is this: the way he freely comes to people today is through the proclamation of his word, the celebration of the sacraments, and the life and witness of the Christian community."[48] We are personally engaged by the elements of the rite which we recognize and to which we are able to relate on a human level. This is essential, because for worship to be 'authentic'—a favorite term of Weil's—it must encompass those forms of expression that engage us in our entirety: body, mind and spirit. Authentic worship is not so much about designing new forms of ritual in order to express a particular truth in a new context as it is an attempt to integrate sacramental awareness with authentic communal tradition. For all its creative, generative power,

---

45. Heb 4:14.

46. Heb 8:6.

47. Price and Weil, *Liturgy for Living*, 14–15.

48. Bliese and Gelder. *The Evangelizing Church*, 39.

authentic communal tradition arises out of a particular context, in which its various elements hold a particular significance, whatever fresh and original meaning they may acquire in their new ritual setting. Authentic worship incorporates those symbols and elements which are shared by the particular community, and with which we connect at a deep and personal level. Ronald Grimes explains: "Ritual performs this community-creating role by reminding us of the past, for it bridges a gap between past and present. Worship involves a remembering or making present of past events . . . and, through the representation, renewing the community's identity . . . In other words, ritual makes clear that we are parts of a tradition, of ideas and loyalties that have been handed over and reinterpreted over time."[49]

As Grimes rightly observes, "imagining ritual cannot transpire merely 'in the head' but is embodied and social."[50] Sacramental rites aim at human transformation and must therefore take our humanness into consideration. Meaning that reaches right down into the bone and marrow, as Grimes would say, is not something that can simply be fabricated by a committee or conjured up at will. Moreover, rituals are as much a function of time and place as they are transmitters of timeless truths. The actions and language employed in liturgical rites are both symbolic and functional. Unless we are fully sensitive to the power of both our traditional symbols and the newer ones, and of how and when they might best be employed, unless all the faithful are allowed to be participants and not merely spectators or by-standers, unless the environment of our rituals seeks to convey the Gospel's life-giving message, such rituals may inspire us, but will not necessarily leave us different people.

Through prayer and liturgy we attempt to give expression to the essentially inexpressible; through word and music, through body language and symbol, we seek to convey our understanding of the world, of the meaning of our place in it, and of the mystery of the divine. In turn, as we open ourselves up to God in our worship we find our hearts and imaginations shaped and stirred by the movement of the Holy Spirit through our participation in the liturgy. In the words of the old dictum, *lex orandi lex credendi*: roughly, "the way we pray shapes the way we believe."[51] The

---

49. Grimes, *Deeply into the Bone*, 13.

50. Ibid., 4.

51. This ancient Latin axiom is generally attributed to Prosper of Aquitaine (c. 435–442), a monk who served as secretary to Pope Leo the Great, from his work *The Defense of St. Augustine* (c. 440).

transformational power of our sacramental worship lies in the fact that it is not simply a commemoration or celebration of Christ's saving work, although these are certainly essential elements. It is, in the words of Nathan Mitchell, "not something we do for God but something God does in and for us."[52] Unquestionably, it is the means by which we remember and celebrate what God has done for us, but more than that, it is a means through which together we participate in this saving work through our shared identity as members of Christ's body. To use Rahner-like terminology: through our sacramental liturgies both God's self-gift and our free response to that gift are acknowledged and celebrated.

Attempting to understand sacraments apart from their liturgical context would surely prove as fruitless as examining each particular note of a piano concerto in isolation in order to better comprehend its emotional impact upon the listener. In the same way, to attempt to understand sacraments in a purely sterile theoretical/intellectual context overlooks the vital social dimension out of which they arise, that context in which they continue to effect their saving work.

This notion of corporate worship is central to the Catholic tradition from which Anglicanism derives. Certainly, we can worship God anywhere and in any place, as the unchurched are fond of declaring. However, what is also true is that in order to participate fully in the life of God we need to participate in the means by which God's grace is given its fullest tangible, perceptible expression: the *ekklesia* or church. Through the church the grace of God in the incarnate Christ is symbolized and therefore effected, or made actual, in the world. "To speak in this way of Christian worship," says Weil, "is to point to its fundamental sacramentality. The sacramental nature of certain specific liturgical actions is a sign of the underlying sacramentality of the Church itself." For this reason, he goes on to say, "this definition [of sacraments] must be understood . . . within the wider framework of the Church's life . . . or else there can result a separation of sacramental theory from sacramental practice, and of individual piety from the corporate experience."[53] Therefore, any inquiry into the nature of sacraments is sure to prove more illuminating when viewed within the context of the worshipping community.

Where once we tended to regard sacraments as though they were things to be examined and discussed in a detached and almost scientific

52. Mitchell, "The Spirituality of Christian Worship," 6.

53. Weil, *Sacraments and Liturgy*, 2.

manner, our current sacramental theology now reflects—however imperfectly—the truth that, in the words of Tad Guzie, "Sacraments are lived before they are put into categories and conceptualized."[54] We are increasingly coming to appreciate the fact that sacraments are *liturgical actions*. As the Catechism of the Catholic Church reminds us, "A sacramental celebration is a meeting of God's children with their Father, in Christ and the Holy Spirit; this meeting takes place in the form of a dialogue, through actions and words."[55] This simple statement perfectly reflects the significant shift sacramental theology has undergone in only a generation or so.

Sacrament and "Church": A Question of Origins

At this point, it would be helpful to address, albeit briefly, the question of the origin of the sacraments. How many sacraments are there? Two? Seven? Anglicans and Roman Catholics take the number seven for granted (seven sacraments, in the case of Roman Catholics, or two sacraments and five sacramental rites, in the case of Anglicans), yet for centuries, apart from baptism and the Eucharist, which were widely accepted everywhere as being of dominical[56] institution, there was no official consensus as to exactly what fell into the category of sacrament. The number of sacraments varied widely at various periods of history (depending upon the authority one consulted) from two to as many as twenty five or forty, as did, of course, the definition of sacraments. Fixing the number of what may properly be called sacraments to the now-familiar seven was the consequence of several factors. One, of course, was a need for order and regularity on the part of the church, a tightening up of the definition of sacrament which could be agreed upon everywhere. Another factor was the need to guarantee the sure and certain effectiveness of the sacraments as means of grace by unquestionably establishing their institution at key moments in the life of Christ. The Old School model of sacramental theology has tended to attach a great importance to their dominical institution—that is, their direct institution by Christ—attempting to locate in the Scriptures the precise time and place at which each was established: e.g., the sacrament of marriage at the wedding at Cana.[57]

---

54. Guzie, *The Book of Sacramental Basics*, 52.
55. *Catechism of the Catholic Church*, 1153.
56. Originating from or related to Jesus Christ.
57. As a matter of interest, while there are records of nuptial blessings dating back

The institution by Christ of each particular sacrament, a doctrine central to traditional sacramental theology since the twelfth century, was something that, in the periods of the Reformation and following, the Roman Church and the reformers attempted to prove or disprove, as the case may be, by pointing to specific chapters and verses in scripture. Contrary, however, to what was for a long time commonly-accepted teaching, our sacramental rites did not simply spring into existence, more or less ready-formed. Rather, it would be more accurate to say that in much the same way that our central theological doctrines (such as the Trinity) evolved over time as the church considered its many-faceted experiences of God in creation, the initial understanding of the sacraments shared by the early church was one which arose only gradually, under the guidance of the Holy Spirit, as Christians began to reflect together in a systematic way on the revelation of God's grace communicated to them through their experiences of the risen Christ.

Over time, the early Christians came to realize that in certain situations and in particular settings, such as the community's breaking of the bread and the sharing of the cup, Christ was with them in a very powerful, direct and special way. These important ritual observances were more than simply a conducive environment for the community's reflection on God's saving work in Jesus Christ. They served as a means not only by which Christ was present to them then and there, but through which, in remembering Christ's saving work, and locating their own experiences within the framework and context of those saving acts, they in turn were able to share in Christ's very life. "In other words," says Kenan Osborne, "the reality of sacramental life and action in the Church preceded any theoretical discussion of sacraments."[58]

Clearly, then, an insistence on being able to pinpoint the origin in scripture (in isolation from their essential lived context) of each particular sacramental rite reveals a lack of insight into the process by which they arose. This type of "blueprint sacramentology," as Schanz refers to it, has fallen into question in more recent times as we have become increasingly more aware of the complex historical and cultural contexts out of which the various sacramental rites developed.

---

as far as the fourth century, not until the Council of Trent in the sixteenth century was marriage accorded sacramental status.

58. Osborne, *Sacramental Theology*, 6.

Where does that leave us in regard to the question of their institution? The answer is that *yes*, unquestionably, Christ is their source. However, this is not the same thing as claiming that the sacraments were all instituted during our Lord's lifetime in some deliberate and formal manner. Instead, it might be more helpful (and accurate) to say that all the sacraments or sacramental rites have their source in Christ, given that Christ is the true, 'primordial' sacrament of God. That is to say, in his life and ministry, through his words and teachings, Jesus Christ became the real, perceptible, tangible sign of God's loving and saving grace in creation, of God's self-giving. Through his personal example our Lord showed us the ways in which the ordinary things of this world—oil, water, bread, wine— and our human encounters—could be transformative experiences because they could be the means of God's self-revelation. It is Christ, in fact, whom we encounter—and who encounters us—in every sacrament.

At the heart of our sacramental rites is the remembrance of God's saving deeds, and in most particular, the Paschal Mystery. While the outward elements of our liturgical prayer—ceremonial garments, music, texts, gestures, and so on—may reflect the particular culture, environment, or era of the society in which they originate, the impulse that gives rise to them is our own response to God's gracious self-giving. In the words of the Catechism, "We praise God . . . because God's being draws praise from us."[59]

Sacraments are celebrations of what God has done, is doing and will do for us. They possess the components not just of acknowledgment and of anticipation, but also of *anamnesis* (remembrance). However, this remembrance goes far beyond the mere recalling or re-enactment of these important foundational events. It involves a special kind of "active remembering,"[60] says Dennis Smolarski, enabling us to experience these salvific events in such a way that we are able to enter into them. "By remembering in God's presence what has been done for us through the power of the Spirit," says Richard Norris, "we participate in those events. They are present for us. Our time is that time. We are there."[61] Moreover, we 'remember' them not simply as individuals but as a celebrating community. In the words of Mary Birmingham, "The liturgy takes us with [Jesus]—in the

59. *Book of Common Prayer*, "Catechism," 857.
60. Smolarski, *Sacred Mysteries*, 175.
61. Norris, *Understanding the Faith of the Church*, 135.

liturgy's anamnesis we remember these events, and in the remembrance, we are there and it is now."[62]

Such is the power, remarks Timothy Sedgwick, of our sacramental worship and of the symbols it employs "to give expression to the meaning of a relation or an event, and in expressing such meaning to form 'the hearers of the word' so that their understandings and actions may more fully express and realize that meaning."[63] The very term by which the Episcopal Church identifies the greater body to which it belongs—the Anglican *Communion*—reflects the fact that our identity as church obtains from being united in Holy Communion, by which we are made "one body, one spirit in Christ, that we may worthily serve the world in his name."[64]

Anglicans often speak of the corporate nature of the church's worship—an apt depiction indeed, for in the words of the familiar post-Eucharistic prayer, we are "very members incorporate" in the mystical body of Jesus Christ, our Lord.[65] Clearly, therefore, sacraments are not private affairs. While the mystery of salvation is indeed a personal mystery—one that involves each one of us in a very particular way—it is not a solitary mystery. We are saved as a covenant people, as we are reminded time and time again, in order that God's salvation may reach to the ends of the earth.[66] The church does not exist for herself alone, or for the purpose of her own self-perpetuation, but in order to point beyond herself to her source, her Creator, who has called God's holy people forth to be effective public symbols of the grace of God as revealed in Christ. She serves, says Rahner, as "the ongoing presence of Jesus Christ in time and space, as the fruit of salvation which can no longer perish, and as the means of salvation to an individual in a tangible way and in the historical and social dimension."[67]

Sacrament and "Church": A Question of Origins

We have briefly examined the way in which a fuller, more authentic understanding of sacraments reveals their essential dynamic, relational nature to

62. Birmingham, *Word & Worship Workbook for Year B*, 705.

63. Sedgwick, *Sacramental Ethics*, 45.

64. *The Book of Common Prayer*, Holy Eucharist Rite II, Eucharistic Prayer D, 372.

65. Ibid., 372.

66. Isa 49:6.

67. Rahner, *Foundations of Christian Faith*. Quoted in Skelley, *The Liturgy of the World: Karl Rahner's Theology of Worship*, 143.

a degree extending far beyond the familiar Catechism definition of "out-ward and visible signs of inward and spiritual grace." A brief (but neces-sary) review of the evolution of the church's sacramental rites of healing reflects the way in which our understanding of them has developed over the centuries in an ever-evolving theology of health and ecclesiology.

The origins of the church's sacramental rites of anointing can be traced back to the Old Testament, where not only individuals, but holy objects, such as the tabernacle with its furnishings, utensils, altar and ritual items were anointed, and set apart for the Lord's service,[68] so that they might be "most holy; [and] whatever touches them [might] become holy."[69] Anoint-ing was associated with the commissioning of prophets,[70] the ordination of priests,[71] and the investiture of kings.[72] The detailed instructions for the creation and ritual application of this holy oil of anointing call attention to its sacred function: "you shall make no other like it in composition; it is holy, and it shall be holy to you."[73]

While Jewish law as laid out in the Old Testament prescribes the use of holy oil only for certain special individuals—"It shall not be poured upon the bodies of ordinary men."[74]—we know from such nonlegal citations such as Isaiah 1:6, which speaks of "bruises and sores and bleeding wounds" that have not been "pressed out, or bound up, or softened with oil," that common, ordinary olive oil was widely used for treating injuries in biblical times in Israel, as it was in many other ancient cultures. In the New Testa-ment, the account in Luke's gospel of the Good Samaritan, who tended the injuries of the hapless traveler who had been attacked by robbers, "pouring on oil and wine"[75] on his wounds, attests to the fact that at the time of Jesus, oil was commonly used for medicinal purposes.

There is no question but that ministry to the sick—including the unc-tion of the sick—was a central feature of the life of the early church in keep-ing with Jesus's own example and his commission to the disciples to preach the gospel, to cast out unclean spirits and to heal the sick. In Mark's gospel,

68. Exod 40:9.
69. Exod 30:32.
70. 1 Kgs 19:16.
71. Exod 28:41; 29:7; Lev 8:12; 21:10.
72. 1 Sam 10:1; 16:3; 1 Kgs 1:39; 2 Kgs 9:6; 11:12.
73. Exod 30: 32.
74. Ibid.
75. Luke 10:34.

for instance, we read that when the Twelve were sent out by Jesus "they . . . anointed with oil many that were sick and healed them."[76] Matthew's gospel recounts how Jesus commissioned the twelve to "heal the sick, raise the dead, cleanse lepers, [and] cast out demons."[77] Luke tells us that the twelve disciples "went through the villages, preaching the gospel and healing everyone."[78] The numerous accounts of healing with which the gospels and the Acts of the Apostles abound are proof that the theme of healing is central to the New Testament, just as it is clear that Jesus was regarded by his contemporaries as an extraordinary healer, judging by the number of people who either presented themselves to him or else were brought to him to be healed.

Such healings served not only as demonstrations of the compassion of God, but were meant to witness to God's ongoing work of restoration and redemption in creation. It is important, Polkinghorne reminds us, "to understand miracles within a consistent pattern of God's action,"[79] that is, to see how these miracles direct our attention beyond themselves to a divine reality at work. They point to the fact that there is something greater taking place than simply the mending of broken bodies and the healing of injured limbs. They are signs of the inbreaking of God's Kingdom; they point to Jesus, who is ushering in this kingdom, and demonstrating its nature. *The Ministry of Healing*, the report of the 1924 Lambeth Conference,[80] describes the healing miracles of Jesus not as private matters between the individual and God, but "*public* acts, *corporate* matters, *public* effective signs."[81] While they reveal the compassion of Christ for all suffering humanity, as evident in the ministry of healing and reconciliation given by Christ to the church, they are, in fact, both a call to conversion, as well as prophetic signs, a symbolization and a setting into motion of God's restoring activity by which all creation will one day be made whole and new.

---

76. Mark 6:13.

77. Matt 10:8.

78. Luke 9:6.

79. Polkinghorne, *Science and Providence*, 57.

80. Lambeth Conference: a meeting of Anglican bishops from around the world, "for the purpose of taking common council and adopting reports and resolutions of an advisory nature for the guidance of its national Churches, Provinces, and Dioceses," which takes place every ten years. See Harper, *The Episcopalian's Dictionary*, 96–97.

81. Episcopal Church, *Report of the Joint Commission on the Ministry of Healing*, 14.

Two passages in particular in the New Testament clearly provide a biblical warrant for the church's tradition of anointing with oil and the laying on of hands for healing. One, of course, is the oft-quoted letter of James, and the other, the above-mentioned passage from Mark. The passage from James particularly testifies to the early church's notably holistic view of anointing not simply as medicine for the body, but, in the words of the popular hymn, for "the sin-sick soul."

> Is any among you sick? Let him call for the elders of the church, and let them pray over him, anointing him with oil in the name of the Lord; and the prayer of faith will save the sick man, and the Lord will raise him up; and if he has committed sins, he will be forgiven. Therefore confess your sins to one another, and pray for one another, that you may be healed. The prayer of a righteous man has great power in its effects.[82]

What is particularly interesting about this passage is not simply that it provides us with evidence of the importance of the ministry of healing in the early church, but that importance is attributed to the presence of the elders, the representatives of the community. Particularly noteworthy from the modern-day church's point of view is the fact that up until the seventh century the authorization to anoint was not restricted to the clergy. In the early church, in the same way that Communion was made available to the faithful to take home with them, oil presented by the faithful and blessed by the bishop during the Eucharist was available for the purpose of anointing oneself or taking to the homebound when necessary. Clearly, then, the presence of the elders is not for the purpose of making oil for anointing available. Rather, says Thomas Talley, their responsibility is to anoint and pray as *representatives of the community*.[83] The letter of James states, "Therefore confess your sins to one another, and pray for one another, that you may be healed."[84]

At this point in history the role of the presbyter was not unlike that of the elder in the Jewish community, namely, that of counselor and administrator. The threefold order of ministry—bishop, priest and deacon—would not take the form with which we are accustomed today until around the end of the apostolic age.[85] So the presence of the elders here is not so much

---

82. James 5:14–16.

83. Talley, "Healing,: Sacrament or Charism?," 523.

84. James 5:14–16.

85. *Apostolic Age* or *Apostolic Era*: "The period of the Christian church, regarded

a sacerdotal, or priestly function, as it is a testimony to the early church's understanding of the corporate aspect of illness: the fact that the suffering of one member affects the well-being of the whole body. In addition, says Talley, "the sickness or dying of a Christian needs above all to be held within the community, and . . . the presbyters are summoned as the constitutive representatives of the community . . . Their function [in this period] is not to heal nor is it yet to administer last rites, but to protect the sick member from dereliction and separation from the ecclesial body."[86]

The apostolic age is marked by numerous reports of miraculous healings, which are never seen as an end in themselves, but instead regarded as signs of Christ's "victory of life and peace"[87] over the powers of death and darkness. There is little indication of a formal ministry of healing in the earliest years of the church, although it is apparent that the practice of anointing continued to hold a place of importance in the life of the community.[88]

While there is no indication of an official liturgy for anointing at this early date, by the third century we find in an early liturgical treatise known as *The Apostolic Tradition*—attributed to the Greek-born presbyter and prolific author, Hippolytus of Rome—a prayer for the blessing of the oil of the sick, the earliest example available of such a prayer. There is little evidence that it was used to anoint the dying. A little later, the blessing for the oil of the sick found in the sacramentary[89] of St. Serapion of Thmuis[90] indicates that at this time the blessed oil was held to be "a medicament of life and salvation, unto health and soundness of soul and body and spirit, unto perfect well-being."[91] It was the power of God working through the blessed oil which was considered to be important, not the individual applying it. Still

---

as definitive by many, bounded by the resurrection of Jesus Christ (c. AD 35) and the death of the last apostle (c. AD 90?). The ideas and practices of this period were widely regarded as normative, at least in some sense or to some degree, in many church circles." McGrath, *The Christian Theology Reader*, 703.

86. Talley, "Healing: Sacrament or Charism," 523.

87. *The Book of Common Prayer*, 456.

88. Not only did anointing figure in the pastoral care of the sick, but it was also used in the initiation of catechumens, and also for exorcisms.

89. *Sacramentary*: a liturgical book containing the prayers and sacramental rites of the Church.

90. C. AD 360. Bishop of Thmuis in the Nile Delta, around the region of Alexandria, Egypt, contemporary of Athanasius.

91. Palmer, *Sacraments and Forgiveness*, 280. Quoted in Gusmer, *And You Visited Me*, 13.

later, in the fifth century we see the emergence of the sacramental status of the anointing of the sick when it is referred to as a *genus sacramenti* ("a kind of sacrament") by Pope Innocent I.

From the eighth to the twelfth century, several significant changes took place in the church's practice of the anointing of the sick. First, because of the tendency on the part of many of the uneducated faithful to treat the blessed oil almost like a magic potion, the responsibility of its administration eventually became the sole prerogative of the clergy. Laypeople were no longer allowed to anoint. Under Emperor Charlemagne,[92] whose desire for political (and correspondingly) religious uniformity within the newly created Holy Roman Empire expressed itself in, among other things, the establishment of a standardized Roman rite, a formal ritual for anointing was created. This found its way into the section of the newly revised sacramentary containing rites for the dying. The anointing of the sick became a sacrament reserved for the gravely ill, and the emphasis shifted from anointing for healing to anointing as preparation for death, and the spiritual graces associated therewith, most specifically, the forgiveness of sins. An increasing tendency on the part of the church to equate sin with sickness resulted in what had originally been a sacrament of healing taking on an increasingly penitential nature. It was now generally administered after the sacrament of penance, which, because of the often formidable penalties entailed by that sacrament at this time, was frequently postponed until death was imminent. By the twelfth century the church's sacrament of healing had effectively been transformed into "extreme unction" (literally, "last anointing").

As a result of the influence of the later Scholastic theologians,[93] who were concerned in particular with the supernatural grace of the sacrament, there was a corresponding *de*emphasis in respect to its healing effects, which were generally considered as little more than a means of allowing one to depart the world with a minimum of physical discomfort. It was under the title of extreme unction that anointing found its way into Peter Lombard's[94] *Senteniarum libri quattuor* or *Four Books of the Sentences*, that

92. c. AD 742–814.

93. I will say more about this later in the section on the sacramental models.

94. Peter Lombard (c. 1100–1160). Born near Novaro, in Lombardy, studied in Bologna, Rheims, and at the School of St. Victor in Paris, taught in Paris at the Cathedral School, made Bishop of Paris in 1159. His *Senteniarum libri quattuor*, which drew upon Scripture and the writings of the Church Fathers, became a standard theological reference during the Middle Ages.

major medieval textbook of theology in which the number of sacraments, which had varied widely throughout the centuries, at last became fixed at the now-familiar number of seven.

At the Council of Florence, in the fifteenth century, under Pope Eugenius IV, in the doctrinal statement prepared by the council, which defined the essential elements of anointing, extreme unction was officially listed as the fifth sacrament. It was to be given only to the gravely ill—those in danger of dying—who were to be anointed on the senses (eyes, ears and nostrils), as well as the hands and feet, for the healing of the soul (and in some cases, the body). In addition, the minister of the sacrament was to be a priest. Later, the Council of Trent, in the sixteenth century, would issue a document noting the relationship of extreme unction and penance, both instituted by Christ, both of which carried the assurance of the forgiveness of sins, and both of which as a result, Martos observes, "brought courage and confidence to the dying and occasionally even bodily health to the sick."[95] At this time such questions as the age at which one might be allowed to receive extreme unction, and whether or not it was permissible to anoint someone who seemed to be dead, increasingly occupied canon lawyers, along with the question of the graces extreme unction imparted and whether its purpose was the removal of venial sins[96] or original sin.

In the aftermath of the Protestant Reformation, the sacrament of extreme unction, like many of the other sacraments of the Roman Church, came under fire from Protestant reformers who disputed its institution by Christ, and who maintained that the sacramental rite of unction had in fact arisen in the early church (although whether it was actually meant for the purpose of healing or whether or not it was intended for the benefit of the dying was a further point of dispute among the reformers). In the minds of many of the reformers, such as Calvin, the sacrament of anointing was the outmoded relic of a bygone age, and one with which too many abuses—such as the anointing of the dead—had come to be associated to merit its continuance. Most strenuously, the reformers challenged the official teaching of the Catholic Church, which declared that the sacrament of extreme unction could remove sins or confer grace. Those reformers who did endorse the anointing of the sick contended, moreover, that there was

95. Martos, *Doors to the Sacred*, 341.

96. "One commits *venial sin* when, in a less serious matter, he does not observe the standard prescribed by the moral law, or when he disobeys the moral law in a grave matter, but without full knowledge or without complete consent" (*The Catechism of the Catholic Church*, 1862).

no scriptural basis for limiting the ministers of anointing to the clergy. The response of the bishops at the Council of Trent was to declare that it was the Church's right to determine the appropriate ministers of the sacraments.

In contrast to the concerns of the reformers, the bishops of the Council of Trent, says James Empereur, "were convinced that the problems with extreme unction were more pastoral than theological, and so were concerned with clarification and improvement of the way the sacrament was administered."[97] Significantly, while it continued to regard unction as a sacrament for the dying, the Council of Trent did not choose to restrict its use solely to preparation for death, but declared that "it comforts and strengthens the soul of the sick person. It gives him great confidence in the divine mercy," so that he might more easily bear "the inconvenience and trials of his illness" and resist "the temptations of the devil." On an even more hopeful note, it affirmed that "this anointing occasionally restores health to the body if health would be of advantage to the salvation of the soul."[98]

The *Rituale Romanum* of 1614—the Roman Catholic Church's official sacramentary—both simplified and standardized the rite of extreme unction, making it more suitable for use in the case of those near death. Later, in 1747, in the papal constitution *Pia Mater*, Pope Benedict XIV resolved the controversy over whether the primary effect of anointing was the forgiveness of sins or the removal of the remnants of sin by declaring that "those who received the sacraments with the proper disposition were fully absolved both from their sins and from any punishment that was due for them."[99] Aside from these clearly defined metaphysical effects, says Martos, "At least to those who received it while conscious, extreme unction could indeed be a sign of God's mercy and forgiveness . . . And to those who saw the rite being performed it could be a similar sign, bringing some consolation to the bereaved that those whom they lost through death were assured of eternal life. In this sense it was a transition ritual, a rite of passage, which enabled the dying to enter the final phase of their life with inner strength and peace, which enabled friends and relatives to make the emotionally difficult transition from living with their loved ones to living without them."[100]

97. Empereur, *Prophetic Anointing*, 67.
98. Denzinger and Schoenmettzer, *Enchiridion symbolorum*; quoted in ibid., 81.
99. Martos, *Doors to the Sacred*, 342.
100. Ibid., 342.

In the post-Tridentine period, in the minds of the general public (both Roman Catholic and Anglican), the anointing of the sick continued to retain its association with 'last rites.' However, in the centuries between the Council of Trent and the Second Vatican Council, there was a gradual and widespread rethinking—both officially on the part of theologians and unofficially on the part of the clergy who anointed—of the question of just how gravely ill one had to be to merit anointing. Empereur observes, "In effect, what happened was a broadening in the interpretation of the kind of danger of death required for the administration of this sacrament. Such a growing benign interpretation ultimately undermined the thinking that supported this sacrament as extreme unction."[101]

Modern advances in biblical scholarship called into dispute many of the medieval interpretations of the critical biblical texts upon which the church's theology of the sacrament of unction had been grounded. In addition, a growing awareness of the limitations under which traditional sacramental theology had for so long labored due to its scholastic methodology, says Fink—most notably, its lack of a sound ecclesiological base— "exposed the scholastic mode of reflection as no longer adequate to the task of understanding the church's sacramental life."[102] The evolution of modern sacramental theology "from its preconciliar scholastic garb to its contemporary theological 'shape,'"[103] Fink observes, was the result of a number of converging factors, such as the "liturgical movement of the nineteenth and twentieth centuries, [and] the advance in biblical scholarship in both Protestant and Catholic circles."[104] There was, as well, an ever-increasing appreciation of the biblical and patristic foundations of the church's sacramental rites, which gradually led to a shift in focus from the more objective *quid pro quo* ("do this in order to receive grace") orientation to a more interpersonal mode by which sacramental liturgy serves as a means of "saving dialogue"[105] between God and humankind. As well, out of this refreshed theological perspective arose a greater understanding of the important public and participatory dimension of the sacramental rite of anointing.

A glance at earlier forms of the *Book of Common Prayer*'s Office for the Visitation of the Sick, such as that contained in the first Prayer Book

101. Empereur, *Prophetic Anointing*, 70.

102. Fink, *Praying the Sacraments*, 47–48.

103. Ibid., 46.

104. Ibid., 48.

105. Ibid.

of 1549, makes it clear that their focus was not so much that of physical recovery as on helping the faithful to prepare themselves for death, on ensuring that the sick "may be alwayes in a readiness to dye, whensoever it may please almighty God to call them." In the 1549 rite, Empereur notes, "The theological emphasis moves in the direction of viewing sickness as a visitation of God to try or punish the person. Repentance and patient submission is the response that is expected by one who shares in the suffering of Christ through baptism."[106]

Nor is the tone of any of the other Visitation Offices before the nineteenth century much more encouraging. In the 1789 Prayer Book, for instance, the minister is instructed to advise the sick person to put his affairs in order and to draw up his will, if he has not yet done so, "for the better discharging of his conscience, and the quietness of his Executors."[107] The common expectation was that if one was being anointed, the situation must be very grave indeed, and with the obvious limitations of the medical sciences at the time, there was little one could do but prepare oneself for the inevitable.

However, as physician and author Herbert Benson observes, somewhere around the latter half of the nineteenth century, the speedometer of medicine "jumped from 0 to 100 miles per hour"[108] due to groundbreaking new scientific and medical discoveries by the likes of Louis Pasteur and Robert Koch. Prior to the mid-nineteenth century, says Larry Dossey,

> people did not understand that the diseases that carried them away were related to microorganisms. The "germ theory" of disease did not come into use in the English-language medical literature until around 1870. In addition to threats from infectious diseases, people faced broken bones, cancer, metabolic diseases, endocrine disorders, cardiovascular ailments, and so on. The result was that people were burdened by a sense of mystery, vulnerability, chronic dread, and resignation—the certainty that "this is the way things are and always have been" . . . Then, beginning roughly in the

---

106. Empereur, *Prophetic Anointing*, 66.

107. There was an 1892 Prayer Book, but it was almost identical with the 1789 edition. In both cases, in regard to the drawing up of a will, the rubrics add: "*But men should often be put in remembrance to take order for the settling of their temporal estates, whilst they are in health.*"

108. Benson, *Timeless Healing*, 113.

decade of the 1860's . . . medicine began to change radically and dramatically by becoming more scientific.[109]

The ushering in of this scientific era of medicine, which brought with it a greater likelihood of recovery from illnesses and physical conditions that had hitherto invariably proved fatal, required the church to reconsider the essential pastoral context out of which the sacramental rite of unction had originally arisen, namely, the care of the sick.

In addition, just as medical advances were changing the once fatalistic aspect of unction, so also the social sciences were making their mark upon it, not merely by raising considerations about the psychological dimensions of physical illness, but by providing theologians with a new vocabulary with which to discuss sacramental theology. In his essay "Renewing Worship: The Recovery of Classical Patterns," Geoffrey Wainwright notes: "In the twentieth century, the human sciences have devoted sustained attention to the complex systems of symbols—words, gestures, objects, even institutions—by which communities describe, interpret, and fashion reality, express and form their thoughts, emotions, and values, and communicate across time and space in ways that both build and convey traditions as well as allowing and reflecting social relations in the present.[110]

Other factors, such as the growing popularity of the charismatic movement, with its positive emphasis on the gifts of the Spirit, and on healing and renewal, posed a dramatic challenge to the familiar equating of the anointing of the sick with 'last rites.' Within the Anglican Communion, the subject of the church's ministry of healing took on an increasing importance which was reflected at several Lambeth Conferences and General Conventions,[111] resulting in numerous reports and studies within the Anglican Communion that, in particular, acknowledged the complementary roles of medicine, the social sciences, and the church's own ministry of healing. "As a result of their encounter with Pentecostal spirituality," reads one Church of England report to the House of Bishops, "Anglican laity as well as clergy (like charismatics in other denominations) began to pray for others with a sense of expectancy that spiritual gifts of healing will be manifested."[112]

---

109. Dossey, *Reinventing Medicine*, 17–18.

110. Wainwright, "Renewing Worship," 45–56.

111. The General Convention, which takes place every three years, is the national legislative body of the Episcopal Church.

112. Church of England, House of Bishops, *A Time to Heal*, 12.

In the Roman Catholic Church, out of the liturgical revisions emerging from the Second Vatican Council, the term "extreme unction" was replaced by "Anointing and Pastoral Care of the Sick," in order to restore to the sacrament its original pastoral perspective. Now it was no longer reserved only for those who were at the point of death. Henceforth, according to the Constitution on the Sacred Liturgy, "as any one of the faithful begins to be in danger of death from sickness or old age, the fitting time for him to receive this sacrament has certainly already arrived."[113] In contrast to its previous once-and-for-all character, the anointing of the sick could be repeated if necessary, depending on the circumstances. Furthermore, the rites of anointing were to be revised in order to "correspond to the varying conditions of the sick who receive the sacrament."[114] Other elements were added that would serve to dramatically transform it and make it more pastoral and less penitential, more hopeful in nature. The liturgical revisions of Vatican II and of our present *Book of Common Prayer* are representative of a widespread ecumenical concern to reestablish, not simply the original emphasis on health and healing, but the ecclesial nature of all the sacraments, including the Anointing of the Sick.

Conclusion

The purpose of this study, as noted, is to examine certain of the Episcopal Church's past and current sacramental rites of healing in order to consider the ways in which they do—or do not—support the gradual, cumulative and ongoing spiritual conversion, renewal and growth of both individuals and of the assembly of faith in such a way as to form a 'ministering/sacramental community' whose mission it is to serve God through participation in Christ's redeeming work. To this end I have attempted, firstly, to explain what we mean when we speak of 'sacraments,' and to define the role they play in the life and worship of the church in the Catholic tradition of which the Anglican faith is a part. In doing so I have attempted to describe, briefly, the shift in sacramental theology set into motion in the decades prior to and following the Second Vatican Council, which might be described not

113. Pope Paul VI, Constitution on The Sacred Liturgy/Sacrosanctum Concilium, III, 76, 4 December 4, 1963. Hereafter, all references to the *Constitution on the Sacred Liturgy* will appear in the text as SC, followed by the appropriate section and chapter number(s).

114. Ibid.

so much as a *revision* of the church's sacramental theology as a *renewal* of it, a recovery of the appreciation of the church's own essential sacramental nature, and the way in which that sacramental nature is expressed through the church's liturgy.

In the next chapter, I will attempt to compare and contrast preconciliar and postconciliar[115] understandings of sacraments by drawing up two contrasting models of sacramental theology by which to analyze and critique our rites of healing. With the help of these contrasting models, I will explore, briefly, the way in which the communal dimension of the Church's rites of healing—and pastoral care in general—became increasingly narrowed in focus over the centuries, to be gradually reduced by an increasing emphasis on personal salvation with a corresponding de-emphasis on the corporate aspect of healing. Finally, I will examine the gradual reappearance of the communal dimension in the Episcopal Church's sacramental rites of healing up to the present day.

115. The term *conciliar* generally describes that which results from, relates to, or is generated by a council. For the purposes of this study the council in question is the Second Vatican Council (1962–1965), and the term *conciliar* pertains in particular to that historical period, which was a time of remarkable liturgical and theological change and renewal not just for the Roman Catholic Church but for the church throughout the world. Accordingly, the term 'preconciliar' means "prior to the Second Vatican Council," while 'postconciliar' means "subsequent to the Second Vatican Council."

2

The Old School and New School Models of Sacraments

Introduction

THERE ARE BASICALLY TWO ways in which to undertake a study of the sacraments. The first is a *sacramenta in genere*, or sacraments-in-general, approach. This method begins with a general theology of the sacraments, explains what all of the sacraments share in common and then proceeds to arrive at one or more general principles which can be applied to them all. The second approach regards sacraments from a more 'holistic' perspective, with a focus not simply on what each one does and how it does it, but with a consideration for the context from which each arises: the mystery of salvation. In order to evaluate the Episcopal Church's current sacramental rites of healing, I have chosen to contrast and compare two particular models of sacramental theology, which, following the example of Tad Guzie, I will refer to as the Old School model and the New School model.[1]

For the purposes of this study, the 'Old School' model is characterized by the sacramental/liturgical mindset that prevailed prior to the Second Vatican Council. The Old School model is dominated by the theology of Scholasticism,[2] a method of philosophical and theological speculation which from the thirteenth to the twentieth centuries characterized Roman Catholic theology. The two models differ chiefly in the fact that the

1. Guzie, *The Book of Sacramental Basics*, 1–2.
2. Particularly the later Scholastics.

Old School model is distinguished by a markedly objective, philosophical approach, which, says Fink, "asked the sorts of questions of sacraments that were more fitting to scientific objects: who made it? where did it come from? what constitutes it to be what it is? when did it cease to be? who may use it? when? and for what purpose?" [3] The New School model on the other hand, regards sacraments in a more dynamic, relational way, as part of a process by which believers are led to a personal encounter with Christ, and which arise in part out of the church's reflection on its lived experience of the Paschal Mystery, "in which, by hearing [Christ's] Word and celebrating his Sacraments, we share in his victory over life and death."[4]

In order to better understand its effect upon the church's sacramental theology, one needs to appreciate the historical context out of which Scholasticism arose. During the Middle Ages,[5] many of the great works of classical literature, long thought to have been lost, began to find their way back to the West via Arabic translations, by way of Moorish Spain. "We think of Italy as the birthplace of the Renaissance," says Jacob Bronowski. "But the conception was in Spain in the twelfth century, and it is symbolized and expressed by the famous school of translators at Toledo, where the ancient texts were turned from Greek (which Europe had forgotten) through Arabic and Hebrew into Latin."[6] Within the next hundred years or so (from approximately 1150 to 1250), all these Greek, Arabic, and Jewish classical works, zealously assembled from Greece, the Middle East, and Asia, were to have a profound impact upon Christian philosophy and theology. The effect of this sudden explosion of knowledge (much of it from faulty renderings of the originals, which were then translated with varying degrees of accuracy into Latin) on Western sacramental theology cannot be overestimated. In the Latin West, the consequence of this flood of information, and in particular, the scientific and metaphysical works of Aristotle, was to inspire theologians to seek to achieve a similar intellectual clarity in matters theological.

The distinctive Western optimism in the power of human reason to master not just the laws of nature, but the nature of the divine, is reflected in

---

3. Fink, *Worship: Praying the Sacraments*, 47.

4. *The Book of Common Prayer*, The Great Vigil of Easter: The Lighting of the Paschal Candle, 285.

5. Approximately AD 500–1500, the period following the fall of the Roman Empire and preceding the period of the Renaissance.

6. Bronowski, *The Ascent of Man*, 177.

the confidence with which the Scholastics sought to apply the Aristotelian method not just to mathematics and physics but also to theology. In the process, says Colin Morris, the exposition of doctrine became "no longer, as in the past, primarily the responsibility of bishops or monks. They had been superseded as theologians by a new force in the church: the masters, who taught in the cathedral schools of the twelfth century and the universities of the thirteenth."[7] Scholasticism, observes Fink, "employed a specific model in its reflection and examination of the sacraments. It looked on them as 'objective realities,' quasi-scientific objects, which could be observed and analyzed from without."[8]

The Aristotelian philosophical vocabulary employed by the Scholastics, says Martos, "was replete with technical terms such as 'substance' and 'accident,' 'matter' and 'form,' 'power' and 'activity' [as] medieval thinkers did their best to understand their meanings and then use them to develop philosophical explanations of the Christian mysteries."[9] This desire to scrutinize the sacraments in a scientific manner was due, in no small part, I believe, to the fact that at the heart of the sacraments lies the mystery of salvation. The temperament of the West is one that is notoriously impatient with mystery—a trait that has proven beneficial when channeled into the field of scientific exploration, but has more often proven disastrous in respect to sacramental theology. The problem with such an academic approach, Duffy points out, is that "we can forget that sacraments are not about theory but about a Spirit-empowered experience of Christ within his community, the Church."[10] Clearly, to attempt to reduce the church's sacraments into neat little formulas and definitions without regarding them in the context of the celebrating community is to ignore the all-important truth that these sacraments are not 'things' to be received, but celebrations of the church, the body of Christ, who is the primary sacrament of all.

---

7. Morris, "Christian Civilization (1050–1400)," in McManners, *The Oxford Illustrated History of Christianity*, 215.

8. Fink, *Worship: Praying the Sacraments*, 47.

9. Martos, *Doors to the Sacred*, 61.

10. Duffy, *Alternative Futures for Worship*, 29.

The New School Model

If the Old School model is characterized by a tendency to regard the various sacraments in a detached and philosophical manner, as quasi-objective, metaphysical realities rather than graced encounters, as we will see, by contrast, that the New School model, shared by both Anglicans and Roman Catholics, regards sacraments as *liturgical celebrations*, acts of the Church in assembly by which, through our encounter with the Risen One, says Fink, "we are drawn into Christ's own truth. Our imaginations become shaped by the truths of Christ. Our affections take on the affections of Christ. And the behavior we enact together is Christ's own behavior toward God . . . and toward those whom he names as friends."[11]

In order to better appreciate the impact this shift in perspective has had on sacramental theology, it is helpful at this point to compare and contrast some of the significant ways in which the one model differs from the other, and in particular, to consider them both from an historical perspective. To this end, we will consider the following:

1. The Models on Sacraments and Grace
2. The Models and Church
3. The Models and Liturgical Celebration
4. The Models and the Scope of Sacramental Effects
5. The Models and the Relation of Word and Sacrament

11. Fink, *Worship: Praying the Sacraments*, 9.

12. Hughes, "Sacraments and Ordination." Note also that the introduction to Guzie's *The Book of Sacramental Basics* summarizes this particularly well.

13. Temple, "The Sacramental Universe." In *Nature, Man and God,* 485.

The Models on Sacraments and Grace.

Old School Model	New School Model
Grace is an *it*, an "infused quasi-substance (Catholic) or imputed judicial decree (Protestant)."[12]	Grace is not an *it*, but relationship with God. Rather than "something other than God, imparted by Him, [grace] is the very Love of God (which is Himself) approaching and seeking entry to the soul of man."[13]
Matter is base and profane until transformed by the sacramental liturgy; "Liturgical practice *suppresses* and *spiritualizes* the material nature of the symbolic elements."[14] Sacraments convey grace to a world in which it is normally lacking: the Old School model "portrays the presence of grace as an intervention of God at definite points in space and time. The presence of grace is restricted to very limited circumstances and events."[15]	"[The] 'secular' world is from the outset always encompassed and permeated with the grace of God's self-communication . . . God's self-communication is present in our world and our history in two forms: as an offer made to our freedom and as the acceptance or rejection by our freedom of this offer."[16]
No intrinsic relationship between the sacramental *sign* and the *grace* imparted by it: "All previous theories of sacramental causality, Catholic or Protestant, tend to treat the relationship between sacramental sign and the grace conveyed as arbitrary and extrinsic."[17]	Intrinsic relationship between the sacramental sign and the grace conveyed by it: "the symbol is the external manifestation of the form, but gives that form a way of actualizing itself in reality."[18]

The Catechism tells us that sacraments are "given by Christ as sure and certain means by which we receive [God's] grace."[19] But what is grace? Turning again to the Catechism, we find grace defined as "God's favor toward us, unearned and undeserved; by grace God forgives our sins, enlightens our minds, and strengthens our wills."[20] Grace is, in fact, one of the most important attributes of God as we understand God; it is the "gracious, nurturing, forgiving, calling-to-account in relationship"[21] aspect of God's love, attested to again and again in the Hebrew Scriptures. One finds it, for instance, celebrated throughout the psalms ("God will send forth his steadfast love and his faithfulness"[22]), in the prophets ("I knew that thou art a gracious God and merciful, slow to anger, and abounding in steadfast love."[23]), and in other passages in which God's *graciousness* is used to describe God's desire to draw humankind into personal and intimate relationship. This is not the language of metaphysics, but of encounter, and such an encounter cannot but leave us changed.[24]

In the New Testament, while the term *grace* retains its earlier sense of favor, it begins to acquire a greater complexity of meaning. The word by which the early Christian writers most often chose to translate the word *grace*—the Greek word *charis*—refers not simply to the favors bestowed upon one, but, as Robert Gleason points out, conveys the sense of "a certain internal power by which one is able to perform marvelous things,"[25] God's power at work within, as in Acts 11:23, which describes Barnabas's visit to the church in Antioch: "When he came and saw the grace of God, he was

14. Ibid.

15. Skelley, *The Liturgy of the World*, 56.

16. Ibid.

17. Ibid.

18. Callahan, "Karl Rahner's Theology of Symbol," 196.

19. Catechism, 858.

20. Ibid.

21. Neelands, Course lecture for TRT 3566F, "Studies in Anglican Theology," Trinity College, Toronto, September 16, 1999.

22. Ps 57:3.

23. Jonah 4:2.

24. As Vorgrimler reminds us, "'encounter' here means more than simply a momentary meeting. It has a mystical meaning, i.e., human beings unite themselves as intensively as possible with the person and destiny of Jesus Christ" (*Sacramental Theology,* 80).

25. Gleason, *Grace*, 42.

glad; and he exhorted them all to remain faithful to the Lord with steadfast purpose. "

In the writings of St. Paul, grace becomes an important part of the new language of salvation, where it serves to describe not simply God's gracious self-giving, but God's self-giving *in Christ* as the result of God's desire to effect salvation for all, even the most seemingly undeserving, as in Romans 3:23, in which Paul writes that "since all have sinned and fall short of the glory of God, they are justified by his grace as a gift." This theology of grace arises out of Paul's distinctive message to the early Christian communities, proclaiming that God justifies all sinners apart from the law, through God's grace in Christ.

Grace as personal relationship with God, or grace as the influence or power of God working within: the early church struggled to resolve the apparent tension created by these two understandings of grace. In the Eastern church, the emphasis placed by the Greek church fathers on the supreme gift of grace as God's divine self-giving, says Schanz, embraced a more biblical understanding of grace as God's presence in humankind: "The Fathers of the East laid special stress in sacramental theology on the divinizing aspect of sacramental grace. Christ is our supreme model of divine sonship; and through the sacraments . . . fashions and models us as second sons, endowing us with the graces of sonship of the eternal Father in the power of the Holy Spirit."[26] Thus, he says, "Eastern theology emphasized a more personal dimension of grace, with God making himself present as friend."[27]

However, if the emphasis in the East was on the gift of grace as God's divine self-giving and the mode of God's indwelling, in the West, in contrast, one finds an increasing emphasis on the question of exactly *how* that grace is able to effect its transformation within men and women. In the writings of Tertullian[28] one finds the first attempt at expressing a formal theological doctrine of grace, although it is not until St. Augustine[29] that a clearly articulated doctrine of grace actually begins to emerge.

The term *grace*, St. Augustine points out, is derived from the Latin *gratia*, meaning "gift," originating as it does in God's generous self-offering,

26. Schanz, *The Sacraments of Life and Worship*, 66.

27. Schanz, *Introduction to the Sacraments*, 56.

28. Quintus Septimus Florens Tertullian (160–215), born in Carthage, North Africa, Father of Latin Theology.

29. Augustine of Hippo (354–430), born Tagaste in North Africa. Bishop of Hippo Regius in North Africa, one of the Doctors of the Church.

which awaits our faithful response. But how free *are* human beings to choose to accept this precious gift? Augustine and others like him, says Schanz, "grappled with the tension between God's grace as an *influence* upon the human person, his mind and will, and human freedom, which God's grace leaves intact."[30] On account of Adam's disobedience, says Augustine, human nature became tainted and weakened by sin. As a result, despite the gift of free will bestowed upon us by the Creator, our minds have become darkened and our wills corrupted. We are incapable of *not* sinning, and we are dependent on God's grace to redeem us. Augustine quotes John 15:5: "for apart from me you can do nothing."

Accordingly, it is only through God's grace that we can be saved, for it is God's grace that leads us to repentance, making it possible for us to be pardoned. The grace of God through Jesus Christ, Augustine explains, is "that by which alone men are delivered from evil, and without which they do absolutely no good thing, whether in thought, or will and affection, or in deed; not only in order that they may know by the manifestation of the same what should be done, but moreover in order that by its enabling they may do with love what they know."[31] This gift of grace, in other words, works to transform us from within so that we are freed from the thrall to sin, and given divine assistance in order to lead holy lives.

What emerges in Augustine, moreover, is an understanding of justification by grace through faith, which becomes a process of *growth* in grace, and he quotes: "for God is at work in you, both to will and to work for his good pleasure."[32] It is a picture, says David Neelands, of grace at work within and without: God offering us grace, causing us to delight in that grace, humankind "floating in the grace to the vision of God, God allowing us to share in God's nature, and finally rewarding us by crowning his gifts in us with glory."[33]

By and large, says Alister McGrath, the theologians of the early Middle Ages were "content to regard grace as a shorthand term for the graciousness or liberality of God."[34] By the late Middle Ages, however, the notion of grace gradually takes on an increasingly abstract, somewhat impersonal quality,

---

30. Schanz, *Introduction to the Sacraments*, 56.

31. *Admonition and Grace*, 2:3. In *The Essential Augustine*, 176.

32. Phil 2:13.

33. Neelands, Course lecture for TRT 3566F.

34. McGrath, *Christian Theology: An Introduction*, 3rd ed., 451.

due in no small part to a growing tendency on the part of the manuals[35] to break down each of the sacraments separately in order to interpret them in philosophical categories.

St. Thomas Aquinas, in many ways the greatest disciple of St. Augustine, in an attempt to effect a harmony between the question of God's sovereignty and humankind's free will, is the first to categorize grace in terms of *actual* grace[36] (*gratia gratis data*, or "grace which is freely given") and *habitual* grace[37] (*gratia gratis faciens*, or "grace which makes pleasing"). It is clear, says Aquinas, "that man cannot prepare himself to receive the light of grace except by the gratuitous help of God moving him inwardly."[38] Actual grace, according to Aquinas, refers to a series of divine actions or influences upon human nature, while habitual grace is a substance, a disposition or quality in the soul, "something which [happens] to human nature, allowing it to be acceptable to God,"[39] thus enabling God to transverse the great gulf between God and sinner. What Aquinas has done, in fact, is to establish an intermediary step "by which," says McGrath, "the soul is made ready for the habitation of God,"[40] a development that would later come under fire by theologians such as William of Ockham, who called into question the idea that God's grace was incapable of reaching sinners directly without this intermediate cause.

What concerned Ockham and others was the implied separation of nature and grace, the emphasis on grace as an extra, a supernatural power infused directly into believers through the sacraments, rather than as something already present in creation by means of God's self-communication. The obvious implication of such a theory, they felt, in contrast to the universality of grace that one finds celebrated throughout the scriptures—the

35. From *manuale*, (Latin, "a book of handy size"). The *Manuales* (also known as *Rituale, Agenda, Sacerdotal, Ordinarium*) were liturgical books compiled in the Middle Ages for the use of parish clergy. They contained prayers, blessings, and formularies for the administration of the pastoral offices.

36. "Actual grace is the divine energy setting the soul in motion towards some particular goal beyond its reach . . . it does not live in the soul but acts upon it in a sense from outside; it sets intellect and will in motion without becoming a permanent quality of either" (Sheed, *Theology for Beginners*, 141).

37. *Habitual* or *sanctifying* grace: "The gift of God inhering in the soul, by which men [sic] are enabled to perform righteous acts. It is held to be normally conveyed in the Sacraments" (ibid.).

38. Thomas Aquinas, *Summa Theologica*, Pt. I–II, Q. 110, Art. 6.

39. McGrath, *Christian Theology*, 451.

40. Ibid.

notion of a world filled with grace—was a theology of grace by which God's self-communication is understood as something essentially supplementary to the world, something that finds its expression in particular separate and discrete events, topping off nature, as one critic observes, like the icing on a cake.[41]

Ultimately, the original understanding of grace in terms of divine encounter would begin to give way to a markedly different notion of grace characterized by almost juridical overtones. That is, there was less of an emphasis on the nature of grace as divine love and more of a stress on grace as "the interior action of God upon the soul [which] not only cures man of his weakness and allows him to lead a good moral life, [but also] elevates him so that he can merit before God."[42] "Disputes on infant baptism, the status of heretics, remaining in the state of grace without continual acts of faith and charity, etc.," says George Worgul, caused the church in the West to rethink its theology of grace, and the result was an ever-increasing distinction between uncreated grace[43] and created grace[44] which, Worgul notes, "often neglected the earlier vision of grace as an interpersonal relationship."[45]

While Thomas Aquinas's own writings convey a vision of the human being dwelling in grace, they were reinterpreted in a way, says Gleason, that "emphasized the objective nature of grace. In them there is less mention of grace as divine love, the divine mercy, God himself leaning over man in a dialogue relationship." Instead, he says, there is an insistence upon the fact that grace is a reality within the soul, "something extra . . . added from without."[46] It is worth noting, says David Neelands, that much of this had to do with a misreading of Aquinas. "The whole of theology of grace, as summed up in Aquinas, can be encompassed in a great circle, which has to do with the exodus and the reditus[47] from God and back to God. It's the

---

41. Unsigned review of *Surnaturel*. Online: http://henridelubaconline.blogspot.com/.

42. Gleason, *Grace*, 62.

43. God's self-communication.

44. "Uncreated grace is God himself as present in the recipient; created grace is a divine gift, other than God but above our natural powers, freely given to us by God. The precise characteristics of created grace vary according to the circumstances of the recipient, particularly with the individual's fundamental response to God's offer of self" (Donovan, *A World of Grace*, 66).

45. Worgul, *From Magic to Metaphor*, 154.

46. Ibid., 61.

47. Returning, turning back.

principle that God is the alpha and the omega, that all things start with God and return to God. And all of theology can be summed up in terms of that golden circle."[48] Unfortunately, although Aquinas was enormously popular as a teacher in his own time and ever after, he fell into the hands of bad commentators—mostly his own disciples—and some of them very highly placed—who interpreted his works in ways he would never have intended. "In traditional scholastic theology," says Lambert Leijssen, "the sacraments were defined as 'efficacious means or causes that communicate the grace that they stand for.' Aristotelian epistemology and metaphysics formed the philosophical context for theological reflection, with categories such as *materia-forma*, substance-accident and *causa*. These means were made available to the faithful through the ministry of the sacraments. Sadly, it gave rise to a distorted understanding of the sacraments as automatic dispensers of grace—'grace machines.'"[49]

Sacramental grace, in the light of this new redemptive emphasis, is less like divine friendship than like a kind of spiritual medicine bestowed by God upon a fallen humanity in order to provide it with something it lacks, an echo of which we can infer from the words of the General Confession found in previous editions of *The Book of Common Prayer*: "and there is no health in us."[50]

The biblical notion of the *graciousness* of God—"abundant in steadfast love," "compassionate and gracious," "merciful"—gradually became obscured by an emphasis on the *will* of God: grace was now something to be conferred by God at God's pleasure when the appropriate conditions were met; i.e., the correct form and matter, the proper disposition on the part of the recipient, and so on. The biblical notion of a world alive with the grace of God gave way to that of a sinful world nearly devoid of grace save for occasional sacramental moments. It was a theology of grace, says Skelley, that "viewed sanctifying grace as a created modification of the human soul, whereas the Scriptures speak of it as the gift of God's Spirit." Grace, in this

---

48. Neelands, Course lecture for TRT 3566F.

49. Leijssen, *With the Silent Glimmer of God's Spirit*, 9.

50. General Confession, 1928 *Book of Common Prayer*. Earl H. Brill writes: "The most recent revision of *The Book of Common Prayer* . . . has eliminated from the General Confession the phrase ' . . . and there is no health in us.' For that statement seemed to deny the persistence of God's image in us. Anglicans, then, believe that though sin is an undeniable fact which can be overcome only by God's grace and forgiveness, nevertheless God has not totally absented himself from the life of sinful humanity" (*The Christian Moral Vision*, 11).

respect, he says, "was seen as something that is produced through efficient causality. Grace was identified with some change that took place in believers. Consequently, grace was seen as something separate from God and as something made by God." [51] In time, he says, "as Aquinas was interpreted and reinterpreted, an increasing determination to break down divine mystery into precise philosophical categories led theologians to focus a disproportionate degree of attention on the causal nature of the sacraments, and to objectify the grace they conveyed. This emphasis placed on 'causality' resulted, inadvertently, in attributing to the grace of the sacraments in the minds of many of the faithful an almost magical quality that worked quite apart from the individuals participating in them." [52]

The grace associated with a sacrament became known as its fruit: sacraments were fruitful if the recipient of the sacrament actually received the grace offered by God through them. By the beginning of the thirteenth century onward, says Vorgrimler, this particular concern with the fruitfulness of the sacraments resulted in a determination on the part of theologians to establish the minimum conditions under which this could occur. As a result, "the sacramental prayers (by which the Holy Spirit is invoked) were replaced by indicative formulas. The sacraments were transformed from symbolic liturgical actions and life-events to extremely brief, punctual gestures. In this shortened form it was no longer possible to accommodate any expressions of self-obligation to service and witnessing in the world." [53]

Aquinas had stressed the importance of the sacrament as a sign with the awareness that signs effect what they signify by the fact that they signify it. In other words, he understood that grace—the invisible, spiritual reality—must be realized by being expressed, made visible and perceptible, and that one could not rightly separate the rite and the grace that was able to manifest itself by being signified. He had declared *Deus non alligavit gratiam sacramentis:* [54] *God's grace is not linked exclusively to the sacraments.* [55] Nevertheless, the Old School model, says Guzie, became characterized by a tendency "to see the initiative of God toward us as linked within the

51. Skelley, *The Liturgy of the World*, 54.

52. Worgul, *From Magic to Metaphor*, 154.

53. Vorgrimler, *Sacramental Theology*, 54–55.

54. Thomas Aquinas, *Summa Theologica*, Pt. I–II, Q. 113, Art. 3.

55. Although God, observes Vaillancourt, "has indeed made the sacraments a privileged means of revealing himself and signifying his presence" (Vaillancourt, *Toward a Renewal of Sacramental Theology*, 62).

church's sacramental system so intimately that grace is liable not to happen for a person unless a sacrament is received."[56]

This diminished theology of grace was the result, further, of a later form of medieval realism known as Nominalism, or the Modern Way, which was distinguished by the principle that only actual physical particulars are real, and that the metaphysical realities so fundamental to scholastic theology were little more than philosophical conventions, with no actual ontological[57] basis. As a result, it created a seemingly insurmountable chasm between the realms of faith and reason that effectively devastated the foundations of Scholastic theology.[58] The uncertainty of metaphysics, Martos points out, not surprisingly corresponded with a similar lack of confidence in the sacramental theology that had for so long guided the Western Church: "Sacramental theology . . . could no longer depend on philosophy for its explanations, and so it turned to canon law. The words of the canonists were still the words of the great scholastics, but now they had legal rather than theological meanings. Matter and form were the things that were necessary for validity. Validity was what was required to cause the sacramental reality. The sacramental reality gave power in a legal sense . . . "[59] The result was "a mechanistic and minimalistic attitude toward the seven sacraments." In time, says Martos, "the reformation demolished what remained of the medieval synthesis and abolished what had become misused and misunderstood sacramental practices in large portions of Europe."[60]

"In many ways," says McGrath, "the Reformation may be regarded as a rediscovery of the Pauline writings, and especially of the doctrine of justification by grace through faith."[61] In the early sixteenth century, the young Augustinian priest and theology professor Martin Luther, while reading through the epistles of St. Paul, was struck by what seemed to him to be an understanding of God's grace completely at odds with that of the theological and sacramental system of his day. He concluded that over the centuries the church had lost sight of that which was central to Paul's doctrine of

56. Guzie, *The Book of Sacramental Basics*, 1.

57. Referring to or based upon being or existence.

58. "Nominalism," in Cross and Livingstone, *The Oxford Dictionary of the Christian Church*, 978–79.

59. Martos, *Doors to the Sacred*, 73.

60. Ibid., 80.

61. McGrath, *Studies in Doctrine*, 390.

salvation, namely, that "since we are justified by faith, we have peace with God through our Lord Jesus Christ. Through him we have obtained access to this grace in which we stand."[62] Grace, as St. Paul assures us, and St. Augustine reminds us again and again, is a free gift of God that, when received, unites the soul of the believer with Christ, much in the manner, as Luther would say, as a bride to the bridegroom.[63] The good works arising out of this union are the response of a grateful heart to a gracious God, rather than an attempt to win some heavenly reward or to evade divine punishment. There is nothing, Luther determined—neither pious works nor alms nor penances, nor ascetic practices, nor the intercessions of the saints and martyrs—that a believer can achieve or perform that might oblige God to reward him with justification.

The Scholastic theories pervading the church's sacramental theology, contaminated by superstitious practices totally incompatible with Scripture, Luther felt, had led to a distorted understanding of the nature of the sacraments, and in particular, of the grace they conveyed. A sacrament was an outward and visible sign of God's grace, to be sure, but for Luther, as Martos explains, "it was the faith of the believer in God's power and goodness that made it an effective sign and enabled the person to receive God's grace through it."[64] Faith, by which the Christian life is begun, said Luther, justifies not as a work or as a quality or as knowledge, but as assent of the will and firm confidence in the mercy of God.

Accordingly, grace was not something funneled down from heaven to one class of believers in order to be doled out on behalf of another, but freely available to all. Inevitably, says Patrick Collinson, the subsequent emphasis placed by Luther on the "priesthood of all believers" meant that the "sacramental economy of the church together with the hierarchical priesthood, guardians of doctrine and of the souls of the church's members, was radically undermined, since in Luther's perception the mass and all other devotions were 'works' with a false motivation."[65]

The Protestant reformers, with their emphasis on justification by grace through faith, and on the centrality of God's word, called for a return

62. Rom 5:1–2.

63. "Martin Luther, *Commentary on Galatians*, quoted in Mursell, *The Story of Christian Spirituality*, 171.

64. Martos, *Doors to the Sacred*, 84.

65. Patrick Collinson, "The Late Medieval Church and Its Reformation (1400–1600)." In McManners, *The Oxford Illustrated History of Christianity*, 259.

to a more Augustinian understanding of grace, and a rejection of what they felt to be an unscriptural—and even at times, nonsensical—underpinning of current sacramental theology. The response on the part of the Roman Church has often been described as a theological entrenchment. Addressing what it considered to be Protestant heresies, it embarked upon a counter-reformation that resulted in a tightening up and nailing down of the Church's teachings on such matters as Scripture and tradition, original sin, justification and sanctification, the veneration of saints, and of course, the sacraments. In addition to the many positive reforms resulting from this undertaking, one of the more unfortunate consequences was a narrowing of perspective that would significantly impact the Roman Church's understanding of grace and sacraments for centuries to come.

In the end, says Gary Shogren,

> The Reformation brought about a revival of Augustinian theology, finding its expression in the slogan *sola gratia*: salvation is of God's gracious inclination toward us from beginning to end, and does not depend on works nor Church nor sacrament.[66] It has its beginning in the gracious election of some to salvation, without regard to merit or spiritual inclination, and leading to the gift of regeneration. Calvin in particular dismissed the medieval view of grace as "magic" (*Institutes* 4:14.14–17).

> The Council of Trent rejected the Reformers' understanding of grace. Prevenient grace and free will could lead one to initial faith in Christ and baptism. Through the sacraments, grace would be given to start the process of justification and holy living.[67]

The unfortunate tendency to overlook the interpersonal dimension of grace, which one could say was characteristic of the Old School model (whether Roman Catholic or Protestant), persisted well into the late nineteenth century, and even beyond,[68] at which time a combination of factors,

66. Not an entirely accurate translation of Luther's own theology, actually. Luther believed that outside of the Church there was no salvation. However, "although Luther also considered the sacraments to be necessary, the decisive factor is faith in that salvation which is offered and given to us through the Word and sacrament" (Lohse, *Martin Luther*, 180).

67. Gary S. Shogren, "Grace (NT)," in Freedman, ed., *Anchor Bible Dictionary*, 2:1088.

68. Teilhard de Chardin, for example, who entered his theological training in the early twentieth century, found himself confronted by the late Scholasticism of the Suaresian system, "under which [he] was formed and against he reacted, [according to which] there is no inner link between human action and the divine gift of grace; the only link is

including the rediscovery and reexamination of crucial primary sources—
including the works of Aquinas—and important advances in biblical and
historical scholarship began to call such impersonal interpretations of
grace into question.

One should note also that if traditional Scholastic theology erred in
the overobjectification of grace, the Protestant tradition (as a recent study
by the Church of England points out) has tended to err in the opposite
direction: "One . . . difficulty with traditional Protestant approaches has
been the way in which in their overspecification of the content of faith
they themselves had been in constant danger of introducing a new system
of merit, one based this time on intellectual belief rather than practical
works."[69]

As noted in *An Episcopal Dictionary of the Church*, "Anglican theology, notably represented by Richard Hooker, has emphasized the gratuitous
nature of grace and the importance of participation in the economy[70] of
God's salvation, especially as known in the life of the Church where grace
is sacramentally represented and made known."[71] At the same time, the
Church of England's report, *The Mystery of Salvation*, cautions us not to
forget, in our desire to ensure that our liturgies are doctrinally sound, that
'authentic' liturgy requires more than theological correctness: when we
place an inordinate stress in our sacramental rites on either faith or merit,
we lose sight of the fact that the grace of God is first and foremost God's
own gracious initiative.

Out of the liturgical reformations of the late nineteenth and the twentieth centuries and following, came the gradual recovery of the older, more
biblical notion of grace, as reflected in the New School model's understanding of grace neither as thing, nor secondary cause,[72] but as relationship with

an arbitrary decree of God." (Francisco de Suarez [1548–1617] was a Jesuit theologian
and an advocate of Congruism, which holds that God brings about the salvation of the
elect by bestowing upon them the 'medicinal' graces of which they will need to make use,
and without which, said Suarez, they fall into sin and lose their souls.) See Murray, *The
Thought of Teilhard de Chardin*, 3.

69. Church of England, Doctrine Commission of the General Synod, *The Mystery of
Salvation*, 132.

70. Economy/*oikonomia* of salvation: "This historical saving activity of God, the
oikonomia . . . takes place in a theological framework: it originates in the overflowing
love of the Father and, in glorifying him, leads back to him, in order that he may be 'all
in all' [1 Cor 15:28]" (Vorgrimler, *Sacramental Theology*, 28).

71. Armentrout and Slocum, "Grace," in *An Episcopal Dictionary of the Church*, 224.

72. That is, as some sort of metaphysical reality that brings about a change in another

God; in the words of Michael Skelley, "a gift of God rather than a gift from God."[73]

Guzie, reflecting on this theology of coexistence, notes that one's life as a Christian "can be understood only in relation to the *whole body* of which Christ is the head." He goes on to say: "I do not possess grace in such a way that I can speak of 'my' grace. I *share* in the life of the graced *body* which is the church."[74] Or, to quote Vorgrimler: "Of essential importance is the insight, consequent on the theology of grace that has been presupposed, that liturgy is made possible and empowered by God; it is God who incorporates those who entrust themselves to God in the liturgy into the great homeward movement to God."[75] Whereas previously the grace conferred by the sacraments had been described in more or less ontological terms—as though the grace of God were a metaphysical quality bestowed upon individuals which possessed the power to inform the soul—the New School model speaks of the way in which the grace of the sacraments transforms the believer by effecting within a deeper relationship with Christ and with the church which is the ecclesial body of Christ.

The almost magical way of thinking about sacraments, that until recently prevailed, is effectively dispelled when we regard them in the light of the Incarnation, by which they are revealed to be a means of Christ's continuing presence in and among us. No longer is it a matter of how sacraments cause grace—as though symbol and grace were unrelated—but of the ways in which they are instrumental in allowing grace—God's own self-communication—to express and manifest itself. Fink captures the distinction succinctly: "Symptomatic of this radical shift in rhetoric is the contrast between the way sacraments are identified in the [Roman Catholic Church's] 1917 Code of Canon Law and in the revised code of 1983. In the former they are listed under the heading *de rebus* (on things); in the latter, under the title 'The Office of Sanctifying in the Church.'"[76]

In the words of Anglican Archbishop William Temple, "A sacrament . . . conveys not only God's meaning to the mind, but God himself to the whole person of the worshipper. No doubt it is 'Grace' which is commonly spoken of as thus conveyed; but Grace is not something other than God,

---

entity.

73. Skelley, *The Liturgy of the World*, 56.

74. Guzie, *The Book of Sacramental Basics*, 60.

75. Vorgrimler, *Sacramental Theology*, 22.

76. Fink, *Praying the Sacraments*, 46.

imparted by Him; it is the very Love of God (which is Himself) approaching and seeking entry into the soul of man."[77] The power of the sacraments to transform and renew lives lies in the fact, says Macquarrie, that "in all the sacraments . . . we are receiving Christ, receiving his grace, which means his presence in our lives."[78] In situations critical to salvation, the grace of God is mediated through Jesus Christ by the power of the Holy Spirit to individuals who, says Vorgrimler, "enfold their (new) decisions in the liturgical symbolic actions of the Church and for that very reason are prepared to accept from the Church the assurance of salvation."[79] "The gracious influence of God," says Gleason "penetrates the center of man's existence, gradually forms all the regions of his humanity, and continually urges him to realize the full development of his powers through the total gift of his heart in filial love. By delivering him from fatal self-obsession, by involving him in a mysterious, personal encounter with Christ, it redirects his fundamental drives, desires, and the liberty of his will . . . In grace it is God Himself who comes to meet man."[80]

We would do well to remember that many of the liturgical practices and traditions that for centuries served to obscure rather than proclaim the true nature of the sacraments reflect an unfortunate (and often popular) misinterpretation of the church's doctrine and canon law. The almost magical light in which the sacraments were, for so long, often popularly perceived, was, as Martos points out, never sanctioned by the Church's hierarchy or canon law, nor even evident in its official manuals of sacramental theology. The teachings of the Council of Trent and of Thomas Aquinas, according to Richard McBrien, have more often been misconstrued (and misrepresented) than understood. The Catholic tradition, he notes, "has always been insistent that the grace of God is given to us, not to make up for something lacking to us as human persons, but as a free gift that elevates us to a new and unmerited level of existence."[81]

While the Scholastics' preoccupation with the question of how the sacraments work revealed a failure to appreciate the interpersonal nature of grace, this is not to say, however, that we cannot benefit from many of the insights to be found in the traditional theology of the sacraments. A

77. Temple, "The Sacramental Universe." In *Nature, Man and God,* 484–485.

78. Macquarrie, *A Guide to the Sacraments,* 38.

79. Vorgrimler, *Sacramental Theology,* 76.

80. Gleason, *Grace,* 187.

81. McBrien, *Catholicism,* 150.

balanced synthesis of traditional and contemporary approaches that demonstrates a "respect for and deep probing of the church's *tradition* of teaching on the sacraments," Kevin Irwin points out, is more helpful than one that either overobjectifies sacraments or conversely, one that indulges in over-generalizations, and focuses on an "overly horizontal notion of grace"[82] that fails to do justice to the sacred mystery out of which sacraments arise.

Rather than serving as instruments for conveying something previously lacking, but now brought about by God—namely, grace—it is more accurate to say that sacraments are a means by which God's grace is *expressed* and therefore *realized*. By means of the sacraments, God's saving grace, spiritual in nature, is rendered tangible and perceptible. Rahner writes: "The world is permeated by the grace of God . . . The world is constantly and ceaselessly possessed by grace from its innermost roots, from the innermost personal center of the spiritual subject. It is constantly and ceaselessly sustained and moved by God's self-bestowal . . . Whether the world gives the impression, so far as our superficial everyday experience is concerned, of being imbued with grace in this way, or whether it constantly seems to give the lie to this state of being permeated by God's grace which it has, this in no sense alters the fact that it is so."[83]

A sacramental *world*: the very notion seems to challenge—perhaps even threaten—many of our familiar assumptions about sacraments. A large part of the problem lies in the Old School model by which we became accustomed to think of the grace of the sacraments as something apart from God's self, something imparted by God to the world at particular times and places, under particular circumstances and as the result of particular events. The New School model, in contrast, regards grace not in the nature of some metaphysical reality, but as relationship with God. To quote Norris, "For God to be truly 'with us' is *grace*; for us to come into God's company is the result of *grace*."[84] By this model we come to understand humanity to be, in the words of Hughes, "graced sinners whom the sacraments enable to grow in God's love within our relation to one another in the Church."[85]

82. Irwin, ""Recent Sacramental Theology," 593–608.

83. Karl Rahner, "Considerations on the Active Role of the Person in the Sacramental Event," in *Theological Investigations,* 14:166–67; quoted in Skelley, *The Liturgy of the World,* 57.

84. Norris, *Understanding the Faith of the Church,* 187.

85. Hughes, "Sacraments and Ordination."

The Models and Church

Old School Model	New School Model
The church is an *it*: a hierarchical structure whose ministry is primarily the work of ordained clergy, who are assisted by members of the laity.	The church is a *we*: "the Body of which Jesus Christ is the Head and of which all baptized persons are members"[86] and in whose ministry all members share.
The church is the 'dispenser' of the sacraments.	The church—the assembly of the faithful—'celebrates' the sacraments; moreover, it functions as a kind of sacrament, making Christ present in the world in a very real and tangible way when it acts or speaks as church.
Preoccupation with the question of how and when God is present in the sacraments.	Renewed focus on how the assembly of the faithful can be fully present. "What happens to the people who celebrate with bread and wine?"[87]

"The first Christians," says William Bausch, "had no idea of 'going to church' to receive the sacraments." Instead, "They had every idea of 'being' church, and celebrating those mysteries and festivities that brought them into contact with the risen One in their midst."[88] During the era of the domestic church, roughly AD 100–313, as Christianity began to take on a distinctive character—"urban, Gentile and Hellenized," as Edward Foley describes it—its organization continued at first to remain "more familial than institutional."[89] That is, while the structure of organization might vary somewhat from community to community, a sense of the shared ministry of all believers appears to have been integral. As they found themselves expelled from the synagogues and, in time, from the Jewish community in general, the first Christians gathered in borrowed rooms and private homes, where "they devoted themselves to the apostles' teaching and fel-

86. *Catechism*, 854.

87. Guzie, *The Book of Sacramental Basics*, 35.

88. Bausch, *A New Look at the Sacraments*, 1.

89. Foley, *From Age to Age*, 27.

lowship, to the breaking of bread and the prayers."[90] The objects employed in their liturgical celebrations were, for the most part, ordinary everyday eating and drinking vessels, their preparations, by today's standards, were simple, and a complementarity, or mutuality, of ministry was the norm. St. Paul describes it thus: "When you come together, each one has a hymn, a lesson, a revelation, a tongue or an interpretation."[91] What we find is a picture, says John Drane, of a fellowship of faith that regards itself "not as an organization, but as a living organism."[92] Although the term *sacrament* would, at that time, have been foreign to these first Christian communities, as Clare Wagner observes, by nature they were remarkably sacramental, for they were "animated by resurrection faith, by the Spirit continually given them by the risen Christ. They embodied the presence of the risen Jesus; therefore they were sacramental and their actions as communities were sacramental. People in those early communities—while never using nor knowing the word sacrament—did understand that it was the presence of the risen Christ which they desired, and felt responsible, to keep alive in the world."[93]

"From the beginning," says Ross Mackenzie, "the spread of Christianity was largely the work of its laity . . . It was to the community as a whole that the apostolic commission of witness and mutual service was entrusted. They prayed as a community, celebrated the baptismal or eucharistic liturgy as a community, and shared in bringing the good news about Christ to non-Christian friends and strangers."[94] They were not simply witnesses to Christ's saving work but a part of it. The ministry of the church, Christ's body, was understood to be the work of all the baptized, to which each member was able to contribute in his or her own way, as St. Paul's letters illustrate.[95] As an example, St. Paul's letter to the church in Rome[96] addresses the Roman Christians as "fellow workers" and "workers in the Lord," all of whom "are led by the Spirit of God."[97]

90. Acts 2:42.

91. 1 Cor 14:26.

92. Drane, *Introducing the New Testament*, 393.

93. Wagner, "Current Trends," 160–69.

94. Ross Mackenzie, "Christian Passages." In Mackenzie, *Education for Ministry, Year Three*, 223.

95. Cf. 1 Cor 12:8; 12:28; Rom 12:6; Eph 4:11.

96. c. AD 56–57.

97. Rom 8:14.

Firsthand testimony, says Stoutzenberger, suggests that these earliest Christian communities were envisioned along the lines of a large circle, with Christ, from whom the church draws its identity, at the center, and within this large circle, many smaller circles of belonging, and of concern and service.[98] By the end of the first century, however, one can already begin to discern a growing distinction between the various members of these communities. Drane notes, for instance, "In an earlier chapter of 1 Clement,[99] two groups of people are distinguished within the congregation. No longer are all equal as brothers and sisters in Christ. Instead, we find the notion of 'clergy' and 'laity.'"[100] Moreover, as these small Christian communities were able to move into larger, more formal, more permanent worship spaces, the very arrangement of these new liturgical settings, which segregated clergy and laity as effectively as actors and audience are separated by the footlights, would begin to undermine the former notion of *koinonia*.[101]

As Christianity made the shift from a small persecuted sect to an imperial state religion, the young Church began to adapt as its new architectural model the Roman *basilica*.[102] These new arrangements afforded a greater dignity to Christian worship, but at the same time the shift from the informal, family-like setting of the house church to these more formal, institutional worship settings would have a profound effect on the way in which the members of the community thought of themselves. As Foley

98. Stoutzenberger, *Celebrating Sacraments*, 71.

99. Clement, Bishop of Rome (c. AD 96). The epistle 1 Clement, which is considered to be genuine, was written c. 95–96 in response to reports of internal strife in the Church at Corinth.

100. Drane, *Introducing the New Testament*, 395–96.

101. ARCIC I Final Report, "Elucidations on Authority in the Church": "Union with God in Christ Jesus through the Spirit is the heart of Christian koinonia. Among the various ways in which the term koinonia is used in different New Testament contexts, we concentrate on that which signifies a relation between persons resulting from their participation in the one and the same reality (cf. 1 John 1:3). The Son of God has taken to himself our human nature, and he has sent upon us his Spirit, who makes us . . . truly members of the body of Christ . . . Moreover, sharing in the same Holy Spirit, whereby we become members of the same body of Christ and adopted children of the same Father, we are also bound to one another in a completely new relationship. Koinonia with one another is entailed by our koinonia with God in Christ. This is the mystery of the Church." Anglican/Roman Catholic Joint Preparatory Commission. "ARCIC I Final Report, "Elucidations on Authority in the Church." (Sept 1981).

102. *Basilicas*: Roman civic buildings, generally, large, rectangular, roofed halls, situated in the *forum*, or public square, with an *apse*, or arch at one end, where the magistrates would be seated on a slightly raised platform.

explains: "One of the results of moving from borrowed rooms to permanent worship structures was the transference of the name traditionally given to the community, *ekklesia*, to the building itself. While this change in terminology did not indicate that the community no longer considered itself the true *ekklesia* or foundation of living stones, it did anticipate a time when such consciousness would be lost among the baptized. Eventually, only the building would be recognized by the vast majority of believers as 'the church.'"[103]

Lisa Maughans notes that "English speakers perhaps suffer from their Germanic ancestors' choice of the term *church*, which derived from the *place* Christians gathered (German *kirche*, from the Greek term for a place 'belonging to the Lord,' *kyriake*, or *kyriakon*). *Church* for the first Christians meant the *people* (Greek *ekklēsia*; Latin *ecclesia*: "assembly"), who always remain in some sense assembled. *Church* communicated a living and dynamic relationship among the members and with God himself. Gentile converts might associate *church* with town assemblies (*ekklēsiai*) where citizens gathered for political and juridical deliberation. Greek-speaking Jews across the Mediterranean world knew that *ekklēsia* in the Septuagint[104] . . . referred to the visible 'assembly' of the covenant people."[105]

The doctrine of the church, which had not been a major issue in its formative years, faced as it had been at that time with the question of survival, took on a new importance as it began to emerge as an official institution. By the end of the first century we find evidence of a hierarchical structure remarkably unlike that of the first Christian communities described in the Acts of the Apostles. The evolution of this new ministerial structure was, in part, a response to dangers from without—for instance, persecution by Imperial Rome—and from within, in reaction to the threats of heresy and schism, and in particular, in response to the ever-present threat of Christianity's being turned into a private cult, under the sway, and subject to the whim of, individual charismatic leaders.[106] It arose, as well, as a result of the need for the establishment of recognized authorities capable of quelling

---

103. Foley, "The Domestic Church: 100–313," in *From Age to Age*, 29–30.

104. A Greek translation of the Hebrew Bible (or Old Testament), dating from the third century BC. Sometimes abbreviated as LXX. *Septuaginta* is Latin for the number seventy.

105. Driver, *Christ at the Center*, 146.

106. Reader's Digest Editorial Staff, *After Jesus*, 104.

divisions and settling disputes necessary to the preservation of order as the church's numbers swelled dramatically.

Having survived rejection and persecution in the course of its first three centuries, Christianity would, ironically, eventually become the victim of its own success. In Harmon Smith's words, "the establishment of Christianity as the official state religion by Constantine brought, as we would now expect, the routinization of the liturgy and its appropriation as a means to ends other than its own.[107] This, in turn, led to the domestication of the sacrament so that increasingly it became, as it were, the church's possession."[108]

As an exhausted and crumbling Roman Empire succumbed to the hordes of invaders who swept over its frontiers and across its borders in the fifth century, out of the ruins of this long-established civilization would arise the states of modern Europe, a new civilization for which, as Will Durant observes, the foster mother would be the church.[109] At the end of what we have come to call the Dark Ages,[110] the missionary fervor of the Western Church proved so successful that entire tribes and nations—nearly all of Europe—became Christianized. However, this flood of new converts would prove to be a mixed blessing. The lengthy and painstaking traditional catechumenal process, by which the first Christians had been prepared to take their place in the church's life and ministry, would inevitably collapse under the sheer weight of the numbers of new converts. The result was a "superficially Christianized"[111] population, many of whom had had their new faith imposed upon them by their newly converted chieftains and rulers, most of whom were ill prepared, and a great many for whom this new faith was intermingled with elements of their old pagan religions.

The church that emerged from the Dark Ages was dramatically different from that of the earlier Christian communities. "Partly as a result of the exigencies of the time," says W. T. Jones, "partly because of the ambition of its rulers, it had grown into a great . . . institution. . ."[112] By the twelfth and

---

107. That is, a unifying faith for a unified empire.

108. Smith, *Where Two or Three Are Gathered*, 61.

109. Durant, *The Story of Civilization*, 4:43–44.

110. That is, the early part of the Middle Ages, the period roughly extending from the collapse of the Roman Empire around the end of the fifth century to about AD 1000.

111. Robert A. Marcus, "From Rome to the Barbarian Kingdoms," in *The Oxford Illustrated History of Christianity*, 85.

112. Jones, *A History of Western Philosophy*, 2:145.

thirteenth centuries, the friendly, informal atmosphere of the first Christian communities had given way to a hierarchical, highly clericalized model of the church, its worship conducted in Latin—a language now unfamiliar to the ordinary worshiper (and almost as foreign to many of the poorly educated rural clergy). Its sacramental theology was burdened by a determination to analyze the sacraments in an academic, overly objective fashion, with an emphasis on particular details and a corresponding neglect of their essential context (that of the celebrating community) that resulted, says Martos, in "an experience of rituals reduced to their bare essentials" and an "all too often . . . mechanistic idea of sacramental causality."[113]

One of the casualties of the harsh and catastrophic interval of the Dark Ages, during which time a vast body of literature and learning was lost or destroyed, was the historical context so essential to an authentic understanding of the nature of sacraments and church. In centuries to come, the resulting ecclesial amnesia would have a serious impact on sacramental theology as theologians attempted to reconstruct the origins of the sacraments independent of the lived experience of the assembly of faith.

This hierarchical, institutional model effectively downplayed the role of the laity. The ecclesial dimension, Guzie observes, "was important to the great scholastics, but it came to be almost totally neglected in the later middle ages."[114] By then, says Foley, the laity had become "most decisively distanced from the [sacramental] action,"[115] a fact that expressed itself not simply in the church's liturgies, but in other features such as her architecture. For instance, Foley notes, however beautiful they may have been, the rood screens[116] that featured so prominently in churches throughout England and Europe from around the fourteenth to the sixteenth centuries, were actually designed as a sort of buffer zone to segregate the assembly from the area where the monks or clerics prayed, effectively blocking the congregation's view of the sanctuary.[117]

Scholastic theology, says Fink, lacked a strong ecclesiological base, and as a result "it . . . replaced the Augustinian image of the *totus Christus*

---

113. Martos, *Doors to the Sacred*, 69.

114. Guzie, *The Book of Sacramental Basics*, 59.

115. Foley, "The Prelude to Reform: 1073 to 1517," in *From Age to Age*, 92.

116. Rood screen: An ornamented, often elaborately designed wooden, wrought iron, or stone screen surmounted by a rood (a cross, specifically, the cross of Christ's crucifixion) which separates the nave of the church from the choir or chancel.

117. Foley, "The Prelude to Reform: 1073 to 1517," in *From Age to Age*, 96.

(Christ in the midst of the church, together with the church that is gathered into union with him) by an image of *Christus solus* (Christ alone, present in the ministry of the priest, and acting on behalf of the people)."[118] Perhaps most telling of all, in regard to the loss of the sense of being church, was the development, as early as the seventh century, of the private mass and the votive mass (offered for special intentions), Eucharistic celebrations in which the priest was the sole actor and the congregation (if they were present at all) were relegated to the role of spectator. Guzie notes, "The loss of awareness of *being church* brought with it a decline in sacramental practice. Communion was no longer an essential part of the eucharistic action for most people, and the sacraments were no longer an action in which the whole assembly felt engaged . . . The sacraments thus became 'things' which you 'went to church' (the building) to 'receive.'"[119]

Sacramental theologian Tom Richstatter observes that over time there arose an understanding of the church's sacramental liturgies as the sole responsibility of the clergy. To this way of thinking, "The priest becomes the one who puts matter and form together. The priest can 'do it' all by himself (e.g. Mass). The priest administers the sacraments; the rest of the Church *receives* sacraments. The priest says Mass; the [congregation] *hear* Mass. The sacraments are removed from their ecclesial context . . . [and] become 'private' events." Strictly speaking, of course, says Richstatter, it was understood, from a theological perspective, that these liturgical events were not truly private, "and so there developed the theory that the priest, in himself, made the whole Church present." When a lone priest celebrated a sacrament in the absence of the congregation, therefore, while for all appearances it was a private event, it only *looked* private. "Private Confession and Private Mass, while they might appear private, were theologically public."[120]

The determination of the Scholastics to break down divine mystery into philosophical categories gradually led to a reductionist approach to sacraments marked by an emphasis on particulars and a corresponding neglect of their ecclesial dimension. Among other things, this resulted in liturgical practices that were 'frozen' in time—forced to remain unchanged in order to protect the doctrine they expressed—in addition to 'scholarly' interpretations of the sacraments often colored by popular piety,[121] as well

118. Fink, *Worship: Praying the Sacraments*, 47–48.

119. Guzie, *The Book of Sacramental Basics*, 33.

120. Richstatter, "General and Introductory Materials: Part 3 Theological Issues, Chapter d31, Sacrament."

121. Meaning, interpretations which are more of a reflection of the popular

as the uncritical acceptance of long-standing conventions regarding the origin and nature of the sacraments which owed more to tradition and centuries of liturgical practice than fact.

The response of the Roman Church to the doctrinal challenges of the Protestant reformers found its most profound expression in the Council of Trent (1545–1563). This was not merely a reaction to the Protestant Reformation, but an internal reform undertaken by the Roman Church itself, addressing many of the abuses that had come under attack by the reformers. Observes Thomas Bokenkotter: "when it was finished, even critics had to admit the job was well done. Trent ranged over the issues raised by the protestants and defined the Catholic position in such clear and trenchant language that thenceforth everyone knew exactly where the Catholic Church stood. For the next four centuries, the authority of the Council of Trent was virtually unchallengeable within the Catholic Church."[122]

While more than half of the doctrinal decrees issued by the Council of Trent, Bokenkotter notes, were related to the theology of the sacraments, they were mainly concerned with addressing the challenges raised by the reformers. "For the most part, they simply reasserted the medieval Church's understanding of the sacraments. The number of the sacraments, they declared, were seven—no more and no less—although not all of the same dignity or necessity. No allusion at all was made to the complex history behind the gradual recognition of this number of sacraments."[123] Moreover, while clarifying the Church's official doctrine on the sacraments regarding such things as number, causality, validity, proper disposition, and so on, the notion of the assembled church itself as a kind of sacrament, notes Fink, would not be recaptured for some four hundred years, an unfortunate state of affairs which the limitations of biblical scholarship at this time, as well as the unfortunate scarcity of firsthand historical data regarding the nature of the early church, served to reinforce.

The institutional church came to assume the role of the guardian and dispenser of the sacraments, channeling grace, as it were, from God through the ordained clergy and down to the laity, who were relegated more or less to the role of spectators at clerical celebrations. Sacraments became things to be administered by the few to the many, to be received rather than celebrated. The sacraments, now valued for their guarantee of eternal life and

---

imagination than of sound doctrine.

122. Bokenkotter, *Dynamic Catholicism*, 181–82.

123. Ibid.

salvation from eternal punishment, had come to be regarded as something bestowed *by* the church rather than constitutional *of* it.

"Until the mid-twentieth century," says Martos, "the Roman Catholic Church's understanding of its seven sacraments was largely independent of historical facts . . . And the sacramental rites themselves were assumed to have remained substantially unchanged for nineteen hundred years, even though there was no direct evidence that this was actually so."[124] By the late nineteenth century, however, equipped with a wealth of important religious and historical primary and secondary resources, and with exegetical tools unavailable to previous generations, scholars and theologians were able to begin a painstaking reexamination of the origins of the church's sacraments and worship. As a result, Monika Hellwig writes, "we became aware of the sacramental activity of the church in its historical developments, shaped by human ingenuity and perversity, taking unfortunate as well as happy turns."[125] The results of this new scholarship called for a dramatic re-examination and reenvisioning of the church's sacramental rites. For Roman Catholics, as Geoffrey Wainwright notes, a good deal of this recovery of the fullness of sacramental celebration took the form of the scraping away of centuries of ritual accretions; while for Protestants it manifested itself in the recovery of a richer appreciation of the relationship of word and sacrament.[126]

Why has it taken us so long to begin to recover from this tragic ecclesial amnesia? In all fairness, it must be noted that until relatively recently, many of the crucial and relevant historical and theological documents were, to a considerable extent, simply unavailable to the general public. "It's not as though . . . theologians intentionally decided to ignore historical facts in developing their explanations of the sacraments," Martos points out. "Many of the facts were simply unknown, buried in the archives of the Vatican and other old libraries. More importantly, though, the reason they did not bother to dig through these documents was that they believed the truths of faith were changeless and unaffected by history."[127]

Much of the liturgical renewal that was to follow from the Vatican II Council was the result of the gradual recovery of an understanding of the Church itself as a kind of sacrament: "a sign and instrument . . . of

124. Martos, *Doors to the Sacred*, xiii–xiv.

125. Hellwig, "New Understanding of the Sacraments," 375.

126. Wainwright, "Renewing Worship."

127. Martos, *Doors to the Sacred*, xiv.

communion with God and of unity among all men [*sic*]."[128] and "'the universal sacrament of salvation,' by which Christ is 'at once manifesting and actualizing the mystery of God's love for men [*sic*].'"[129] As the ARCIC II report, *Salvation and the Church*, explains: "the Church is . . . called to be, and by the power of the Spirit actually is, a *sign*, *steward* and *instrument* of God's design. For this reason it can be described as a sacrament of God's saving work."[130] The full and proper expression of the church in its role as a sacrament of the ecclesial Christ, "the Christ who is sacramentally present upon earth as *church*,"[131] is that of the assembled community of faith, no matter how large or how small.

While it is true that the "Church makes the sacraments," it is also true that the "sacraments make the church." Clearly, the church is not an *it* but a *we*: the body of Christ, of which all baptized persons are members. The Church, says Rahner, serves as "the ongoing presence of Jesus Christ in time and space, as the fruit of salvation which can no longer perish, and as the means of salvation to an individual in a tangible way and in the historical and social dimension."[132] Every sacrament possesses both a personal and a public aspect, and both aspects point beyond themselves to Christ, who is the ultimate sacrament.

Consider, says Vorgrimler, the ecclesial dimension fundamental to each of the sacraments: "in baptism, the acceptance into the Church as the Body of Christ and *thereby* the remission of all sins; in the Eucharist, the communion with the Church as a community of love and *thereby* the communion with Jesus himself; in penance, the reconciliation with the Church injured by sin and *thereby* the eradication of the sin by God."[133] One could add: in the sacramental rite of unction, the re-incorporation of the individual whose life has been fragmented and disrupted by his or her sickness-situation into the church, which shares in Christ's "victory of life and peace," *thereby* healing through sharing in the wholeness of Christ."

128. *The Catechism of the Catholic Church*, 775.

129. Ibid., 776.

130. Second Anglican/Roman Catholic International Commission. "Salvation and the Church: An Agreed Statement."

131. Fink, *Praying the Sacraments*, 114.

132. Rahner, *Foundations of Christian Faith*; quoted in Skelley, *The Liturgy of the World*, 143.

133. Vorgrimler, *Sacramental Theology*, 92.

The recovery of our ecclesial consciousness has taken us several centuries, and has encompassed a Reformation, Counter-Reformation, two major liturgical movements (one in the nineteenth century and the other in the twentieth), numerous church councils (most particularly, the Second Vatican Council), a number of minor reform movements, as well as several ecumenical endeavors. Nevertheless, Weil points out, this recovery of ecclesial consciousness is still in progress: "In spite of decades of liturgical renewal, we Anglicans have not paid enough attention to the central place held by the assembly in scripture and the Christian tradition . . . Many lay people still see themselves primarily as listeners and observers in worship."[134] The faithful participation of the assembly, the body of Christ, in the liturgy is as essential to a fruitful celebration of the sacraments as the proper matter and form.

While there is a growing appreciation for the importance of the role of all the baptized in the celebration of our sacramental liturgies—witness, for instance, the increasing number of eucharistic ministers and lectors, and the growing number of liturgy-planning committees—there persists, to a disheartening extent, a tendency to regard the sacraments in the old minister/recipient light. This is all the more regrettable when one considers that authentic liturgy is only possible when every member of this mystical body, each of whom has been equipped by the Holy Spirit for its building up, is allowed to realize his or her identity as church in the liturgy by which God calls us to share in God's very life. If the sacraments are truly liturgical acts, then serious consideration must be given to the role of all the baptized as ministers. Such a reorientation leads us away from the Old School model's preoccupation with questions concerning the manner in which Christ is really present in the sacraments and towards the New School model's focus on how Christ is present in and as the assembled church who celebrates the sacraments. The old notion of the congregation as bystanders is revealed as inadequate—or better yet, inauthentic—when one considers the sacraments as the means by which the church realizes her true nature in remembering, celebrating, and participating in the saving events at her heart. As Vorgrimler reminds us, "It would be wrong to think that the liturgy makes God the Father present. Instead, it is *we* (also) who in and by means of the liturgy are made present to God the Father, are brought before his face: *through* his son Jesus *in* the Holy Spirit."[135]

134. Louis *A Theology of Worship*, 36.

135. Vorgrimler, *Sacramental Theology*, 25.

These many centuries later, we Anglicans are beginning to recover a consciousness of the church as the priesthood of all believers, all of whom share in Christ's eternal priesthood. Just so, we need to learn to regard our sacraments and sacramental rites in this new, more dynamic light, and this requires a model of sacramental theology capable of expressing this new understanding.

The Models and Liturgical Celebration

Old School Model	New School Model
Sacraments are quasi-private rituals and the responsibility of the ordained.	Sacraments are liturgical actions, which are "not private actions, but the celebrations of the church."[136]
A view of sacraments as *things* which can be examined out of context in an artificial and quasi-scientific manner.	A renewed appreciation of the dynamic and relational nature of sacraments.
Clergy-dominated liturgical rites in which the faithful are relegated to the role of spectators and recipients.	Liturgical celebrations in which the "full and active participation"[137] of all the faithful is the desired aim. A mutuality of ministry in which each order is allowed to "fulfill the functions proper to their respective orders."[138]

In speaking of the fundamental sacramentality of Christian worship, Weil observes: "The principle of the Incarnation implies that an act of worship, the offering of praise and honor to God because of his ultimacy in regard to all that exists, should signify the engagement of the whole person and the whole created world in a divine/human encounter." Accordingly, he says, "it is impossible to discuss sacramental theory apart from liturgical practice."[139]

---

136. *SC* I, 26.
137. *SC* II, 14.
138. *The Book of Common Prayer,* "Concerning the Service of the Church," 13.
139. Weil, *Sacraments and Liturgy,* 2–3.

Nevertheless, before Vatican II, says Jean Lebon, it was enough then to know the letter of canon law; the spirit of the celebration was secondary: "The ideal of the liturgist was to perform the 'ceremonies' detailed in the official books as scrupulously as possible. These official books were no more than extremely detailed descriptions of what had to be done."[140]

By the nineteenth century, says Weil,

> the Church had generally lost a true liturgical sense. Religious practice was understood . . . as an individual, inward matter which, for those so inclined, had external expression in the official, authorized public liturgy, that is, according to the rites of the official books . . . It is easy to find evidence among nineteenth-century writers that the liturgy was viewed as a private act surrounded by public ceremonial, the coinciding of private acts of piety by the number of people gathered. One may see the early sources of this in the unbalanced clericalism of the high Middle Ages, that is, from the twelfth century onwards. The clerical domination of the liturgy crowned a gradually developed passivity among the laity with their total exclusion from any active participation. This clerical domination, ironically, was not really addressed effectively at the Reformation, and an individualistic piety continued in various forms. By the nineteenth century ceremonial, rites, and other external matters were viewed as secondary to the private prayer of the individuals gathered. Not surprisingly, the especially pious even saw the ritual as a negative factor, a distraction from true prayer.[141]

As the Middle Ages gave way to the historical period known as the Renaissance, with its distinctive emphasis on the individual, the grace of the sacraments came to be regarded more and more in individualistic terms, a regrettable situation which prevailed until relatively recently. In the words of Beguerie and Duchesneau, "for many Christians sacramental celebrations were above all acts of personal piety. Of course, taking communion, making confession and receiving the last rites nourished faith, but they were not seen as something involving the whole community. It was a matter between God and the believer, albeit through the intermediary of a priest."[142] One of the distinguishing characteristics of the Old School model is an individualized piety with little or no appreciation for the social dimen-

140. Lebon, *How to Understand the Liturgy*, 20–21.
141. Weil, *Sacraments and Liturgy*, 92.
142. Beguerie and Duchesneau, *How to Understand the Sacraments*, 65.

sion fundamental to the church's liturgical celebrations. Liturgy, to this way of thinking, was sacred drama, and the laity became largely relegated to the role of audience. It was not necessary for the liturgy to be theologically meaningful or even comprehensible to them. If few of the faithful could actually understand the Latin of the Mass, they were to be content with the air of mystery and sanctity that it lent to the proceedings. Their role, as has been wryly observed, was to "pray, pay and obey." Participation in the liturgy, for the laity, became largely confined to following the service in one's missal or prayer book, or simply listening, and it was not uncommon, while the celebrant presided, for the faithful to occupy themselves with their own private devotions. Participate? It was sufficient, many of the faithful had come to believe, simply to be present while the priest celebrated the Mass; liturgy, after all, was the job of the clergy. This mindset is epitomized in the encyclical of Pope Pius X, *Vehementer Nos*, given at St. Peter's in Rome in 1906: "It follows that the Church is essentially an *unequal* society, that is, a society comprising two categories of persons, the Pastors and the flock, those who occupy a rank in the different degrees of the hierarchy and the multitude of the faithful. So distinct are these categories that with the pastoral body only rests the necessary right and authority for promoting the end of the society and directing all its members towards that end; the one duty of the multitude is to allow themselves to be led, and, like a docile flock, to follow the Pastors."[143]

More recently, this Old School mode of thought finds expression in the type of objection voiced by Monsignor Klaus Gamber, well-known critic of the Novus Ordo,[144] to the exclusive use of the vernacular in the Mass as a means of encouraging the active participation of the faithful. Why, he asks in *The Reform of the Roman Liturgy*, does the congregation have to understand *all* the liturgy? Why could the use of the vernacular not have been limited to Scripture readings, general intercessions and "the singing of good Church hymns and songs"?[145] Would that not be sufficient? In a similar vein, Michael Davies, another outspoken critic of post–Vatican II liturgical reform, joins in lamenting the fact that the increasing involvement of the laity on liturgical planning committees has "'dragged the dignity of

143. Pius X, *Vehementer Nos* (11/02/1906)."

144. Novus Ordo Missae (Latin: *New Order of the Mass*), generally abbreviated as Novus Ordo, unofficial term for the revised liturgy of the Mass following the Second Vatican Council.

145. Gamber, *The Reform of the Roman Liturgy*, 60.

our Lord's institution down to the embarrassing level of the home-made'" as a result of the fact that "the promotion of the active participation of the faithful [has] given rise to the widely-held opinion that 'the liturgy must be made by the community's work.'"[146]

If the Old School model is represented by a highly clericalized liturgy and a conspicuously individualistic piety, the New School model could be said to be marked by the recognition of the fact that it is the whole assembly of the faithful that celebrates the sacraments. One of the most important developments in the field of contemporary sacramental theology is the recovery of the social dimension of the church's liturgies: the concept of sacraments as *liturgical actions*, and moreover, as *actions of the church in assembly*. No longer can we attempt to understand sacraments in isolation in the sterile environment of the 'theology lab,' nor can we presume it to be enough to fulfill the minimum requirements in regard to sacraments, nor to think of sacraments as something administered by one individual for another, like holy medicine.

The recovery of the notion of sacraments as authentic liturgical acts, in the context of corporate worship, allows us to regard them in a truly dynamic way, and forces us, in our liturgical explorations, to consider well the complexity and interrelatedness of the various elements of our worship: for instance, the integration of body and mind in our liturgies; the involvement of all the baptized in such a way as to allow each order of ministry, in the words of the Prayer Book, to "fulfill the functions proper to their respective orders";[147] the combination of the many other elements to be considered (time, location, vestments, artwork, language, music, worship aids, and the like). As Weil observes: "Sacraments are not purely intellectual activities. They are celebrated by specific human persons in a specific social context and all this multiplicity of factors shapes their participation in the meaning of the sign . . . From this perspective, it is impossible to discuss sacramental theory apart from liturgical practice."[148] Our current sacramental theology now reflects more and more the fact that sacraments are *liturgical actions*, realities to be experienced rather than simply studied, celebrated rather than simply administered.

---

146. From a sermon delivered by then-Cardinal Joseph Ratzinger to the German Bishops Conference, 1979. See Davies, *Pope Paul's New Mass*, 240.

147. *The Book of Common Prayer*, "Concerning the Service," 13.

148. Weil, *Sacraments and Liturgy*, 2–3.

"The recovery of the classical substance and forms of Christian worship," says Geoffrey Wainwright, "was an aim, and to a considerable degree the achievement, of the modern liturgical movement in both its Catholic and its Protestant manifestations. Never an end in itself, the recovery subserved the active, intelligent participation of the people of God in worship that expressed the gospel and the faith in their purity and their richness."[149] Under the scrutiny of contemporary scholarship, many of the scriptural interpretations underlying much of our earlier sacramental theology have been called into question. In addition, many of the customs and traditions so familiar to the church's liturgy that for centuries were believed to be the practices of the primitive church have been revealed to have originated no later than the Middle Ages or the period of the Renaissance.

The introduction to Section III, "The Reform of the Sacred Liturgy," in The Constitution on the Sacred Liturgy states that "In order that the Christian people may more certainly derive an abundance of graces from the sacred liturgy, holy Mother Church desires to undertake with great care a general restoration of the liturgy itself. For the liturgy is made up of immutable elements divinely instituted, and of elements subject to change." The latter, it goes on to say, "not only may but *ought* to be changed with the passage of time if they have suffered from the intrusion of anything out of harmony with the inner nature of the liturgy or have become unsuited to it."[150]

149. Wainwright, "Renewing Worship."
150. *SC* III, 21 (italics added).

The Models and the Scope of Sacramental Effects

Old School Model	New School Model
An understanding of sacraments—and sacramental rites—as rituals which take place only within the time of the celebration. A 'vertical' perspective of the sacramental process that focuses on the moment of celebration.	Sacraments as a means of personal transformation which begins with God's prevenient[151] grace and unfolds throughout the successive stages of our lives. Both a 'horizontal' and a 'vertical' perspective of sacraments. A recognition of sacraments as a means of growth, renewal and conversion allowing Christians at every age and in every stage of life to reclaim their mission to carry on the work of Christ as his ministers in the world.
Sacraments are, for the most part, limited in scope: e.g., marriage, reconciliation, unction for healing, etc.	"As an extension of the work of Christ [sacraments] lead to mission and service, providing effective grace for the individual as related to the community."[152]

One of the characteristics of the Old School model is a tendency to regard sacraments as rituals that confer grace almost automatically at the time of the ritual, to be received or not by the faithful, depending on various factors (such as proper disposition, etc.). We might think of it as a vertical perspective of the sacramental process, focusing on the moment of celebration. The later Scholastics, says Martos, "erected an elaborate intellectual system of theological terms that had little or no reference to the lives that people actually led or to the religious experiences that they actually had. The sacraments that were received were spiritual realities in the soul that were neither experienced nor known except in virtue of the sacramental rites."[153]

151. Coming before, preceding.
152. Hughes, "Sacraments and Ordination."
153. Martos, *Doors to the Sacred*, 71.

This development marked the loss of the sense of the sacraments as a 'way' or a process unfolding throughout the stages of a believer's life—an understanding that had been integral to the early church. Sacraments, for the early Christians, were not limited to the moment of celebration. The sacramental process, leading to the moment of celebration and then beyond, was one that began with conversion (the response of faith to God's prevenient grace), was nourished by evangelism, and proceeded by degrees to the moment of celebration.

Furthermore, this moment of celebration was not regarded as an end in itself, but as part of an *ongoing* process of conversion, the gradual re-forming of one's human character after the pattern of Christ, effected through the Holy Spirit. The scope of the sacrament of penitence, for instance, was not confined to the moment of confession and the pronouncement of absolution. It was a process that, from around the second to the fifth centuries, involved confession, penance, reconciliation and restoration to the community of faith from which one had been estranged by sin. It was a process that took place in successive stages, which in turn were marked by various liturgical rites. Baptism, likewise, was not something whose scope was considered to be limited to the time of celebration. The rite of baptism was the highlight of a long process of conversion marked by one's enrollment as a catechumen, in the course of which, says Duffy, the process of interaction between the baptized and the catechumens who were preparing for baptism sought to "renew the commitment of the baptized while evoking commitment from the nonbaptized candidates."[154]

How then was this sense of the sacraments as an ongoing process of conversion and transformation lost? The problem, says Fink, lies in the Scholastic theology that tried to make sense of them.

> The scholastic theology of sacraments simply did not have a mechanism, nor even the language, to relate participation in sacraments to the ongoing transformation into Christ. It did, of course, name "sanctifying grace" as an increased share in the life of Christ, but beyond affirming it, there was little in scholastic theology to describe just what that meant or how it took effect. It did speak as well of "actual grace," which is the help the sacraments give for living one's life, but even here there was little intrinsic connection drawn between the actual enactment of the sacrament and the grace that ensued. Sacraments were envisioned episodically, that is, as individual experiences with their own specific value and

154. Duffy, *A Roman Catholic Theology of Pastoral Care*, 20.

effect, and not within the process view that ongoing transformation into Christ calls for.[155]

In contrast to the episodic perspective of the Old School model depicted above, the New School model has recovered an understanding of *sacrament-as-way*, that is to say, sacraments as part of a life-long transformational journey. The individual who receives the sacrament participates in a relationship with Christ shared by all other members of Christ's body, the church, and both, Fink reminds us "must undergo a continual process of transformation into Christ."[156] Thus, according to a recent Church of England study, "the reception into the community is the beginning of a journey of growth into the pattern of Christ . . . This journey will pass through different stages of maturity and responsibility; there will be crises, reversals and renewals which it may sometimes be appropriate to acknowledge and support in a public way."[157] The unfolding of the various stages of the sacraments begins with the call to conversion; their fullness is experienced in the living out of them. The catechumenate is a prime example of this: the call to conversion, the preparation, the celebration (the sacrament of baptism), and the living out of the new life into which the individual has been initiated. In other words, Beguerie and Duchesneau observe, "The time which precedes the celebration and that which follows it are also part of the sacrament . . . Liturgical celebrations are not the 'whole' of the sacramental life. They are its 'source and climax.'"[158]

Sacraments, as we have seen, are not private actions but public, liturgical actions, celebrations of the church. As such, we must ask ourselves what purpose they serve in God's *oikonomia*—God's divine economy. According to the Old School model, the sacraments—holy matrimony, reconciliation, unction, etc.—are, for the most part, limited in scope. Each sacrament occupies its own particular sphere of influence, so to speak. For instance, the traditional emphasis in the sacramental rite of holy matrimony has long been chiefly on the relationship between the husband and wife, with, of course, a stress on the importance of the role of the couple in raising their children in the love and knowledge of God. However, all sacraments possess

155. Fink, *Worship: Praying the Sacraments*, 11.

156. Ibid., 14.

157. Church of England, Archbishops' Council. "Initiation Services: Commentary by the Liturgical Commission," Liturgical Commission and the General Synod's Revision Committee on the Initiation Services.

158. Beguerie and Duchesneau, *How to Understand the Sacraments*, 35.

both a horizontal and a vertical dimension. To illustrate, in the sacramental rite of marriage, while the couple who are united in holy matrimony have come to celebrate the love that exists between them and to publicly enter into a "solemn and public covenant" with one another, the union into which they enter also has a broader aspect, both private and corporate. In the words of Bernard Cooke, "Christian marriage is the woman and the man in their unfolding relationship to each other as Christians; they are sacrament for each other, sacrament to their children, and sacrament to all those who come to know them. The meaning of what they are for each other should become for them and others a key part of what it means to be human."[159]

Accordingly, in contrast to previous liturgies, the Episcopal Church's new marriage rite reflects a broader and more eschatological[160] dimension, one that is expressed in the bidding of the new couple to be "a sign of Christ's love" to the world.[161] The relationship into which husband and wife enter is to mirror its ideal, the relation of Christ to the church. As they continue to grow in love they become, with God's grace, reflections of Christ's own self-giving in order that they "may reach out in love and concern for others."[162] Even this most seemingly private of sacramental rites, therefore, clearly possesses an essential corporate and ecclesial—and ultimately, forward-looking, eschatological—dimension.

Similarly, our rites of healing should communicate a similar dimension, central to the New School model's awareness of the scope of sacramental effects. Lizette Larson-Miller explains: "As healing overcomes death and reveals the promise of immortality, and the oil (particularly perfumed oil) is symbolic of the 'oil of paradise,' so the sick person witnesses to our future fulfillment in concrete and specific ways . . . In relation to this eschatological role, the rite must not 'be limited to consoling words and strengthening gestures,' but it must also proclaim this 'liberation' of a new

---

159. Cooke, *Sacraments & Sacramentality*, 93.

160. Eschatology is the branch of theology relating to "last things." It is concerned not just with death, the Last Judgment and the end of the world, but also the second coming, the resurrection of the dead, etc. The Eucharist is our foretaste of the eschatological heavenly banquet, just as the liturgy for Christian marriage signifies to us "the mystery of the union between Christ and his Church" (423) and the Blessing of the Marriage concludes: "bring them to that table where your saints feast forever in your heavenly home"(*The Book of Common Prayer*, 430).

161. *The Book of Common Prayer*, 428.

162. Ibid., 429.

vocation and new future, as well as the reality of the suffering Christ and the suffering Christian in Christ."[163] All our sacramental rites invite us to look beyond the immediate horizon of their effects in order that we too may become "a sign of Christ's love"[164] to the world. This truth is powerfully expressed in *the* great sacrament of healing, the Eucharist: "Deliver us from the presumption of coming to this Table for solace only, and not for strength; for pardon only, and not for renewal. Let the grace of this Holy Communion make us one body, one spirit in Christ, *that we may worthily serve the world in his name.*"[165]

The Models and the Relation of Word and Sacrament

Old School Model	New School Model
Little sense of the relationship between word and sacrament. Liturgies rich in material symbolism but marked by the mediocre quality of the proclamation of the word of God, or else word-heavy liturgies in which the role of the sacramental rite is treated as subordinate to the proclamation of the Word.	Through the sacraments the church enacts God's Word. Both word *and* sacrament serve to elucidate the underlying mystery, and are allowed to do so in a way that enables the faithful to be thereby engaged.

"Whether within the biblical text or beyond," observe Brown and Loades, "words can and do . . . function sacramentally, despite all their apparent clash and dissonance. For it is precisely through meditation upon such images that our participation in the Word made flesh is most effectively deepened. Chewing the eucharistic elements and chewing the words should thus not be seen as opposed activities. Words, no less than the Word himself, can be fully sacramental."[166] The account in the gospel of Luke of the two disciples on the road to Emmaus[167] describes this essential rela-

163. Larson-Miller, *The Sacrament of Anointing of the Sick*, 68.

164. *The Book of Common Prayer*, 428.

165. Ibid., Eucharistic Prayer C, 372.

166. Brown and Loades, "Introduction: The Divine Poet," in *Christ: The Sacramental Word*, 20; quoted in: "Case Study 4.23."

167. Luke 24:13–49.

tionship most profoundly. Luke tells us that on the evening of the day of Jesus's resurrection, two of his disciples are returning home to the village of Emmaus, about seven miles from Jerusalem. They have heard the women's account of the miraculous encounter at the empty tomb and of the glad tidings of the angelic messengers, but "these words seemed to them an idle tale, and they did not believe them." As they walk sadly along, they are joined by a mysterious stranger, who asks them what it is they have been discussing. *Haven't you heard about this Jesus of Nazareth*, they reply, and proceed to relate to him these recent events, unable to recognize that it is their Lord walking alongside them, even after he explains to them "in all the scriptures the things concerning himself." It is not until later, when they sit down together at the table, and Jesus takes the bread, blesses, breaks it, and gives it to them, that their eyes are opened and they recognize him. Later they ask one another, "Did not our hearts burn within us while he talked to us on the road, while he opened to us the scriptures?" Yet until word and symbolic act were combined, they were unable to recognize the Lord in their midst.

Over the centuries an appreciation for the crucial relationship between word and symbol in the sacraments began gradually to slip away. The reason for this lies, in part, in the intellectualizing the rites underwent at the hands of the later Scholastics in their attempt to pin down exactly what sacraments were and how they effected the grace that it was agreed they conveyed. The focus was drawn away from the context of the underlying divine mystery out of which the rituals had arisen and toward, instead, the various *details* of the rituals themselves. As Bausch explains: "In the process of analyzing them, the mystery was stripped to what some thought were the bare essentials. Then these essentials were put in the concrete form of laws and rubrics. Now there was a quick and easy measurement of their validity. It was made easier to say, *this* is a sacrament; *that* is not.' It was easier to figure out precisely where grace resided and what to do to get it. Every person with rubrical savvy could call it forth."[168]

However, it was not always so. "The writings of the Fathers of the Church," says Vaillancourt, "who describe the sacramental practice of the early centuries attribute great importance to proclamation or revelation as a dynamic factor in the sacramental process."[169] In the fifth century, for instance, St. Augustine, who defined a sacrament as "a sign of sacred real-

168. Bausch, *A New Look at the Sacraments*, 7.
169. Vaillancourt, *Toward a Renewal of Sacramental Theology*, 91.

ity" and as "a visible word" or communication from God, declared: "*Accedit verbum ad elementum et fit sacramentum*."[170] Aquinas would explain some eight centuries later:

> Now Augustine says (De Doctr. Christ. ii) that "words are the prin-
> ciple signs used by men"; because words can be formed in various
> ways for the purpose of signifying various mental concepts, so that
> we are able to express our thoughts with greater distinctness by
> means of words. And therefore in order to insure the perfection
> of sacramental signification it was necessary to determine the sig-
> nification of the sensible things by means of certain words . . . The
> sensible elements of the sacraments are called words by way of a
> certain likeness, in so far as they partake of a certain significative
> power, which resides principally in the very words . . . Conse-
> quently it is not a superfluous repetition to add words to the visible
> element in the sacraments; because one determines the other. [171]

The Word of God, Vorgrimler says, "(always clothed in human words), however it is communicated, is not limited to demonstrative or informative function: it effects what it says; it brings what it announces."[172] Unfortunately, as Christianity made the transition from struggling sect to official institution, the proclamational role of the sacraments became less of a consideration in its liturgies. Vaillancourt notes: "[The Church] be-came less preoccupied with revealing its own mystery than with showing Christians all the implications of a mystery with which they were assumed to be already familiar."[173] In time, the preoccupation of the canonists with the causal power of the sacraments would overpower any sense of the sac-ramental rite as a word-event: a means by which that which is articulated in words—the mystery of salvation—is given tangible expression, and by which proclamation becomes encounter. The result, Bouyer points out, was a ritual service that gradually declined "under the ever-increasing burden of its verbal trapping,"[174] and that clearly demonstrated a lack of appre-ciation for the important revelatory and performative aspect of the words themselves. He describes a typical Mass of the Middle Ages in which, while

---

170. "The Word touches the element and the sacrament is made," or alternately, "The Word touches the element and becomes the sacrament." Augustine, *On the Gospel of St. John*, 80, 3.

171. Thomas Aquinas, *Summa Theologica*, Pt. III, Q. 60, Art. 4.

172. Vorgrimler, *Sacramental Theology*, 77.

173. Vaillancourt, *Toward a Renewal of Sacramental Theology*, 91.

174. Bouyer, *Rite and Man*, 60.

observing the rubrics, "the priest hurries through the required gestures, stammers through words which are supposed to be essential, but which no one could hear even if they wanted, and which are treated as if they no longer aimed at any kind of intelligibility."[175] Just as unfortunate, says Schanz, was the "fossilization of the Roman Mass in the Latin tongue." While the retention of Latin may have been inspired, he observes, "by the political desire to employ every possible expedient of unity," by the seventh century, "Latin made impossible the earlier dialogue format of the primitive liturgy. People no longer understood what was said at the altar. . . "[176]

Several centuries later, Martin Luther would declare: *Fides ex auditu*: "So faith comes from what is heard, and what is heard comes by the preaching of Christ."[177] Essential to a sound and lively faith, he understood, was knowledge of the word of God, which for Luther and the reformers meant that the Bible had to be available to the faithful in a language, as Cranmer would say, "understanded [*sic*] of the people," not in an ancient tongue comprehended only by the privileged classes, guarded and meted out by the ecclesial authorities.[178]

The emphasis by the Roman Church on the *power* of the sacraments at the cost of their essential revelatory dimension, says Schanz, was a contentious issue for the reformers. Regrettably, however, their typical response— to place an even greater stress on the proclamation of the word and to further downplay the role of ritual and symbol—tended to demonstrate a corresponding lack of appreciation for the essential relationship of word and sacrament.[179] "Simply reversing the general trend of thought," says Bouyer, "they passed from the correct conception that true religion cannot lose itself in unintelligibility to the much more questionable position that a religion is true to the extent that it is immediately and wholly intelligible . . . This very soon gave rise to . . . the desire . . . to reduce everything to an obvious meaning, without any mysteries."[180]

Little wonder that the conflict between the Roman Catholic Church and the reformers is often characterized as a word/sacrament dichotomy:

175. Ibid.

176. Schanz, *The Sacraments of Life and Worship*, 275.

177. Rom 10:17.

178. Luther notes that he himself was twenty before he ever saw a Bible.

179. This is all the more unfortunate, considering that Luther described a sacrament as a word that is not simply pronounced but acted out.

180. Bouyer, *Rite and Man*, 59.

on the one hand, an emphasis on the sacraments (and in particular, their causal power), with a corresponding deemphasis on the word, and on the other hand, a strong emphasis on the centrality of the word, with a decreasing emphasis placed on the significative power of the sacraments. In the words of Macquarrie, "If catholics [*sic*] have erred in the direction of an exaggerated objectivity, protestants [*sic*] have sometimes been guilty of making our human faith the foundation of the sacrament."[181] Both sides suffered from the same theological handicap, if it can be called that, in that consciously or otherwise, both were still struggling to understand the sacraments apart from their essential ecclesial context, and divorced from their essential proclamatory role, approaching them as though word and sacrament served two different functions, rather than being a part of the same dynamic. In this regard, whether Roman Catholic or Protestant, the Old School model can be distinguished by a failure to appreciate the importance of the relationship of word and sacrament, an unfortunate state of affairs that manifests itself in two very different ways.

The first, says Schanz, regards "the service or liturgy of the word [as] subordinate and merely preparatory to the essential sacramental act,"[182] and expresses itself in what we might call ceremony-centered liturgies. These are liturgies rich in material symbolism, but in which the mediocre quality of the proclamation of the word of God—whether in reading, preaching or in the celebration of the sacraments—makes it clear that little if any consideration has been given to the fact that *both* word and sacrament are symbolic means of conveying the mystery of salvation, that both are vehicles of God's communication, meant to engage us and transform us through our faithful response. Proclamation, in such circumstances, may take the form of formulas—ritual words, often hurriedly pronounced,[183] or sometimes even inaudible,[184] whose meaning is all but lost on the congregation—or else they may take the form of doctrinally correct but spiritually

---

181. Macquarrie, *A Guide to the Sacraments*, 53.

182. Schanz, *Introduction to the Sacraments*, 60.

183. One reason why the sacramental formulas were often so quickly and mechanically pronounced was on account of the desire to stress the fact that the sacraments 'work' *ex opere operato* and not owing to the merits of the celebrant.

184. In *Pope Paul's New Mass*, Michael Davies laments the fact that the "silent canon," which decreed that the Eucharistic Prayer was to be recited by the presider in a low, even inaudible, tone of voice, is, in the new Roman Rite, "not simply no longer obligatory, but forbidden" (380).

unengaging "moral prescriptions" that have been all but stripped of their symbolic power.

At the other extreme, we find what might be called word-heavy liturgies in which the role of the sacramental rite is regarded as subordinate to the proclamation of the word. Such liturgies are distinguished by an emphasis on exposition and a corresponding deemphasis on ritual and symbolism. Here we find liturgies in which preaching is given pride of place, and the accompanying ritual actions and symbolism serve, Bouyer notes, as "mere clothing of abstract ideas."[185] The texts of these word-heavy liturgies, he says, "devitalized by the very stress that has been placed upon them,"[186] often seem oddly disconnected somehow from the action taking place, and appear to have been drawn up for instructive purposes with little if any sense of the symbolic power of the words themselves. In such liturgies the words accompany the action, but fail to illuminate, to engage, or to draw the faithful into the saving event in any real, meaningful way. They may instruct, but they are unable to truly *express* the nature of the underlying saving encounter, or else they may express the nature of the saving event, but in a kind of language, says Donald Reeves, that is meaningless to outsiders, or to anyone without a certain degree of theological sophistication.[187] As Macquarrie explains:

> Striking a right balance between the verbal and the non-verbal elements of a sacrament is not easy, as history shows us. In the Protestant churches, the stress has been on the verbal, the ministry of the word, written and spoken. This makes for services of worship that are often drab, with a lengthy sermon as the principle item. It makes heavy demands on the preachers, and their formation tends to be primarily academic. It tends to make Christianity something to be heard and understood, rather than lived. On the other hand, where the sacramental action is excessively stressed, the sermon tends to be hurried and often has little substance, so that in the absence of words, the sacrament may lose its point and become a superstitious or merely mechanical observance.[188]

If the Old School model is marked by the lack of a proper sense of the relation between word and sacrament, the New School model, in contrast,

---

185. Bouyer, *Rite and Man*, 61.

186. Ibid.

187. Reeves, *For God's Sake*, 77.

188. Macquarrie, *A Guide to the Sacraments*, 25–26.

manifests in its liturgies an appreciation for the complex proclamatory and symbolic function of both word and ceremony in the sacramental event. Not only do word and symbol together serve to elucidate the underlying mystery, but they are allowed to do so in a way that enables the faithful to be thus engaged. In other words, the proclamation of the word of God is not just a preparatory step leading up to the celebration of the sacraments, nor do the words of the liturgy simply fill an instructional or edifying function, or serve as "pleasing ritual noises."[189] In addition, a sensitivity to the use of symbolic language—poetic language, ritual language, imagery, metaphor, formal pronouns, rhyme schemes, archaisms, and so on—even in the course of liturgical revision enriches the worship experience by allowing the faithful to 'connect' with the liturgy on a level that, as Susanne Langer would say, invites insight rather than merely a rational or even emotional response.

Honoring the connection between word and sacrament acknowledges the importance of both as a means of God's self-communication. We can draw a parallel from human experience. A romantic love between two individuals without any perceptible means of expression is an exercise in frustration; conversely, mere physical expression without communication, in some way, of the love underlying it, is all but meaningless. Just so, together, through word, symbol, and ritual God's self-communication is conveyed to human beings through the sacraments in a way that is not just an expression or a proclamation of God's saving grace for humankind, but a means by which we *encounter* that grace in Christ through the power of the Holy Spirit.

In truth, the perceived dichotomy of word and sacrament proves false. Word and sacrament, in fact, are not two different things, but rather, two vital expressions of God's own sacrificial self-giving through Jesus Christ, by which we enter into engagement with the Living God. Thus, Jesus Christ, the Word Incarnate, becomes for us the sacrament of God, the perfect expression and image through which God's grace is communicated to us. Richard Norris observes: "So the sacraments . . . are part of the very constitution of the church. The church cannot be itself apart from the hearing of God's Word through the Scriptures and the proclamation of their message. No more, however, can it be itself apart from the grace by which this Word gets internalized—by which the ekklesia is enabled to agree from the inside

189. Perham, *Lively Sacrifice*, 74.

with Christ who is its life. And that, by God's grace, is what happens in the carrying out of the sacraments."[190]

Towards a New Understanding of Sacrament

So, then, with the aid of traditional terminology, how might we define sacraments anew? Drawing upon and expanding on the definition given in the Catechism, we might begin by saying that a sacrament is
a liturgical action of the assembled Church, rooted in the Paschal Mystery, and *derived from the life and ministry of Christ* ("given by Christ").

Furthermore, in the sacraments
by tangible and perceptible signs, by which God's love is proclaimed, manifested and encountered ("outward and visible signs"), *the faithful recall, celebrate and respond to the offer of God's grace* ("inward and spiritual grace").

Through the sacraments
the body of Christ is transformed and built up that it might glorify God by sharing in Christ's redeeming mission and ministry, "being sanctified by the power of the Holy Spirit" ("as sure and certain means which we receive that grace").

This is the heart of the theology of the sacraments. The very nature of the love of God is such that it needs to be expressed in order to actualize itself in creation, and it needs to be expressed in ways perceptible to human beings in order that they might respond to and participate in it. God is present in Christ Jesus, who is himself the revelation of the love of God. By means of these worldly realities—the sacraments—the mystery of salvation is able to take on flesh and blood, and manifest itself in the midst of our human existence.

190. Norris, *Understanding the Faith of the Church,* 217.

3

From the 1549 Visitation Office to a Public Service of Healing

Introduction

THE PURPOSE OF THIS study, as previously noted, is to look at the Episcopal Church's sacramental rites of healing in order to discern how well they help to nurture our faith and to assist our growth into the likeness of Christ at every age and in every stage of life, and to show, moreover, that our sacramental rites are meant to engage us in a mutuality of ministry. In order to do this we must first look at the sacramental rites out of which our own current liturgies of healing evolved, namely, the earlier Prayer Book Visitation Offices. We have come a long way from that first Visitation Office in the Prayer Book of 1549, but its legacy, as we shall see, is still very much with us. In the previous chapter we compared and contrasted the Old School and New School models of sacramental theology. It may be beneficial, as we examine the evolution of our own Anglican rites of healing, to consider them in the light of these two sacramental models.

Our theology, in typical Anglican tradition, is expressed through our liturgies, and the evolution of *The Book of Common Prayer*'s rites of healing reflects an evolving theology of health and ministry. An examination of these liturgies—not just the texts, but such things as the settings in which they take place, the symbols and the gestures they employ, and the accompanying rubrics—tells us much about the way we understand not just the deeper meaning and place of sickness and suffering in our lives as

Christians, but the importance of our own Christian vocation and witness in every circumstance and at every stage of life.

We have examined both the history and the nature of sacraments, and the ways in which they have been interpreted, reinterpreted, celebrated and received throughout the centuries. The task before us now is to reconsider our own Anglican sacramental rites of healing—and in most particular, those of the Episcopal Church—in the context both of their history and underlying theology.

The First Visitation Offices

The rite for the Visitation of the Sick was adapted and translated by Thomas Cranmer from the Sarum[1] manual for the first *Book of Common Prayer* of 1549. After the opening greeting, upon entering into the "sicke mannes presence," the priest was to immediately launch into a recitation of Psalm 143:

> HEARE my prayer, (o lorde,) and Consider my desire:
> herken unto me for thy trueth and righteousnes sake.
> And entre not into judgemente with thy servaunt: for in
> thy sight shal no man living be justified. . .

This would be followed by anthems,[2] which began: "REMEMBRE not Lord our iniquities, nor the iniquities of our forefathers. Spare us good Lord, spare thy people, whom thou hast redemed with thy most precious bloud, and be not angry with us for ever . . . ", to be followed by the Lord's Prayer, and then versicles and responses, and further prayers in which God's

---

1. Sarum: "From the eleventh century on," says Hatchett, "the Roman rite was the rite of Western Europe, except in the area around Milan and some places in Spain. Various late medieval uses, mistakenly called rites, were variants of the Roman rite characteristic of a particular location or monastic order. These uses were marked by Gallican elements or innovations, or by resistance to particular revisions or innovations. In England," he notes, "just before the Reformation, the most popular uses were those of Sarum, York, and Hereford. By far the most popular was the Sarum, the use of Salisbury Cathedral. Its codification was probably begun with the founding of the new cathedral at Salisbury when Richard la Poore was bishop (1217–1228)" (*Commentary on the American Prayer Book*, 4).

2. Anthem: (From *antiphon*) An anthem is a sacred hymn or choral composition that is generally sung, but which may be spoken. The section of the 1979 *Book of Common Prayer* titled Concerning the Service of the Church states: "The words of anthems are to be from Holy Scripture, or from this Book, or from texts congruent with them." An anthem draws the worshiper's attention to or highlights what is taking place.

mercy and protection was beseeched on behalf of the sick person. There followed a very lengthy exhortation in which the sick person was assured that whatever the reason for illness—"whether it bee to trye your pacience for the example of other, and that your fayth may be founde, in the day of the Lorde, laudable, glorious, and honourable, to the encrease of glory, and endelesse felicitie: Orels it be sent unto you to correcte and amende in you whatsoever doeth offende the iyes of our heavenly father"—it was, in any case, God's visitation, or loving chastisement, upon this individual for his benefit. Therefore he was to bear up under it humbly and patiently, submitting himself to God's will, looking upon this sickness situation as an opportunity for the amendment of life, a preparation for death—"so that accusyng and condemnyng yourselfe for your owne faultes, you may fynde mercy at our heavenly fathers hande, for Christes sake, and not be accused and condemned in that fearfull judgement"—and a sharing in Christ's sufferings.

"The modern reader," observes Gordon Jeanes, "can only wonder at the stamina of the sick in former times. Even the 1552 form, which was much abbreviated from 1549, would tax many a healthy person. Both forms included brief prayers, a lengthy exhortation, an examination of the faith and conscience of the sick person, and if necessary the writing of a will. The sick person might wish to make a special confession, and in 1549 a form of absolution was given for the priest to use in this instance and also 'in all private confessions.'"[3]

In these Visitation Offices the minister repeatedly exhorts the sick person to "beare [his] sickenes paciently, trusting in Gods mercy, for his dere sonne Jesus Christes sake, *and render unto him humble thanks for his fatherly visitation*" (italics added). After the exhortation, in which the sick individual was assured that "there should be no greater coumfort to christian persons, then to be made lyke unto Christ, by suffering paciently adversities, troubles, and sicknesses," the sick person was then reminded of the coming judgment for which he must prepare himself. At this point the minister would "*rehearse the articles of the fayth*," beginning with the Apostles' Creed, until he was assured that the sick person believed every part of it. Then the minister would "*examine whether he be in charitie with all the world.*" That is, says Kelsey, the minister would satisfy himself that the sick individual was "truly repentant and ready to make restitution for

3. Jeanes, "Cranmer and Common Prayer." In Charles C. Hefling and Cynthia L. Shattuck, *The Oxford Guide to the Book of Common Prayer: A Worldwide Survey*, 36.

anything he had done wrong . . . When the minister was satisfied of the sick person's faith, freedom from worldly cares and charity for all, he was to remind the patient to make a will, remembering the church, and pay all debts. Then the Office concluded with a Psalm and brief prayers for mercy and such relief as seemed expedient to God."[4]

The concluding rubrics read, "*If the sicke person desyre to be annoynted, then shal the priest annoynte him upon the forehead or breast only, making the signe of the cross.*" While the first Prayer Book of 1549 contained provisions for anointing, it made, however, no provision for the laying on of hands.[5]

The 1549 Visitation Office included Holy Communion, either in the course of an abbreviated service from the reserved sacrament, or in a full Eucharistic celebration in the home of the individual. Even here, however, in what one would expect to be the most encouraging element of the service, the thrust of the Office was still that last rites. The opening Collect for the Eucharist, for instance, begins: "Almightie everlyving God, maker of mankynde, which doest correcte those whom thou doest love, and chastisest every one whom thou doest receyve . . . "

On the whole, the tone of the Visitation Office was hardly an encouraging one. Its character, as has often been observed, was one of unquestioning and faithful resignation in the face of sickness, and earnest preparation for death.[6] "*Forasmuche as all men be subject to many sodaine perils, diseases, and sickenesses, and ever uncertaine what time they shall departe out of this lyfe,*" the introduction to the 1549 Communion of the Sicke declares, it is the duty of the minister to ascertain that "*they may be always in a readiness to dye whensoever it shall please almighty God to call them. . .*"[7] "The unrelenting gloom of the Visitation Office," says Charles Gusmer, "has been vehemently assailed by the healing literature, especially the exhortations

4. Kelsey, *Psychology, Medicine & Christian Healing*, 13–14.

5. The following 1552 Prayer Book omitted, as well, the *anointing* of the sick, and it was not until the 1928 American Prayer Book that both anointing and the laying on of hands (as an alternative to anointing) were reinstated. (Hatchett, *Commentary on the American Prayer Book*, 464.)

6. This focus on the preparation for a "holy death" resounds throughout the works of the sixteenth- and seventeenth-century Anglican divines, such as Jeremy Taylor, John Donne, and Lancelot Andrewes, who stressed the importance of self-examination and repentance on a daily basis, rather than waiting until the last minute.

7. The Society of Archbishop Justus. The Book of Common Prayer Online. "The 1549 Book of Common Prayer: Visitation of the Sick." Online: http://justus.anglican.org/resources/bcp/1549/Visitation_Sick_1549/.

of a God who rains down sickness upon his disobedient servants."[8] Robert Prichard observes: "The Visitation of the Sick was a cram session for the Last Judgment. It was the moment in which Anglicans were prepared for that which would follow. Their hearts would be opened and their sins revealed. One can understand the petition in the Great Litany: 'From dying suddenly and unprepared, Good Lord, deliver us.' Anglicans were serious about preparing for death. One who died suddenly did not have time to make such a preparation."[9]

While they did not altogether dismiss the possibility of recovery, the first Visitation Offices did not hold out much encouragement in that direction, which was not altogether surprising, considering the state of medicine at the time. People tended to die at a much earlier age, often from ailments that could be easily treated today by the family physician. At a time when only the gentry had access to doctors (who often did as much harm as good), says Herbert Benson, and rich and poor alike were forced to rely upon self-diagnosis and self-medication, or to avail themselves of the "elixirs and salves readily available from street venders and shopkeepers," disease was commonly considered to be "the result of some kind of divine judgment."[10] *Sickness must be God's will,* went this way of thinking. *Better to bear up under it patiently than to question God's judgment.* In the era in which these rites were created, to be sure, there was often little confidence on the part of either patient or physician of recovery in the event of serious illness. The prevailing tone of resignation one finds in the Visitation Offices on the whole unwitting belies the hope of restoration to health and function expressed in the prayer of anointing:

> As with this visible oyle thy body outwardly is
> annoynted: so our heavenly father almyghtye God,
> graunt of his infinite goodnesse, that thy soule inwardly
> may be annoynted with the holy gost, who is the spirite
> of al strength, coumforte, reliefe, and gladnesse. And
> vouchesafe for his great mercy (yf it be his blessed will)
> to restore unto thee thy bodely helth, and strength, to
> serve him, and sende thee release of al thy paines,
> troubles, and diseases, both in body and minde.

8. Gusmer, *The Ministry of Healing in the Church of England: An Ecumenical Liturgical Study,* 60–61.

9. Prichard, Lecture 1B "Sickness, Healing, and Forgiveness." Virginia Theological Seminary. Course lecture for LTG 6, Introduction to Anglican Worship. Spring 2005.

10. Benson and Stark, *Timeless Healing,* 111.

The ambiguous theology of the first Visitation Office, says Stuhlman, "is tellingly revealed in the three ways in which the words 'visit' and 'visitation' are used in [the rubrics]." First of all, the Office itself is titled "The Order for the Visitation of the Sick," and here the word "visitation" refers to the visitation, or pastoral call, made by the minister. Second, the initial collects of the rite ask that God "visit and relieve" the sick or "visit . . . and . . . restore unto the sick person his former health." But third, the word is also used in a more ominous sense. The sick person is informed in the exhortation that sickness is "God's *visitation*" and the Collect at Communion speaks of the sick person as one "*visited* by [God's] hand." "This theology of sickness as God's visitation," says Stuhlman, "which directly relates all sickness to the sin of the person afflicted, contradicts the words of Jesus in John's gospel[11] and can be scarcely be said to be theologically defensible."[12]

However, the ambiguity that Stuhlman notes may be more in the sense, I believe, of an acknowledgment of the universal condition of sin: the predicament of a humanity created in God's image but fallen short of the glory of God. It reveals, as well, an appreciation for the complex relationship of the material and the spiritual in any sickness situation. Human beings are wonderfully and intricately made, "complex creatures of body, mind and spirit," says Mitchell, "[so that] healing must include the entire person . . . [who] needs an opportunity to deal with the sense of sin and separation which often accompanies sickness."[13] The pastoral care illustrated in the Visitation Office, Prichard suggests, is focused not on "a one-on-one relationship between some sequence of acts and the current illness, but upon the general condition of all sinful people."[14]

By the time of the 1552 Prayer Book, the previously noted provision for Communion from the reserved sacrament disappeared altogether, as a result, perhaps, of the uneasiness of many of the reformers about Communion outside of congregational celebrations. One can perceive the influence of one of Cranmer's theological consultants, Peter Martyr,[15] standing as he

11. John 9:3.

12. Stuhlman, *Occasions of Grace*, 161.

13. Mitchell, *Praying Shapes Believing*, 209.

14. Prichard, "Sickness, Healing, and Forgiveness."

15. Peter Martyr (1500–1562), born Pietro Martore Vermigli in Florence. Augustinian abbot and prior, later Regius Professor of Divinity at Oxford. His sympathy with the aims of the reformers resulted in serious repercussions on the part of Rome. After fleeing Italy and seeking refuge first in Zurich and Basel, and later Strassburg, he eventually settled in England, and was one of the consultants for the 1552 *Book of Common Prayer*.

does, says Samuel Leuenberger, in that reform tradition according to which "all that can interfere with the act of faith through a magical interpretation is avoided. Plainly [according to this way of thinking] Jesus cannot be delivered to the patient in the host or in the bread based on a consecration accomplished long before."[16] Martyr's main concern, says Leuenberger, was the fact that the sick person received the consecrated host without hearing the words of institution. "In this," he says, "it becomes clear for Martyr [that] the celebration of holy communion must be an event in the presence of the congregation."[17] He goes on to say: "The BCP of 1552 took this criticism of Martyr seriously. Hence we . . . find later in the prayer book of 1662 that the words of institution are required in the formula for the Communion of the Sick."[18] Hereafter, up until the present Prayer Book, we find provision for Holy Communion from the reserved sacrament replaced by a requirement for the full celebration of the Eucharist with the sick person, with all the obvious limitations and restrictions that might entail.

In the Prayer Book of 1552, the Office for the Visitation of the Sick underwent a revision that reflected the aversion of the reformers—particularly Martin Bucer[19]—towards what they considered to be superstitious rites, such as the anointing of the sick, particularly in light of the abuses long associated with it. Unfortunately, observes Morton Stone, the elimination of the anointing, which was the unifying element of the rite, resulted in the removal of the rite's most positive and hopeful note. As Stone explains:

> As long as that objective and goal was in mind, there were constructive and animating values in the preceding spiritual exercise. The exhortation to patience, designed to eliminate futile resentments and terrors at the illness itself; the examination of faith and conscience, and the setting in order of the patient's affairs, spiritual and temporal; and the conclusive Confession and convincing Absolution: these were all positive and encouraging, so long as they were explicitly preparations for the supreme Sacrament of healing soul and body. Without it, they collapsed under their own weight,

16. Leuenberger, *Archbishop Cranmer's Immortal Bequest. The Book of Common Prayer of the Church of England*, 19.

17. Ibid.

18. Ibid., 20.

19. Like Calvin, who in his *Institutes* (IV, 18) referred to the rite of unction as a "mere hypocritical stage play," Bucer was of the opinion that the anointing of the sick with oil was an outdated relic of the apostolic age, like the gift of speaking in tongues. Martos, *Doors to the Sacred*, 341–42.

and became negative and depressant, since the only goal to which they led was simply death.[20]

One of the distinctive features of these early Visitation Offices is the characteristic Old School lack of appreciation for the important and essential relationship between word and sacrament, evident, in this case, in their wordy and symbolically impoverished liturgies. Here we find an overriding stress given to the proclamation of the word and to the faith of the individual, and a lack of appreciation for the proclamatory power of symbols. In *Religion and the Decline of Magic*, Keith Thomas describes the manner in which the determination of the reformers "to eliminate theatricality from church ritual and decoration" and to establish a distinction in kind between magic and religion shaped a new concept of religion that "deprecated the aspect of the miraculous and elevated the importance of individual faith."[21] In respect to our earlier Visitation Offices, it was, perhaps, a case of good intentions gone awry. This intense emphasis on theological soundness, and on the proper faith and the right disposition of the individual as the main condition for the reception of grace, as Macquarrie has previously noted, "would seem to be a denial of God's action in the sacrament . . . and dangerously close to "making our human faith the foundation of the sacrament."[22]

The highly symbolic gestures of anointing and the laying on of hands, which speak so eloquently of not simply the remission of sins but of reconciliation with God and the renewal of one's baptismal covenant had, by the 1552 Prayer Book, been removed from the Visitation Office, to its obvious detriment. This lack of appreciation for the manner in which such tangible symbols help to effectively convey God's own self-giving revealed, as well, a lack of appreciation for our own human embodiedness. It is all very well (and necessary, of course) to ensure that our liturgical rites are theologically sound, but while human beings are distinguished from the rest of the created order chiefly by their ability to reason, human thought is, as we have observed, by nature largely symbolic, partly because all human thought contains a subjective element; that is, it possesses an essential, personal, embodied dimension. Would not the Creator of such embodied creatures understand this, and seek to convey divine grace accordingly, in a manner that affirms both our complex bodily and spiritual nature? Therefore, a

---

20. Morton C. Stone, "The Anglican Prayer Books," in *The Order of Ministration to the Sick*, 11.

21. Thomas, *Religion and the Decline of Magic*, 76.

22. Macquarrie, *A Guide to the Sacraments*, 53.

"word-heavy" liturgy (to use Macquarrie's term) that regards such tangible symbols with suspicion and apportions them with a miserly hand may earn our respect in regard to its theological content and scriptural soundness but is more suited for angels than human beings, whose understanding of and appreciation for the world—created and divine—is acquired not simply intellectually but also through the senses.

Geoffrey Rowell, in his essay, "The Sacramental Use of Oil in Anglicanism and the Churches of the Reformation,"[23] quotes the Welsh poet David Jones, who regards the Incarnation as the affirmation of our bodiliness, through which God "'placed himself in the order of signs.'"[24] As Jones observes, "theology regards the body as a unique good. Without body: without sacrament. Angels only: no sacrament. Beasts only: no sacrament. Man sacrament at every turn and all levels of the 'profane' and 'sacred', in the trivial and in the profound, no escape from sacrament."[25] Likewise, in "The Text as Material and Sign," Kathleen Staudt speaks of "poetic language simultaneously as an opaque material—like the stone, paint, or tonality of other art forms—and as a communicating sign, mediating something other than language."[26] And finally, as Peter Fink observes:

> to call an event 'sacrament' is to make two claims about an observable phenomena which is constituted by song, prayer, action, touch, word, interaction. The first claim is that this complex perceptible reality is the language God uses to speak the meaning of Jesus Christ and his saving action to the believer. It is proclamation . . . the event itself is the primary mode of communication to the person who worships . . . The second claim is even more far-reaching. It concerns the way in which the saving action of Jesus Christ unfolds concretely in human life . . . all the human dynamics involved in the sacramental ritual are integral to its effectiveness.[27]

23. Geoffrey Rowell, "The Sacramental Use of Oil in Anglicanism and the Churches of the Reformation." In Dudley and Rowell, *The Oil of Gladness*, 134–53.

24. Jones, *Epoch and Artist*, 167. Quoted by Rowell in "The Sacramental Use of Oil in Anglicanism and the Churches of the Reformation." In *The Oil of Gladness*, 150.

25. Ibid. Rowell notes that the phrase "he placed himself in the order of signs," quoted by Jones derives from the French Jesuit theologian, Maurice de la Taille.

26. Staudt, "The Text as Material and Sign," 13.

27. Fink, *Worship: Praying the Sacraments*, 31.

By the period of the Elizabethan Settlement[28] and the adoption of the Thirty-Nine Articles[29] in their final revision in 1571, according to Article XXV, the rite of holy unction—along with the other "commonly called Sacraments" (Matrimony, Confirmation, Penance, and Orders)—was demoted from full sacramental status to the status of "other rites and ceremonies."[30] The Visitation of the Sick was retained in the 1662 Prayer Book, but the *anointing* of the sick, as we have observed, would not be restored to *The Book of Common Prayer* until the 1928 American Prayer Book.

One can appreciate the strange tension under which these Visitation Offices were created. Officially, the Anglican liturgical rites of healing had been downgraded, as we have seen, from full sacramental status to the status of "other rites and ceremonies." The rite of unction had not been rejected outright by the Church of England in the same way that it had been by many of the Protestant reformers, such as Martin Luther (on the grounds that there was no real proof in Scripture of its dominical institution), or by John Calvin (who argued that, *yes*, the early church had exercised a miraculous gift of healing, but by no means did it require the use of blessed oil). Anointing was, in the minds of many of the leading reformers, an obsolete practice, something that had been exercised by the apostles, but which belonged entirely to another age.

28. Elizabethan settlement of 1559: After Elizabeth's accession to the throne, following the death of her sister Mary, "Parliament restored royal supremacy, but under title of 'supreme governor' of the Church. [The] Uniformity Act restored [the] second Edwardian Prayer Book, but compromised on [the] question of [the] real presence: the 1552 phraseology which implied communion was only a symbolic act was supplemented by [the] 1549 words which suggested Christ's body really present in [the] eucharist. Elizabeth's Council had difficulty getting [the] legislation accepted, especially through [the] resistance by [the] Catholic bishops and nobles who forced concessions." Simon Adams, "Government and Politics 1553–1625: Crown, Church and Parliament." In Haigh, *The Cambridge Historical Encyclopedia*, 155.

29. "The Thirty-Nine Articles were the result of a long process in which the Church of England attempted to provide a theological foundation for its existence during the doctrinal conflicts of the sixteenth century. The conflicts arose from the competing views between Protestants and Roman Catholics as well as controversy within the Church of England itself. The Articles are not a creed nor are they a confessional statement such as those produced by the churches of the Reformation. They seek only to provide a basic consensus on disputed points and to separate the Church of England from certain Roman Catholic doctrines which were regarded as medieval abuses or superstitions. At the same time, however, they affirmed other aspects of Christian belief which were held by the Roman Catholic Church." Armentrout and Slocum, *An Episcopal Dictionary of the Church*, "Thirty-Nine Articles, or Articles of Religion," 519.

30. *The Book of Common Prayer*, Historical Documents, Articles of Religion, 872.

The consensus of Bucer and the continental reformers (following the 1549 Prayer Book) was that while the apostles had anointed and healed the sick with oil, and this divine power of healing, like the gift of tongues, had been exercised by the apostles and by many others in the early church, the use of holy oil in this day and age for the healing of the sick was little more than superstitious practice. The Old School fixation on the dominical institution of the sacraments left the architects of the Visitation Office in an awkward position. Unction was no longer an official sacrament, and clearly suspect in the eyes of many, yet some sort of pastoral liturgy was needed for the care of the sick and the dying. The result was a curious (and characteristically Anglican) compromise, as expressed in Article XXV of the Articles of Religion:[31]

> Sacraments ordained of Christ be not only badges or tokens of Christian men's profession, but rather they be certain sure witnesses, and effectual signs of grace, and God's good will towards us, by the which he doth work invisibly in us, and doth not only quicken, but also strengthen and conform our faith in him.

> There are two sacraments **ordained of Christ** our Lord in the Gospel, that is to say, Baptism, and the Supper of the Lord.

> Those five **commonly called Sacraments**, that is to say, Confirmation, Penance, Orders, Matrimony, and Extreme Unction, **are not to be counted for Sacraments of the Gospel**, being such as have grown partly of the corrupt following of the Apostles, partly are states of life allowed in the Scriptures; but yet have not like nature of Sacraments with Baptism, and the Lord's Supper, for that **they have not any visible sign or ceremony ordained of God.**

Article XXV does not actually come out and state that Unction, Confirmation, Penance, Orders, and Matrimony are *not* sacraments, but rather, asserts that they are not "Sacraments of the Gospel." Over the centuries the "five commonly called Sacraments" have unofficially come to be regarded, in many quarters, as 'lesser sacraments,' an *almost-but-not-quite* sort of designation: a means of grace, to be sure, but as the Catechism states, "not necessary for all persons in the same way that Baptism and the Eucharist are."[32] One should, however, keep in mind the fact that, as Peter Toon points out,

31. "The Articles of Religion" (1801), in The Book of Common Prayer, 872.
32. Catechism, 860.

the Articles of Religion were meant to lay down "within the mid-sixteenth-century situation, as much as was necessary to secure Catholic faith and ordered life in the Church of England; and they do not seek to go past the minimum. On the central issues of the gospel they are full and exact. Yet they are as broad and comprehensive as was deemed to be consistent with theological safety."[33]

The uncomfortable compromise was a sacramental rite for the sick that, for the most part, served as preparation for death and judgment. It offered little hope in regard to healing, and not much more in the way of comfort: "Remember not, Lord, our iniquities, nor the iniquities of our forefathers. Spare us, good Lord, spare thy people, whom thou hast re-demed with thy most precious bloud, and be not angry with us forever. . ." This is less a grace-empowered renewal of life than a rehearsal for death.

The rubric in the Visitation Office allowing for private confession continued to appear up through the 1662 *Book of Common Prayer*. The Visitation of the Sick, Prichard notes, "was . . . the one place in which Cranmer retained references to private confession." He continues: "No actual form was provided for confession, however. I suspect that 16th century Anglicans assumed that forms for confession were so well known that it was unnecessary to print them (much in the same way that the Rite II Communion service omits any form of the blessing, assuming that any celebrant will be able to supply what is needed). By the mid seventeenth century, private confession had fallen out of favor, and no one saw any need to provide a form."[34]

Neither the 1789 nor the 1892 American *Book of Common Prayer* contained actual forms for a special Confession and Absolution in their Visitation Offices, although one finds up through the 1892 American Prayer Book a consistent emphasis on the need for repentance and an understanding of illness as preparation for the Last Judgment. "*Then shall the Minister examine whether [the sick person] repent him of his sins and be in charity with all the world; exhorting him to forgive, from the bottom of his heart, all persons that have offended him; and if he hath offended any other, to ask them forgiveness; and where he hath done injury or wrong to any man, that he make amends to the uttermost of his power.*"

33. Peter Toon, "The Articles and Homilies," in Sykes and Booty, *The Study of Anglicanism*, 137.

34. Prichard, "Sickness, Healing and Forgiveness."

By examining the rubrics following the Communion of the Sick in the 1789 and 1892 *Book of Common Prayer*, which indicate that the rite may be used with "*aged and bed-ridden persons who are not able to attend public Ministration in Church*," one can begin to discern a subtle change in tone: death is no longer automatically assumed to follow in the wake of serious illness.

In the early decades of the twentieth century, the 1920 Lambeth Conference, responding to the growing interest in the church's ministry of healing, and concerned about the increasing popularity of Spiritualism, Christian Science, and Theosophy, commissioned the *Lambeth Report on the Ministry of Healing*, which would be released in 1924.[35] The report recommended a revised Order for the Visitation of the Sick that would not only include provisions for a special confession of sin, but would also restore the unction of the sick as "more immediately directed to the complete restoration of the patient."[36]

If earlier Visitation Offices were the product of a state of medicine in which physicians could do little in the event of serious illness other than make the patient as comfortable as possible, the tone of the 1928 Prayer Book is one that exhibits a more positive tenor in accordance with the remarkable developments in the rapidly advancing science of medicine. Now, with an ever increasing likelihood of recovery, the faithful were less receptive to being instructed to resign themselves to death! As *Prayer Book Studies III* notes:

> No longer is it the chief task of the physician to make the patient as comfortable as possible until death overtakes him, or until the indomitable urge of all life towards health has wrought its own cure. He is engaged in a confident battle with sickness and death, with inflexible hope of victory. He will welcome the ministrations of the Church if they are constructive, removing troubles of the mind and soul which impede concentration upon the task of recovery— but not if they give up the fight by merely instilling resignation to the approach of death.[37]

35. This growing interest in the church's ministry of healing was the result of a number of influences, including high church groups such as the Non-Jurors in the eighteenth century, the nineteenth-century Oxford Tractarians, and the Anglo-Catholic party, with its emphasis on the church's sacramental life.

36. Quoted in "The Visitation of the Sick: Unction, Imposition of Hands, and Exorcism," by Harris, in *Liturgy and Worship*, 475.

37. *The Order for the Ministration of the Sick*, 11–12.

Interestingly, as Kelsey observes, "The Office of Visitation in the 1928 *Prayer Book* added a great deal of more comforting material. Some of the emphasis was shifted, leaving more to the discretion of the individual priests, but without suggesting to the clergy any fundamental need for changing their way of thinking."[38]

The Visitation Office in the 1928 American Prayer Book included such new prayers as A Prayer for Recovery and A Thanksgiving for the Beginning of a Recovery, thus restoring the focus of the rite on healing. As Prichard notes, however, "The revisers in 1928 did not eliminate all traces of the earlier emphasis upon preparation for death; they simply tried to separate it from the prayers of the church for healing. They drafted a new litany for use at the time of death in which the older theme dominated. They appended it to the end of the Visitation of the Sick."[39]

Notably, for the first time since the first *Book of Common Prayer* of 1549, the Visitation of the Sick included the anointing of the sick with holy oil. As Stuhlman observes, "With the recovery of the healing ministry in this century, most of the emphasis at first fell on the restoration of health once again, as is evident from the language of the 1928 provisions for unction."[40] The name of the 1928 Office is still that of the 1549 Prayer Book—The Order for the Visitation of the Sick—but a glance at the two different prayers for anointing speaks volumes.

38. Kelsey, *Psychology, Medicine & Christian Healing*, 14.

39. Prichard, "Sickness, Healing, and Forgiveness."

40. Stuhlman, *Occasions of Grace*, 173.

1549 Book of Common Prayer

If the sicke person desire to be annoynted, then shal the priest annoynte him upon the forehead or breast only, making the signe of the crosse, saying thus,

As with this visible oyle thy body outwardly is annoynted: so our heavenly father almyghtye God, graunt of his infinite goodnesse, that thy soule inwardly may be annoynted with the holy gost, who is the spirite of al strength, coumforte, reliefe, and gladnesse. And vouchsafe for his great mercy (yf it be his blessed will) to restore unto thee thy bodily helth, and strength, to serve him, and send thee release of al thy paines, troubles, and diseases, both in body and minde. And howsoever his goodnesse (by his divine and unserchable providence) shall dispose of thee: we, his unworthy ministers and servaunts, humbly beseche the eternall maiestie, to doe with thee according to the multitude of his innumerable mercies, and to pardon thee all thy sinnes and offences, committed by all thy bodily senses, passions, and carnal affeccions: who also vouchsafe mercifully to graunt unto thee gostely strength, by his holy spirite, to withstand and overcome al temptacions and assaultes of thine adversarye, that in no wise he pravaile against thee, but that thou mayest have perfit victory and triumph against the devil, sinne and death, though Christ our Lord: Who by his death hath overcomed the Prince of death, and with the father, and the holy gost evermore liveth and reigneth God, worlde without ende. Amen.

1928 Book of Common Prayer

When any sick person shall in humble faith desire the ministry of healing through Anointing or Laying on of Hands, the Minister may use such portion of the foregoing Office as he shall think fit, and the following:

O BLESSED Redeemer, relieve, we beseech thee, by thy indwelling power, the distress of this thy servant; release him from sin, and drive away all pain of soul and body, that being restored to soundness of health, he may offer thee praise and thanksgiving; who livest and reignest with the Father and the Holy Ghost, one God, world without end. Amen.

I anoint thee with oil (or I lay my hand upon thee), In the name of the Father, and of the Son, and of the Holy Ghost; beseeching the mercy of our Lord Jesus Christ, that all thy pain and sickness of body being put to flight, the blessing of health may be restored unto thee. Amen.[41]

41. *Book of Common Prayer* (1928), 320.

The new rite restored provisions for a special confession (something that had been dropped from the 1789 Prayer Book): *"Then shall the sick person be moved to make a special confession of his sins, if he feel his conscience troubled with any matter; after which confession, and evidence of his repentance, the Minister shall assure him of God's mercy and forgiveness."*[42] However, the American *Book of Common Prayer* would not provide a specific *form* for private confession until the 1979 Prayer Book.

Like the Visitation Offices before it, the 1928 Visitation of the Sick tended to retain its semi-private aspect. Much in the same manner as previous Visitation Offices, the rubrics for the Communion of the Sick in the 1928 rite *imply*, but do not come right out and *recommend*, that individuals other than the minister and sick person might also be present to receive the sacrament.

1549 Visitation Office	1928 Visitation Office
And yf the same daye there be a celebracion of the holy communion in the churche, then shall the priest reserve (at the holy communion) so muche of the sacrament of the body and bloud, as shall serve the siche person, and as many as shall communicate with hym (yf there be any.) *And so soone as he conveniently may, after the open communion ended in the church, shall goe and minister the same, firste to* those that are appointed to communicate with the sicke (yf there be any), *and last of all to the sicke person himselfe.*	*At the time of the distribution of the holy Sacrament, the Minister shall first receive the Communion himself, and after minister unto* those who are appointed to communicate with the sick, *and last of all, the sick person.*

However more positive its emphasis on healing, the 1928 rite was, in the words of the Standing Liturgical Committee that prepared the proposed revised Visitation Office in 1951, "little better than a disorganized miscellany in its accumulated provisions."[43] Described by Mitchell as "the

42. Ibid., 313.

43. Episcopal Church, Standing Liturgical Commission, *Order for the Ministration of the Si*, 13.

least used and the least usable service in the 1928 Prayer Book,"[44] the 1928 Visitation of the Sick, requiring elaborate preparations, was seldom administered, although there was a widespread tendency among the clergy to adapt segments of it in the course of their pastoral visits. Kelsey, writing in 1966, recalls a conference around that time where the Visitation Office had been read "as part of a paper on healing to a group of the rectors of large churches in one of the large Episcopal dioceses in this country. The reactions of these clergy were quite typical . . . None of them had read it through in many years. Yet a majority supported its basic theology and were very hesitant about any need to change it."[45]

"The visible Church of Christ," reads Article XIX of the Articles of Religion, "is a congregation of faithful men [sic], in which the pure Word of God is preached, and the Sacraments be duly ministered according to Christ's ordinance, in all things that of necessity are requisite to the same."[46] What one finds expressed, however, in the Visitation Offices, is more of the old sense of the church as the official dispenser of the sacraments in the person of the church's duly appointed ministers, or of the church as the place in which the sacraments are "duly ministered." There is no real sense of a mutuality of ministry, nothing to suggest to the faithful that they are not just recipients, but co-celebrants in this sacramental liturgy. There is little to imply that the healing and restoration conveyed by God's grace through this sacramental rite is to enable all the faithful in every stage and circumstance to resume the work for which they were baptized.

All of the Visitation Offices, despite the accompanying rubrics that refer to "*those who are appointed to communicate with the sick,*" have the aspect of quasi-private rites. Certainly, much of this has to do with practical considerations pertinent to the time: physical frailty and infirmity on the part of the sick, fear of contagion, poor roads, difficult travel conditions, and the like. Furthermore, such a rite would only be requested when the individual was in dire circumstances, or "*extremitie of syckenes.*" All in all, considering the fact that so much of the Visitation Offices is taken up with preparation for death, there is little wonder that for so long it was, despite its official title, viewed as a 'last rites' service.

Furthermore, there is little in these Visitation Offices, as we have seen, to suggest either that one need *not* wait until one was on the brink of death

44. Mitchell, *Praying Shapes Believing*, 207.

45. Kelsey, *Psychology, Medicine & Christian Healing*, 15.

46. *The Book of Common Prayer*, Historical Documents, Articles of Religion, 871.

to request sacramental ministrations, or that the Visitation Office might be celebrated in the church in the presence of the assembly of the faithful. There is, on the whole, little that points to the essential corporate nature of this rite (other than the rubrics that refer to those "*appointed to communicate with the sicke*"), indicative of the Old School lack of appreciation for the fact that it is the church—all the baptized, the body of Christ—that not only celebrates the sacraments, but actually functions as a *kind* of sacrament, making Christ present in the world in a very real and tangible way when it acts or speaks as Church.[47]

This furthermore, I believe, points to an uneasiness on the part of the church as to what to make of this rite and how best to employ it, or if it is even necessary! Again, as John Richards explains, "The corporate nature of the act can be made real if it takes place in a corporate setting—the Holy Communion being the obvious one . . . Some [Anglican] theologians, however, object to this on the grounds that nothing can be added to the benefits received in the sacrament, while others maintain that the Holy Communion is the supreme means of bringing one to a 'state of grace' in which state alone one is completely open to any specific and individual blessings God has to give."[48]

The development of our liturgies of healing, from the first Visitation Office of 1549 up to the American Prayer Book of 1928, reveals an uneasy tension created by the desire to fashion a sacramental liturgy capable of addressing both the practical and the spiritual situation of the particular individual, while remaining uncontaminated by the sorts of "vanitie and superstition"[49] (erroneous and misleading abuses and practices) that had come under attack by the reformers.

In an attempt to purge the church of all superstitious ceremonies, some of the richly symbolic elements such as the oil of anointing, that

47. Interestingly enough, the 1552 Prayer Book Visitation Office specifies that when the Communion is to take place in the home of the "sycke person," there should be "a good nombre to receive the communion with the sycke person." Consequent Visitation Offices do not specify "a good nombre" and merely state that the sick person should give timely notice to the Minister as regards the number who are to communicate with him. Also worth noting is the fact that in the original 1549 Visitation Office, the rubrics state that "the sicke person shall all wayes desire some, eyther of his owne house, or els of his neighbors, to receive the holy communion with hym; for that shall be to hym a singular great comfourte, and of theyr parte a great token of charitie."

48. Richards, *But Deliver Us from Evil*, 14.

49. 1662 *Book of Common Prayer*, "Of Ceremonies, Why Some Be Abolished and Some Retained."

powerful symbol of the healing power of God's mercy and loving care, and the ancient biblical gesture of the imposition of hands were eliminated. "Now therefore," the minister exhorts the sick person in the 1789 Prayer Book's Visitation Office, "taking your sickness, which is thus profitable for you, patiently, I exhort you, in the name of God, to remember the profession which you made unto God in your Baptism." And yet the sacramental anointing that would have so movingly served as a reminder of one's baptismal anointing is no longer there! This reveals a tragic lack of appreciation for the role such symbols play as graced mediums for the holy mystery through which we are privileged to share with Christ in "that victory of life and peace."

Three Liturgies of Healing: From the 1979 Ministration to the Sick to Enriching Our Worship 2's A Public Service of Healing

This brings us to the present. The chart on the following page summarizes key elements of our three current liturgies of healing found in the 1979 *Book of Common Prayer*, *The Book of Occasional Services* (1991), and *Enriching Our Worship 2* (2000). This chart briefly outlines the various similarities and differences between each, which we will examine in greater detail.

A Comparison of the Three Rites[50]

If the Visitation Offices are characteristic of an Old School model of sacramental theology, one would expect to find the New School model represented by our most current sacramental rites of healing. Just how far we have come in this respect—and how far we have yet to go—will become evident as we examine all three.

50. Episcopal Church. General Board of Examining Chaplains. "Chart: 2006 General Ordination Exam, Background Material: Set. 2. Liturgy and Church Music."

1979 *Book of Common Prayer* Ministration to the Sick	*Book of Occasional Services* A Public Service of Healing [1991]	*Enriching Our Worship 2* A Public Service of Healing [2000]
Greeting or Acclamation	Greeting	Greeting
--------------	Collect	Collect
Sets of Lessons – a. General b. Penitence c. When Anointing is to follow d. When Communion is to follow	Sets of Lessons— a. Old Testament b. Psalms c. New Testament d. The Gospel	Sets of Lessons a. Old Testament b. Psalms c. New Testament d. Gospel
Sermon	Sermon	Sermon
Prayers	Litany of Healing	Litany for Healing
Confession and Absolution	Confession and Absolution	Confession of Sin and/or Need and Absolution
[Blessing of Oil]	[Blessing of Oil]	[Blessing of Oil]
Anthem	Anthem	--------------
--------------	Prayer of Blessing	Introduction to Laying on of Hands
Laying on of Hands	Laying on of Hands	Laying on of Hands
If no Eucharist: Lord's Prayer and final prayer	--------------	If no Eucharist: Lord's Prayer, Prayers after laying on of hands
The Peace	The Peace	The Peace
--------------	If no Eucharist: —Lord's Prayer, Prayer, Blessing and Dismissal	Blessing and Dismissal
If Eucharist follows	If Eucharist follows	If Eucharist follows
Offertory	Offertory	Offertory
Great Thanksgiving, etc.	Great Thanksgiving, etc.	Great Thanksgiving, etc.
Postcommunion Prayer (usual or appointed in rite)	Postcommunion Prayer (usual or appointed in rite)	Postcommunion Prayer (usual or appointed in rite)
Blessing or Dismissal	Blessing or Dismissal	[Blessing] and Dismissal

Items in brackets are optional according to the rubrics.

We begin with the first of our contemporary sacramental rites of healing, the Ministration to the Sick from the 1979 Prayer Book. More than any
previous American Prayer Book, the 1979 *Book of Common Prayer* reflects
an unmistakable New School aspect: a concept of ministry grounded in
the patterns of the early church, as it calls each of the faithful in a most real
sense into participation as a part of this "chosen race, a royal priesthood, a
holy nation, God's own people."[51] The recovery of the concept of the ministry of all the baptized was propelled to a considerable degree by events such
as the social justice movements of the 1960s and '70s, the emergence of
renewal movements such as Faith Alive (with its emphasis on spiritual renewal, personal witness and lay ministry), the Episcopal charismatic movement, and the Total Ministry movement.[52] In addition, it owes a great deal
to the Anglican–Roman Catholic dialogues following the Second Vatican
Council, which raised such issues, says David Holmes, as "the role of the
laity in parish work, the church as community rather than institution, and
the challenges of the modern world."[53] The "new spirit of self-examination
and openness," says Holmes, between Protestants and Roman Catholics is
reflected in the decision of the Episcopal Church's 1964 General Convention to authorize a revision of the 1928 Prayer Book. To give one an idea of
the difference such a revision made, Holmes observes:

> Episcopalians need only compare worship in their parish churches
> to worship under the 1928 *Book of Common Prayer*. In most par-
> ishes they will find at least the following changes. Congregations
> participate more fully in worship: lay people read the lessons and
> prayers, carry the bread and the wine to the clergy for consecra-
> tion, and assist in the administration of the elements. The prin-
> cipal service of a parish is more frequently the holy communion
> (increasingly called "the Eucharist"), and clergy face the people

51. 1 Pet 2:9.

52. The concept of ministry encompassed in the term "Total Ministry," says Timothy
Sedgwick, is rooted in a vision of an emerging church exemplified by "a ministering
community rather than a community gathered around a minister." Episcopal Diocese of
Newark Total Ministry Task Force, "Report of the Task Force on Total Ministry to the
126th Convention of the Episcopal Diocese of Newark. Report of the Task Force on Total
Ministry to the 126th Convention of the Episcopal Diocese of Newark, January 28 & 29,
2000. This theology of ministry, according to the report of the Task Force, flows from the
recognition of the fact that "all ministry, be it lay, diaconal, priestly or episcopal, flows
from the community's experience of God in its midst." It is, in other words, a response to
God's own gracious initiative.

53. Holmes, *A Brief History of the Episcopal Church*, 163–64.

(instead of turning their backs on them) when celebrating it. Parishes emphasize the fullest possible communion of the congregation, including baptized children."[54]

A cursory examination of our previous rites of healing suggests that one of the aspects in which they were most lacking was their underlying ecclesiology, unwittingly creating privatized rituals out of what should have been communal celebrations. More than any previous *Book of Common Prayer*, says Thaddaeus Schnitker, the 1979 Prayer Book "has succeeded in its liturgy in regaining many ideas the Anglican reformers wanted to pursue when they talked about the reintroduction of a liturgy that would correspond to the ideals of the primitive Church."[55] Central to this, says Schnitker, is "a renewed understanding of the sacramentality of the Church for the world in which it exercises through all its members its ministry of grace and reconciliation, and the expression of that sacramentality in the liturgy in which all members in their different functions are equipped with the means to carry out their tasks."[56]

In order for this to come about, it would take not just a rethinking of our theology of health and ministry, but a recovery over the centuries of our sense of church—and in particular, of our understanding of the church's liturgy as the work of all the people of God. We begin to understand our sacraments and sacramental rites in their true light when we cease to regard sacraments as *things* administered by one individual to another, and begin instead to see them as *liturgical acts* that derive from the whole body of the faithful, the church, which is the sacrament of Christ.

The Ministration to the Sick from the 1979 Book of Common Prayer

In case of illness, the Minister of the Congregation is to be notified.

At the ministration, one or more parts of the following service are used, as appropriate, but when two or more are used together, they are used in the order indicated. The Lord's Prayer is always included.

Part One of this service may always be led by a deacon or lay person.

54. Ibid., 112.
55. Schnitker, *The Church's Worship*, 150.
56. Ibid., 155.

Healing Touch and Saving Word

When the Laying on of Hands or Anointing takes place at a public celebration of the Eucharist, it is desirable that it precede the distribution of Holy Communion, and it is recommended that it take place immediately before the exchange of the Peace.

The Celebrant begins the service with the following or some other greeting

Peace be to this house (place), and to all who dwell in it.

Part I. Ministry of the Word

One or more of the following or other passages of Scripture are read

General

2 Corinthians 1:3–5 (God comforts us in affliction)
Psalm 91 (He will give his angels charge over you)
Luke 17:11–19 (Your faith has made you well)

Penitence

Hebrews 12:1–2 (Looking to Jesus, the perfecter of our faith)
Psalm 103 (He forgives all your sins)
Mark 6:7, 12–13 (They anointed with oil many that were sick)

When Anointing is to follow

James 5:14–16 (Is any among you sick?)
Psalm 23 (You have anointed my head with oil)
Mark 6:7,12–13 (They anointed with oil many that were sick)

When Communion is to follow

1 John 5:13–15 (That you may know that you have eternal life)
Psalm 145:14–22 (The eyes of all wait upon you, O Lord)
John 6:47–51 (I am the bread of life)

After any Reading, the Celebrant may comment on it briefly.

Prayers may be offered according to the occasion.

The Priest may suggest the making of a special confession, if the sick person's conscience is troubled, and use the form for the Reconciliation of a Penitent.

Or else the following general confession may be said

Most merciful God,
we confess that we have sinned against you
in thought, word, and deed,
by what we have done,
and by what we have left undone.
We have not loved you with our whole heart;
we have not loved our neighbors as ourselves.
We are truly sorry and we humbly repent.
For the sake of your Son Jesus Christ,
have mercy on us and forgive us;
that we may delight in your will,
and walk in your ways,
to the glory of your Name. Amen.

The Priest alone says

Almighty God have mercy on you, forgive you all your sins
through our Lord Jesus Christ, strengthen you in all goodness,
and by the power of the Holy Spirit keep you in eternal life. *Amen.*

A deacon or lay person using the preceding form substitutes "us" for "you" and "our" for "your."

Part II. Laying on of Hands and Anointing
If oil for the Anointing of the Sick is to be blessed, the Priest says

O Lord, holy Father, giver of health and salvation: Send your
Holy Spirit to sanctify this oil; that, as your holy apostles

anointed many that were sick and healed them, so may those
who in faith and repentance receive this holy unction be
made whole; through Jesus Christ our Lord, who lives and
reigns with you and the Holy Spirit, one God, for ever and ever. *Amen.*

The following anthem is said

Savior of the world, by your cross and precious blood you
have redeemed us;
Save us and help us, we humbly beseech you, O Lord.

*The Priest then lays hands upon the sick person, and says one of the
following*

N, I lay my hands upon you in the Name of the Father, and
of the Son, and of the Holy Spirit, beseeching our Lord Jesus
Christ to sustain you with his presence, to drive away all
sickness of body and spirit, and to give you that victory of life
and peace which will enable you to serve him both now and
evermore. *Amen.*
or this

N, I lay my hands upon you in the Name of our Lord and
Savior Jesus Christ, beseeching him to uphold you and fill
you with his grace, that you may know the healing power of
his love. *Amen.*

*If the person is to be anointed, the Priest dips a thumb in the holy oil,
and makes the sign of the cross on the sick person's forehead, saying*

N, I anoint you with oil in the Name of the Father, and of
the Son, and of the Holy Spirit. *Amen.*

The Priest may add

As you are outwardly anointed with this holy oil, so may our
heavenly Father grant you the inward anointing of the Holy
Spirit. Of his great mercy, may he forgive you your sins,
release you from suffering, and restore you to wholeness and

strength. May he deliver you from all evil, preserve you in all
goodness, and bring you to everlasting life; through Jesus
Christ our Lord. *Amen.*

*In cases of necessity, a deacon or lay person may perform the anointing,
using oil blessed by a bishop or priest.*

If Communion is not to follow, the Lord's Prayer is now said.

The Priest concludes

The Almighty Lord, who is a strong tower to all who put their
trust in him, to whom all things in heaven, on earth, and under
the earth bow and obey: Be now and evermore your defense,
and make you know and feel that the only Name under
heaven given for health and salvation is the Name of our Lord
Jesus Christ. *Amen.*

Part III. Holy Communion

*If the Eucharist is to be celebrated, the Priest begins with the [Peace and]
Offertory.*

*If Communion is to be administered from the reserved Sacrament, the
form for Communion under Special Circumstances is used, beginning
with the [Peace and] Lord's Prayer on page 398.*

*If the sick person cannot receive either the consecrated Bread or the
Wine, it is suitable to administer the Sacrament in one kind only.*

One of the usual postcommunion prayers is said, or the following

Gracious Father, we give you praise and thanks for this Holy
Communion of the Body and Blood of your beloved Son
Jesus Christ, the pledge of our redemption; and we pray that
it may bring us forgiveness of our sins, strength in our
weakness, and everlasting salvation; through Jesus Christ
our Lord. *Amen.*

The service concludes with a blessing or with a dismissal

Let us bless the Lord.
Thanks be to God.

If a person desires to receive the Sacrament, but, by reason of extreme sickness or physical disability, is unable to eat and drink the Bread and Wine, the Celebrant is to assure that person that all the benefits of Communion are received, even though the Sacrament is not received with the mouth.

• • • •

A Closer Look at the Ministration to the Sick

Several features in particular set the 1979 rite for the Ministration to the Sick apart from its predecessors. The first and most obvious feature is the name: *"Ministration to* the Sick," rather than *"Visitation of* the Sick," in keeping with a more positive emphasis, as Armentrout and Slocum point out, on "the healing power of Christ and the connection between the worshipping community and the sick person."[57] As the Introduction to *Prayer Book Studies 24* affirms:

> our attitudes towards sickness in the twentieth century have changed greatly from those of earlier periods. The grim view of illness as punishment for sin and the concept of the "visitation" as a preparation for death, no longer are sound in the light of the advances of medical knowledge and techniques, particularly in the last fifty years, nor has such an approach any foundation in Scripture. The purpose of the Order is to seek through God's help the restoration of the patient to health and to soundness of mind and body, and to give him the comfort and spiritual strength to enable him to endure suffering and all the discomforts of illness with hope and with quietness of mind. At the same time it must be recognized that we cannot fully know God's will in these matters, and that we are really asking God to "fulfill now the desires and petitions of his servants *as may be most expedient for them*."[58]

57. Armentrout and Slocum, "Ministration to the Sick." In *An Episcopal Dictionary of the Church*, 333.

58. Episcopal Church, The Standing Liturgical Commission, *Pastoral Offices*, 11.

Whereas the emphasis in the Visitation Offices was on preparation for death, now one finds two separate rites, one for the Ministration to the Sick (pp. 453–461) and the other for the Ministration at the Time of Death (pp. 462–467), two different services with two different focuses. "The separation of the two elements is a logical one from a pastoral point of view," observes Prichard. "Praying for healing and preparing for death are two very different things, and it makes a great deal of sense to provide resources for both."[59] At the same time, as Mitchell points out, having the one immediately consequent to the other "guards against the . . . error of not dealing with the fact of death and with the certainty that some sick people will not recover."[60]

Clearer in focus, the service for the Ministration to the Sick follows the theological shift established by the 1928 Prayer Book, in which the old emphasis on sickness as visitation by God as chastisement for sin gives way to an emphasis on healing and restoration. The Introduction to *Prayer Book Studies 24* observes that the purpose of the 1979 Office "is to seek through God's help the restoration of the patient to health and to soundness of mind and body, and to give him comfort and spiritual strength to enable him to endure suffering and all the discomforts of illness with hope and with quietness of mind."[61] With this in mind, the drafters of the 1979 rite have, for instance, deleted the Collect[62] and the Epistle[63] from the beginning of The Communion of the Sick in the 1928 Prayer Book, both of which embody the theme of illness as correction or chastisement, and they have added new prayers such as For Recovery From Sickness:

> O God of heavenly powers, by the might of your command
> you drive away from our bodies all sickness and all infirmity:
> Be present in your goodness with your servant N., that his
> weakness may be banished and his strength restored; and that,
> his health being renewed, he may bless your holy Name;
> through Jesus Christ our Lord. *Amen.*

59. Prichard, "Sickness, Healing, and Forgiveness."

60. Mitchell, *Praying Shapes Believing*, 207.

61. Episcopal Church, *Pastoral Offices*, 11.

62. "Almighty, everliving God, maker of mankind, who dost correct those whom thou dost love, and chastise every one whom thou dost receive; We beseech thee to have mercy upon this thy servant visited with thine hand. . . " 1928 *Book of Common Prayer*, 321.

63. Heb 12:5.

While the thrust of the rite is clearly that of healing, at the same time, the Ministration to the Sick acknowledges the reality that medicine and technology have their limits: we are all mortal, and there comes a time when physical healing is not always certain or even possible, a fact reflected in prayers such as In Pain, or In the Morning. Furthermore, it affirms the complementary role played in the work of healing by the medical profession and associated disciplines, as illustrated by prayers such as For Doctors and Nurses and Before an Operation.

One of the improvements of the 1979 rite is the Ministry of the Word, a selection of readings and prayers with a relatively easy-to-use format providing ample opportunity for reflection and pastoral care. The purpose of these Scripture passages is to set the ministry of healing in its biblical context. Their theme is clearly God's love and God's power of healing and restoration.[64]

The Ministration to the Sick is clearly envisioned as taking place (ideally) within the context of a communal celebration of the Eucharist. When this is not possible or practical, the administration of Communion from the reserved sacrament by a deacon or a licensed eucharistic minister[65] provides a valuable opportunity for ministry to the sick and the shut-ins of the parish, "a powerful ministry," says Mitchell, "witnessing to the Church's concern for those unable to attend the parish Eucharist and binding them to the Church in its chief act of worship."[66] Through the Eucharist, in the midst of illness, suffering and setbacks, the sick are able to celebrate and themselves bear witness to the redeeming and restorative power of the Holy Spirit. Through the bread of heaven and the cup of salvation they receive sustenance for the work they have been given to do by virtue of their Baptism. Thus they and all who celebrate with them are reminded that all who share in this bread and this cup are "one body and one spirit, a living sacrifice in Christ, to the praise of [God's] name,"[67] a fact diminished neither by sickness nor by death.

---

64. The small, pocket-sized edition of the rite, *Ministry to the Sick*, published by the Church Hymnal Corporation, is particularly helpful, not simply because of its smaller size, but owing to the fact that the Scripture readings are printed out, thus making it easier for use by celebrant and sick person. (Malania, *Ministry to the Sick According to the use of the Episcopal Church as Set Forth in the Book of Common Prayer*).

65. In accordance with Title III, Canon 3 of the Episcopal Church.

66. Mitchell, *Praying Shapes Believing*, 213.

67. *The Book of Common Prayer*, Holy Eucharist, Prayer D, 375.

The 1979 Prayer Book rite also contains rubrics regarding the administration of Communion "in one kind only"[68] in cases where an individual, for whatever reason, is unable to take either the bread or the wine. While Communion in one kind lacks the fullness of sign of the reception of both eucharistic elements, there are sickness situations in which Communion from the reserved sacrament might preclude the carrying of the wine, for fear of contagion, for instance, or when the communicant is a recovering alcoholic.[69] The Eucharistic doctrine of Concomitance, which maintains that the body and blood of Christ is simultaneously present in each of the consecrated species, affirms that reception in one kind still allows one to experience the fullness of Communion with no diminution in effect. In circumstances in which the individual is unable to consume either the bread or the wine, he or she is to be assured by the Celebrant that "*all the benefits of Communion are received, even though the Sacrament is not received with the mouth.*"[70]

Unlike previous Prayer Books, the Ministration to the Sick includes a form for the blessing of the oil of the Anointing of the Sick.[71]

---

68. *The Book of Common Prayer*, 457.

69. A recent report by Gould available on the website of the Anglican Church of Canada, states that in regard to "Eucharistic practice and the risk of infection . . . it would seem that communion in one kind (the bread) is the best option for those fearful of the cup both from the standpoint of preventing the spread of infection, and from the theological perspective." (Gould, "Eucharistic Practice and the Risk of Infection"). Similarly, the Episcopal Diocese of Olympia's Diocesan Policy on Alcoholism and Substance Abuse states: "For many who have the disease of alcoholism, communion in 'one kind only' is the norm, while others receive by intinction . . . For others, receiving the bread only, and crossing one's arms across your chest and receiving the words of administration only . . . Some individuals have chosen to kiss the Chalice to honor Our Lord, while abstaining from alcohol." Episcopal Diocese of Olympia, Diocesan Executive Council. "Diocesan Policy on Alcoholism and Substance Abuse Adopted by Diocesan Council, May 25, 1989."

70. This is not new to our Anglican rites of healing, and has been included in the rubrics since the 1549 Prayer Book which reads: "*But yf any man eyther by reason of extremitie of sickenesse, or for lacke of warnyng geven in due tyme, to the curate, or by any other just impedimente, doe not receyve the sacramente of Christes bodye and bloud then the curate shall instruct hym, that yf he doe truly repent hym of his sinnes and stedfastly beleve that Jesus Christ hath suffered death upon the crosse for hym, and shed his bloud for his redemption, earnestly remembering the benefites he hath therby, and giving hym hertie thankes therefore; he doeth eate and drynke spiritually the bodye and bloud of our savioure Christe, profitably to his soules helth, although he doe not receyve the sacrament with his mouth.*"

71. It is normative today (although not universally accepted as an Anglican practice)

> O Lord, holy Father, giver of health and salvation: Send your
> Holy Spirit to sanctify this oil; that, as your holy apostles
> anointed many that were sick and healed them, so may those
> who in faith and repentance receive this holy unction be
> made whole; through Jesus Christ our Lord, who lives and
> reigns with you and the Holy Spirit, one God, for ever and ever.
> *Amen.*

The 1928 Prayer Book, which restored anointing of the sick with blessed oil, curiously, made no provision for its blessing. "The intention of the revision [in the 1979 service]," says Hatchett, "is that the local priest bless the oil for the sick in the presence of the people."[72] The practical advantages of such a rubric are obvious. It could be regarded as comparable to the *Additional Directions* in the Prayer Book allowing additional bread or wine to be consecrated by the celebrant "*if the consecrated Bread or Wine does not suffice for the number of communicants.*"[73] In addition, as Richards notes, this might prove a valuable remedy to an unfortunate (but not uncommon tendency) on the part of many of the faithful "to think that the oil has magical properties." Accordingly, he says, "The time of preparation would correct any such errors, and some feel that the consecrating of the oil is best done as a corporate activity within the situation in which it is going to be used . . . in place of . . . previous consecration by the Bishop."[74] At the same time, however, one could argue that with respect to the importance of the corporate aspect, what greater symbol of unity is there for a diocese than its bishop?

One of the surprises of the Ministration to the Sick is the rubrics permitting a lay person or deacon to administer the laying on of hands and, in "*cases of necessity,*" anointing, using oil blessed by a bishop or a priest.[75]

Another significant change that occurred in the course of the reworking of the 1979 Ministration to the Sick is the fact that the Confession,

---

for the oil of anointing to be blessed by the bishop during the Maundy Thursday liturgy at the cathedral.

72. Hatchett, *Commentary on the American Prayer Book*, 465.

73. *The Book of Common Prayer*, 408.

74. Richards, *But Deliver Us from Evil*, 17.

75. In regard to the issue of anointing by laity, the report by the Church of England, *A Time to Heal*, makes the recommendation that "the House of Bishops should consider the issue of anointing and how its use could be explored further, developed and encouraged among the laity; the healing ministry is a wonderful way of sharing ministry between clergy and laity." 358.

previously central to the rite, has been relocated. As Prichard notes, the effect is to make confession "clearly an optional, but detachable part of the Ministration to the Sick, rather than the integral element that it once was."[76] The rubrics in the 1979 rite state that "*The Priest may suggest the making of a special confession, if the sick person's conscience is troubled, and use the form for the Reconciliation of a Penitent.*"[77] This new rite, The Reconciliation of a Penitent, directly preceding the Ministration to the Sick, has two separate, but equivalent forms of service to address the needs and circumstances of the penitent: the very simple, very brief and direct Form One and the longer, more comprehensive Form Two. The latter, Stuhlman comments, "is particularly suited to the circumstances of those who are seriously ill and wish reconciliation and the recovery of their baptismal status after a review of their past life,"[78] and as Hatchett notes, "is particularly appropriate when a person has turned or returned to the Christian faith, or at other possible 'crisis' points in a person's life."[79]

Just as new to the 1979 Prayer Book is the provision not just for the hearing of a confession by a deacon or lay person, but also for a "Declaration of Forgiveness" by a deacon or lay person following the confession.

> Our Lord Jesus Christ, who offered himself to be sacrificed
> for us to the Father, forgives your sins by the grace of the
> Holy Spirit. *Amen.*[80]

This, I believe, shows great pastoral sensitivity on the part of the architects of the liturgy, since an individual's need for reconciliation may arise at some time other than a regularly scheduled clergy visit, and the rapport that develops at times between the sick and nonordained chaplains and other pastoral visitors may play an important role in helping these individuals to come to such a juncture.

76. Prichard, "Sickness, Healing, And Forgiveness."

77. Form One (447–448), says Mitchell, "is simple, direct, and based on traditional Western forms that have been widely used by Episcopalians throughout the years." Form Two (449–452), longer, richer in imagery, "is influenced by Eastern Orthodox forms, and it sets sin and forgiveness within the framework of the baptismal life in Christ." Mitchell, *Praying Shapes Believing*, 200.

78. Stuhlman, *Occasions of Grace*, 172.

79. Hatchett, *Commentary on the American Prayer Book*, 453.

80. *The Book of Common Prayer*, 448 and 452.

Filling in the Blanks

Having said this, it appears to me that where this liturgy is notably lacking is in its paucity of accompanying rubrics, a detail that is particularly striking when one compares the Ministration to the Sick with other of the Episcopal Church's rites and liturgies. Notable also is the nearly total absence of any preliminary instruction or some sort of comprehensive introduction, something along the lines of *Concerning the Service* or *Additional Directions*, which one finds in respect to other pastoral services.

Consider: the liturgy for the Celebration of a Marriage is preceded by nearly a page of introduction ("Concerning the Service," p. 422,) and followed by over a page of *Additional Directions* (pp. 437–38). These briefly explain the underlying theology of the sacramental rite of holy matrimony, and acquaint the reader with the relevant liturgical norms and pastoral considerations. Similarly, the Order for Christian Burial is preceded by a page of introduction ("*Concerning the Service*," p. 468) and followed by "An Order for Burial," a page and a half of ceremonial guidelines and a profoundly moving and oft-quoted "Note" regarding the Paschal nature of the liturgy for the dead (pp. 506–7). No such provision was made in the 1979 Prayer Book for the Ministration to the Sick, all the more remarkable when one considers, as Mitchell observes, that Episcopalians "are liturgical theologians. We read our theology out of *The Book of Common Prayer* and the manner in which we celebrate its services."[81] It is important, therefore, that the rubrics of our liturgies, as much as the 'rites and ceremonies,' reflect and express their underlying theology. Hopefully, future Prayer Book editions will include additional material concerning the theological foundation of this and all our rites, as well as addressing the relevant pastoral considerations. Perhaps something could be created similar to the introductory material found in *Enriching Our Worship 2*.

Where Did "the People" Go?

While one would have hoped otherwise, the rubrics in the Ministration to the Sick refer specifically only to the celebrant and the sick person, with no direct mention of family, friends or community. Likewise conspicuous by its absence is any *encouragement* to the family and friends either to take part in the Ministry of the Word, to participate in the General Confession, or to

81. Mitchell, *Praying Shapes Believing*, 2.

help with the preparations for, and to participate in, the Holy Communion. This is particularly perplexing when one examines the pertinent rubrics in our earlier Visitation Offices. The 1789 and 1892 Visitation Offices note that "*In the times of contagious sickness or disease, when none of the Parish or neighbours can be gotten to communicate with the sick in their houses, for fear of the infection, upon special request of the diseased, the Minister alone may communicate with him.*" The 1928 Prayer Book rubrics state that the sick person who desires to receive Communion at home should give notice to the Minister "*signifying how many there are to communicate with him.*"[82] Such a rubric seems to imply that there will be other members of the faithful present. Despite the 1979 rite's opening Greeting, "Peace be to this house (place) and to all who dwell in it," there is no *direct* reference to the presence of anyone other than the celebrant and the sick person. Consider, in contrast, the General Introduction to the Roman Catholic *Pastoral Care of the Sick*:

> 33. It is thus especially fitting that all baptized Christians share in this ministry of mutual charity within the Body of Christ by doing all that they can to help the sick return to health, by showing love for the sick, and by celebrating the sacraments with them. Like the other sacraments, these too have a community aspect, which should be brought out as much as possible when they are celebrated.

> 34. The family and friends of the sick and those who take care of them in any way have a special share in this ministry of comfort. In particular, it is their task to strengthen the sick with words of faith and by praying with them, to commend them to the suffering and glorified Lord, and to encourage them to contribute to the well-being of the people of God by associating themselves willingly with Christ's passion and death. . . [83]

Or, compare the opening rubrics for the Ministration to the Sick with those of the 1979 Prayer Book's other pastoral liturgies, such as the Celebration and Blessing of a Marriage,[84] which requires at least two witnesses, or the rite of confirmation,[85] in which confirmands are "expected to make

82. 1928 Book of Common Prayer, 321.

83. Catholic Church. National Conference of Catholic Bishops. Bishops' Committee on the Liturgy. Secretariat. *Pastoral Care of the Sick.*

84. *The Book of Common Prayer*, 423–32.

85. Ibid., 413–19.

a *public* affirmation of their faith," or even the liturgy for the Burial of the Dead, whose rubrics state: *"The service should be held at a time when the congregation has opportunity to be present."*[86] In the light of this last example, this specific omission seems especially glaring!

It is even more surprising when one examines a proposed (but never adopted) revision of the Visitation Office prepared by the Standing Liturgical Committee in 1951. The introductory rubrics for the proposed rite state: *"At a private Ministration, it is desirable that one or more lay persons be present, both to join in the responses, and to encourage the patient by the supporting prayers of the Church."*[87]

The subsequent rubrics for this proposed revision make it clear that this is *intended* to be communal worship. It refers to *"the People"* throughout the service, and further states that *"Anyone who is sick in body or mind, slightly or seriously, may receive the Laying-on of Hands and Holy Unction."*[88] This leads me to wonder: what happened? Where did *"the People"* go in the 1979 rite? I cannot imagine a situation in which the sickness and the suffering of one person does not somehow impact upon the lives of others in some way, whether they be family, friends, or caregivers. Why do the rubrics for the Ministration to the Sick make no mention of them, for all intents and purposes? Even in the relative privacy of the sickroom or hospital room, when the rite of unction is allowed to maintain its communal nature, the healing presence and the ministrations of family and friends—a reassuring glance, a smile, a gentle touch upon one's shoulder or arm during the laying on of hands—can speak as eloquently as words.[89]

Such ministrations become prayer, which, after all, is defined in the Catechism as "responding to God, by thought and by deeds, with or without words."[90] God's initiative leads us to seek God in relation to one another. Anglicanism, after all, is an *incarnational* faith and as such, says David Smith, "incarnational Christianity requires direct involvement in healing of bodies and . . . the ultimate healing or 'perfect wholeness' offered by Christ and church is *the creation of community through honest acceptance*

86. Ibid., 468.

87. Episcopal Church, Standing Liturgical Commission, *The Order for the Ministration of the Sick*, 21.

88. Ibid., 37.

89. The objection can be made that the sick person may wish to make a sacramental confession, or may wish to speak privately with the attending priest or minister. In this case, the family and friends would respectfully be asked to step outside.

90. Catechism, 856.

and exchange of suffering."[91] As Lambourne observes: "Those who would join the mystical Body must have communion with a sufferer. Not only in the consecrated elements, not only in the Church, but also in the sufferer does faith know the real presence and by communion with each partake of the spiritual Christ."[92]

Why not challenge the alienation and disempowerment that accompany sickness and debility by enabling the sick person to be a more active participant when this is possible? For instance, why not invite the sick to select the readings ahead of time from a list of suggested lessons, allowing him or her to choose Scripture passages that speak to their particular situation? Why not include rubrics similar to those of the proposed revision mentioned above encouraging the family and friends of the sick to exercise their very important role in the church's ministry of healing? One hopes that future revisions of the *Book of Common Prayer's* sacramental liturgy of unction will consider rubrics similar to those of the proposed 1951 rite, or introductory material similar to that composed by Phobe Pettingell, writing on behalf of the Standing Commission on Liturgy and Music in the introductory chapter, "Praying with the Sick," in *Enriching Our Worship 2*. Here the reader is reminded that "all prayers with the sick should be linked with the people of God in the context of the whole Church. The community of intercessors embraces not only the parish, but also family and friends of the patients and all who are caring for them, as well as the medical community" (p. 17).

A Public Service of Healing from The Book of Occasional Services

This brings us to A Public Service of Healing in *The Book of Occasional Services*. The first *Book of Occasional Services* was produced in 1991 in response to a directive from the General Convention of 1979 to replace *The Book of Offices*.[93] A growing interest on the part of both Anglicans and other Christian faith traditions in the nineteenth and twentieth centuries in the church's healing ministry had led to an increasing demand for a liturgy

91. Smith, *Health and Medicine in the Anglican Tradition* (italics added), 9.

92. Lambourne, *Community, Church and Healing*, 72.

93. "A collection of offices [compiled by the Liturgical Commission in accordance with a resolution of the 1937 General Convention] for specific purposes and occasions 'which occur in the work of the Bishops and other Clergy.'" Armentrout and Slocum, "The Book of Offices." In *An Episcopal Dictionary of the Church*, 54.

of healing that included, among other things, more prayers and scripture lessons than those provided by the 1979 Ministration to the Sick. The result was the creation of A Public Service of Healing (1991).

As the introductory background material provided to the Examining Chaplains in regard to the General Ordination Exams for 2006 makes clear, in both the *Book of Occasional Services* and *Enriching Our Worship 2*,

> the basic intent is to express in liturgical language and actions the theology of healing found in the *Book of Common Prayer* (1979). The focus is on God as creator and sustainer of all life; on Jesus Christ whose compassion and ministry of healing were distinctive marks of his life and mission, and for whom his healings were signs of the coming reign of God; and on the church as the community of God's people and the bearer of Christ's ministry of healing in the world today. The individual healing of body, mind, and spirit is intimately related to the *communal acts* of forgiveness and reconciliation [emphasis mine].[94]

A Public Service of Healing[95]

The service begins as appointed for a celebration of the Holy Eucharist, or with the Penitential Order, or with the following greeting

Celebrant   Grace and peace be with you, from God our Father
             and the Lord Jesus Christ.

People   And also with you.

Celebrant   Let us pray.

The Celebrant says this or some other appropriate Collect

O God of peace, you have taught us that in returning and rest we shall be saved, in quietness and confidence shall be our strength: By the might of your Spirit lift us, we pray, to your presence, where we may be still and know that you are God; through Jesus Christ our Lord, who with you and the Holy Spirit lives and reigns, one God, for ever and ever. *Amen.*

---

94. 2006 General Ordination Exam, Background Material: Set. 2. Liturgy and Church Music. The General Board of Examining Chaplains of the Episcopal Church.

95. Episcopal Church. Standing Liturgical Commission, *The Book of Occasional Services*, 162–69.

One or two Lessons are read before the Gospel.

Between the Lessons, and before the Gospel, a Psalm, hymn, or anthem may be sung or said.

If the Proper of the Day is not used, the Lessons, Psalm, and Gospel are selected from the Table on page 171–173.

A sermon or meditation, or a period of silence, or both, may follow the Gospel.

The service continues with the Creed, or with the Prayers of the People.

For the Prayers of the People a Litany of Healing, as follows, may be used.

Litany of Healing
The Celebrant introduces the Litany with this bidding

Let us name before God those for whom we offer our prayers.

The People audibly name those for whom they are interceding.

A Person appointed then leads the Litany

God the Father, your will for all people is health and salvation;
We praise you and thank you, O Lord.

God the Son, you came that we might have life, and might have it more abundantly;
We praise you and thank you, O Lord.

God the Holy Spirit, you make our bodies the temple of your presence;
We praise you and thank you, O Lord.

Holy Trinity, one God, in you we live and move and have our being;
We praise you and thank you, O Lord.

Lord, grant your healing grace to all who are sick, injured, or disabled, that they may be made whole;
Hear us, O Lord of life.

Healing Touch and Saving Word

Grant to all who seek your guidance, and to all who are lonely, anxious, or despondent, a knowledge of your will and an awareness of your presence;
Hear us, O Lord of life.

Mend broken relationships, and restore those in emotional distress to soundness of mind and serenity of spirit;
Hear us, O Lord of life.

Bless physicians, nurses, and all others who minister to the suffering, granting them wisdom and skill, sympathy and patience;
Hear us, O Lord of life.

Grant to the dying peace and a holy death, and uphold by the grace and consolation of your Holy Spirit those who are bereaved;
Hear us, O Lord of life.

Restore to wholeness whatever is broken by human sin, in our lives, in our nation, and in the world;
Hear us, O Lord of life.

You are the Lord who does wonders:
You have declared your power among the peoples.

With you, O Lord, is the well of life:
And in your light we see light.

Hear us, O Lord of life:
Heal us, and make us whole.

Let us pray.

A period of silence follows.

The Celebrant concludes the Prayers with one of the following or some other suitable Collect:

Almighty God, giver of life and health: Send your blessing
on all who are sick, and upon those who minister to them,
that all weakness may be vanquished by the triumph of the
risen Christ; who lives and reigns for ever and ever. Amen.

or this

Heavenly Father, you have promised to hear what we ask in
the Name of your Son: Accept and fulfill our petitions, we
pray, not as we ask in our ignorance, nor as we deserve in
our sinfulness, but as you know and love us in your Son
Jesus Christ our Lord. Amen.

or this

O Lord our God, accept the fervent prayers of your people;
in the multitude of your mercies look with compassion upon
us and all who turn to you for help; for you are gracious, O
lover of souls, and to you we give glory, Father, Son, and
Holy Spirit, now and for ever. Amen.

*A Confession of Sin follows, if it has not been said at the beginning of
the service.*

*The Celebrant now invites those who wish to receive the laying on of
hands (and anointing) to come forward.*

*If oil for the anointing of the sick is to be blessed, the form on page 455
of the Prayer Book is used.*

The following anthem is sung or said

Savior of the world, by your cross and precious blood you
have redeemed us;
Save us, and help us, we humbly beseech you, O Lord.

The Celebrant says the following blessing over those who have come forward

The Almighty Lord, who is a strong tower to all who put
their trust in him, to whom all things in heaven, on earth,
and under the earth bow and obey: Be now and evermore

your defense, and make you know and feel that the only
Name under heaven given for health and salvation is the
Name of our Lord Jesus Christ. Amen.

*The Celebrant then lays hands on each person (and, having dipped a
thumb in the oil of the sick, makes the sign of the cross on their
foreheads), and says one of the following:*

N., I lay my hands upon you [and anoint you with oil] in the
Name of the Father, and of the Son, and of the Holy Spirit,
beseeching our Lord Jesus Christ to sustain you with his
presence, to drive away all sickness of body and spirit, and
to give you that victory of life and peace which will enable
you to serve him both now and evermore. Amen.

or this

N., I lay my hands upon you [and anoint you with oil] in the
Name of our Lord and Savior Jesus Christ, beseeching him
to uphold you and fill you with his grace, that you may know
the healing power of his love. Amen.

or this

[N.,] I lay my hands upon you [and anoint you with oil] in
the Name of the Father, and of the Son, and of the Holy
Spirit. Amen.

*or prayer may be offered for each person individually according to that
person's need, with laying on of hands (and anointing).*

*Lay persons with a gift of healing may join the celebrant in the laying on of
hands.*

The service continues with the exchange of the Peace.

*If there is not to be a Communion, the service concludes with the Lord's
Prayer and the prayer and blessing given below.*

If the Eucharist is to be celebrated, the Liturgy continues with the Offertory.

*In place of the usual postcommunion prayer (or, if there has not been a
Communion, after the Lord's Prayer), the following prayer is said*

Almighty and eternal God, so draw our hearts to you, so guide our minds, so fill our imaginations, so control our wills, that we may be wholly yours, utterly dedicated to you; and then use us, we pray, as you will, and always to your glory and the welfare of your people; through our Lord and Savior Jesus Christ. Amen.

The Celebrant pronounces this blessing

May God the Father bless you, God the Son heal you, God the Holy Spirit give you strength. May God the holy and undivided Trinity guard your body, save your soul, and bring you safely to his heavenly country; where he lives and reigns for ever and ever. Amen.

A Deacon, or the Celebrant, dismisses the people.

A Table of Suggested Lessons and Psalms

Old Testament
Exodus 16:13–15 (Manna in the wilderness)
1 Kings 17:17–24 (Elijah restores the widow's son to life)
2 Kings 5:9–14 (Healing of Naaman)
2 Kings 20:1–5 (I have heard your prayer . . . I will heal you)
Isaiah 11:1–3a (The gifts of the Spirit)
Isaiah 42:1–7 (The suffering servant)
Isaiah 53:3–5 (With his stripes are we healed)
Isaiah 61:1–3 (Good tidings to the afflicted)

Psalms
Psalm 13 (My heart is joyful because of your saving help)
Psalm 20:1–6 (May the Lord answer you in the day of trouble)
Psalm 23 (You have anointed my head with oil)
Psalm 27 or 27:1–7,9,18 (The Lord is the strength of my life)
Psalm 91 (He will give his angels charge over you)
Psalm 103 (He forgives all your sins)
Psalm 121 (My help comes from the Lord)
Psalm 130 (My soul waits for the Lord)
Psalm 139:1–17 (Where can I go from your Spirit?)
Psalm 145:14–22 (The eyes of all wait on you, O Lord)
Psalm 146 (Happy are they who have the God of Jacob for their help)

New Testament
Acts 3:1–10 (Peter and John heal the lame man)
Acts 5:12–16 (Healings in Jerusalem; Peter's shadow)
Acts 10:36–43 (Apostolic preaching: He went about . . . healing)
Acts 16:16–18 (The slave girl with the spirit of divination)
Romans 8:18–23 (We await the redemption of our bodies)
Romans 8:31–39 (Nothing can separate us from the love of God)
2 Corinthians 1:3–5 (God comforts us in affliction)
Colossians 1:11–20 (May you be strengthened with all power)
Hebrews 12:1–2 (Looking to Jesus, the perfecter of our faith)
James 5:(13)14–16 (Is any among you sick?)
1 John 5:13–15 (That you may know that you have eternal life)

The Gospel
Matthew 9:2–8 (Your sins are forgiven)
Matthew 26:26–30,36–39 (The Last Supper: Not as I will)
Mark 1:21–28 (Jesus heals the man with the unclean spirit)
Mark 1:29–34a (Jesus heals Peter's mother-in-law and others)
Mark 5:1–20 (Healing of Gerasene demoniac)
Mark 5:22–24 (Healing of Jairus' daughter)
Mark 6:7,12–13 (They anointed with oil many that were sick)
Luke 17:11–19 (Your faith has made you well)
John 5:1b-9 (Do you want to be healed?)
John 6:47–51 (I am the bread of life)
John 9:1–11 (Healing of the man born blind)

Comparing the Ministration to the Sick and A Public Service of Healing

There are several noteworthy features of A Public Service of Healing [1991], most particularly the envisioned *setting*. While the Ministration to the Sick is often employed in a sickroom type situation, but *may* take the form of a communal liturgy to be celebrated within the Eucharist, A Public Service of Healing is quite clearly created with a communal liturgy in mind. As such, it may be adapted for an institutional setting—a hospital or nursing home, for instance—as well as the normal parish or home environment. In the words of Mitchell, "It rearranges the prayers to facilitate a large number of people coming forward to be anointed. It also adds more possible readings, a post-communion prayer and blessing, and the litany for healing. This is all in response to the needs of those parishes which have such a service on a weekly or monthly basis."[96]

As the rubrics state, the service is meant to take place within the context of the Eucharist. Calhoun and Fink note the obvious advantages of such a communal setting for the sick, along with their family and caregivers: "A uniquely compassionate community among such people is highlighted and enhanced by a celebration of the sacrament in common; there is a certain communication of mutual understanding and shared faith that helps them to support and pray for one another."[97]

In addition to the material found in the Prayer Book, A Public Service of Healing [1991] provides an opening Acclamation, Collects, an expanded selection of Lessons, an Invitation to those who wish to receive the laying on of hands (and anointing), a Litany of Healing, and a Blessing. The Blessing—"The Almighty Lord, who is a strong tower to all who put their trust in him"[98]—which in the 1979 Ministration to the Sick appears at the *conclusion*, here appears *before* the laying on of hands and anointing. The effect is one of reassurance, both in the power of God to effect healing and to deliver the sick and the suffering from those forces that threaten their sense of bodily and spiritual integrity. In addition, says Russell Newbert, it provides for "an important transitional space before the sacramental action, which allows the participants to respond to the prompting of the Holy Spirit and open themselves up to the healing power of God which is about to be manifested."[99] A space of silence could be added here, as well.

As in the Ministration to the Sick, the Public Service of Healing makes provision for the blessing of the oil of anointing by the priest or the bishop, employing the form found in *The Book of Common Prayer* on page 455. According to Mitchell:

96. The Rev. Dr. Leonel Mitchell, e-mail to author, 27 Apr 2006.

97. Calhoun and Fink, "Alternative 1: Ritual of Anointing for the Long-Term, Seriously Ill," in *Alternative Futures for Worship*, 7:88.

98. "This is an abbreviated version of the blessing which concludes the visitation of the sick in the 1549 Prayer Book, which seems to have no liturgical precedents. Scriptural bases for the blessing are Psalm 61:3, Philippians 2:10–11, and Acts 4:12. The fuller ending in prior editions of the Prayer Book reads 'that there is no other name under heaven given to man, in whom and through thou mayest receive health and salvation, but only the name of our Lord Jesus Christ'" (Hatchett, *Commentary on the American Prayer Book*, 466).

99. The Rev. Russell Anderson Newbert, e-mail to author, 10 Feb 2006. Newbert is the Liturgy and Church Music Consultant on the Episcopal Diocese of Western New York's Board of Examining Chaplains.

The oil may be in oil stocks or in a glass bottle. It is easiest if the oil to be used during the service is in oil stocks set out to be blessed, but it is more effective visually if a bottle of olive oil is blessed and the oil then poured into oil stocks for use. If the bishop is the presider, it is fitting for the bishop to bless sufficient oil for use during the year. The oil to be blessed is held by a server or placed on a small table. The presider stands facing the people and says the prayer with the hands in the orans[100] position, either extending them over the oil or making the sign of the cross over the oil at the words, "Send your Holy Spirit to sanctify this oil." At the conclusion of the prayer, the oil is placed in oil stocks or other vessels and given to the priests who will perform the anointing. Oil not used at the service is kept for future use.[101]

Another noteworthy feature is the rubric preceding the prayer for healing that reads: *"The Celebrant then lays hands on each person (and, having dipped a thumb in the oil of the sick, makes the sign of the cross on their foreheads). . . "* This instruction has been commended by many contemporary Episcopal liturgists owing to the fact that it appears to unite the laying on of hands and anointing into a single gesture, rather than dividing them into two separate signs. According to this school of thought, the alternative—to follow the laying on of hands with an additional gesture of anointing—unintentionally suggests that the one is insufficient without the addition of the other.

There exists a seeming ambiguity about the use of the two signs: the laying on of hands and the anointing with oil.[102] The rubrics imply that the laying on of hands takes precedence over the anointing, the latter of which *appears*, Stuhlman suggests, to be an option neither required nor recommended.[103] Anointing *may* take place, the rubrics suggest, and they proceed to describe how one would do so, without suggesting that this is a necessary action. This may, says Mitchell, "simply reflect pastoral practice in which the laying on of hands by the priest appears as the primary rite, with anointing as an optional supplementary action."[104] Of course, it is

100. Orans: (From Latin for *"praying."*) A prayer posture with open arms and hands extended used by the presider in saying prayers while standing.

101. Mitchell, *Pastoral and Occasional Liturgies*, 85–86.

102. Compare this to official Roman Catholic doctrine, which specifies the "three distinct and integral aspects to the celebration of this sacrament: the prayer of faith, the laying on of hands, and the anointing with oil" (*Pastoral Care of the Sick*, 104).

103. Stuhlman, *Prayer Book Rubrics Expanded*, viii.

104. Mitchell, *Praying Shapes Believing*, 212.

difficult to imagine how one might anoint someone *without* laying hands upon him or her. Mitchell also notes: "Priests often use just the laying on of hand in situations where oil is not available and it is counterproductive to go back to the church to get some. I am sure there are also a few remaining "low church" parishes where oil is considered 'popish' and which use the laying on of hands alone."[105] However, in regard to this, Jennifer Phillips states that at the time of the drafting of the rubrics, "There was no concern with 'popish versus non,' though in my parents' day that was a big preoccupation and debate—the 50s up to the [current] BCP."[106]

Particularly notable is the rubric permitting lay persons *"with a gift of healing"* to *"join the celebrant in the laying on of hands."*[107] This raises two important questions. The most obvious is: how does one decide *who* falls into this category, since the rubrics fail to provide any criteria for determining who such persons may be. Nor is it quite clear what is meant by the suggestion that they *"may join the celebrant in the laying on of hands."* Perhaps, says Mitchell, "They may be members of the Order of St. Luke or other healing fellowships, or others who have this gift. Presumably this means that such persons may join with the priest in laying on hands, not that they may lay hands on some while the priest lays hands on others. If there are many such people they may accompany each of the priests laying on hands and anointing. They may place their hands on the head or shoulders of the persons asking for healing along with the priest."[108]

One can not help but wonder why the families, loved ones and caregivers should not also be invited to take part in the laying on of hands, whether or not such persons possess a discernible *"gift of healing."* Again, Calhoun and Fink suggest that it is not only appropriate, but natural that the same hands that help to care for an individual in their day-to-day life—the hands that help to feed, bathe, dress, tend, and soothe the individual—should be the same hands laid upon that individual's person as they join in prayer.[109]

---

105. The Rev. Dr. Leonel Mitchell, e-mail to the author, 27 Apr 2006.

106. Jennifer Phillips, e-mail to the author, 17 May 2006. The Rev. Dr. Jennifer Philips was a member of the Standing Commission on Liturgy and Music at the time the Ministry with the Sick or Dying was created for *Enriching Our Worship 2*.

107. *The Book of Occasional Services*, 166.

108. Mitchell, *Pastoral and Occasional Liturgies*, 86–87.

109. Calhoun and Fink, "Alternative 1: Ritual of Anointing for the Long-Term, Seriously Ill," in lee and Fink, eds., *Alternative Futures for Worship* 7:91.

The rubrics in A Public Service of Healing [1991] state that "*A Confession of Sin follows, if it has not been said at the beginning of the service.*"[110] We may assume that, considering the communal nature of this service, one is meant to employ the General Confession from Holy Eucharist Rite I or II in *The Book of Common Prayer*. It is a pity that a special, truly communal Confession of Sin was not developed for this. What an important witness it might provide in regard to the ecclesial foundation of this and all our sacramental rites were it to include a confession of sin capable of addressing in a more explicit manner not just our sins against God, or this individual or group of individuals, but all the church whom we have wounded by our sins of commission and omission. Such a communal rite of reconciliation would serve to emphasize the fact that the church is a *community* of healing, and that healing is found—just as reconciliation is found—through restoration to the body whose health and wholeness has been compromised by sin. In this respect, one might adapt the litany of penitence (pp. 267–69) found in the *Book of Common Prayer*'s Ash Wednesday service for this purpose:

> Most holy and merciful Father:
> We confess to you and to one another,
> and to the whole communion of saints
> in heaven and on earth,
> that we have sinned by our own fault
> in thought, word, and deed;
> by what we have done, and by what we have left undone. . .

As noted in the rubrics, the Prayers of the People may be replaced by a Litany of Healing. Mitchell observes: "If it is a Sunday or major holy day service, more general petitions may be included. The celebrant introduces the litany, standing at the chair and facing the people, with 'Let us name before God those for whom we offer our prayers.' The people are encouraged to name audibly those for whom they are interceding. This is the place at which the names of people not present for whom we wish to pray, as well as those who are present seeking healing, may be said aloud."[111]

The introductory rubrics to A Public Service of Healing [1991] state: "*The service begins as appointed for a celebration of the Holy Eucharist or with the Penitential Order.*"[112] The Penitential Order,[113] as Price and Weil

110. *The Book of Occasional Services*, 165.
111. Mitchell, *Pastoral and Occasional Liturgies*, 85.
112. *The Book of Occasional Services*, 162.
113. *The Book of Common Prayer*, 319 (Penitential Rite I—traditional language) and

observe, "with its solemn recitation of the Ten Commandments and the response after each, 'Lord have mercy upon us, and incline our hearts to keep this law' . . . [serves] as an examination of conscience for priests and people together and [constitutes] that approach to the holy God in awe and repentance that the sixteenth century reformers deemed essential."[114] Such a solemn communal acknowledgment of the sin sickness from which all suffer, and for which all require God's healing forgiveness, through the church, which we have wounded, allows us to move gradually from sorrow to joy, from woundedness to wholeness *together*.

A Public Service of Healing in Enriching Our Worship 2[115]

Finally, we arrive at A Public Service of Healing, found in *Enriching Our Worship 2*, which was published in 2000. The former Presiding Bishop's preface to Ministry with the Sick or Dying in *Enriching Our Worship 2* lays out the design behind our most recent healing liturgy.

> *Enriching Our Worship 2* was developed by the expansive Language Committee of the Standing Committee of the Standing Commission on Liturgy and Music in response to a resolution adopted by the 72nd General Convention in 1997. The resolution called on the Commission to develop supplemental liturgical materials for Pastoral Offices of the 1979 Book of Common Prayer. In reviewing the Prayer Book Pastoral Offices, the Commission realized there was a particular need to develop new prayers for ministry with those who are sick or dying, and to provide a rite for the burial of a child . . .
>
> Public services of healing have increasingly become part of the worship life of the Episcopal Church. What had been a private

351 (Penitential Rite II—contemporary language). Both include an opening acclamation, a bidding, confession of sin and absolution, and suitable prayers and the Grace or a blessing. They may include the Decalogue (317–18 or 350) with responses, and sentences of scripture (Summary of the Law, 1 John 1:8, 9, or Hebrews 4:16, 16).

114. Price and Weil, *Liturgy for Living*, 120.

115. In addition to A Public Service of Healing, *Enriching Our Worship 2* also contains Ministry in a Home or Health Care Facility (46–58), Distribution of Holy Communion by Lay Ministers to persons who are ill or infirm (59–63), Prayers for Those Who are Sick (64–70), Prayers for use by a Sick Person (71–92), Additional Prayers (93–95), Ministration at the Time of Death (96–116), A Form of Prayer When Life-Sustaining Treatment Is Withheld or Discontinued (117–27), and The Burial of a Child (131–146).

celebration of laying on of hands and anointing for healing (Visitation of the Sick) with the 1979 Book of Common Prayer has become a public service of healing in many congregations. *Enriching Our Worship 2* includes litanies and prayers—some drawn from traditional prayers and others newly composed—to augment the Prayer Book service.[116]

A Public Service of Healing

This service is suitable for use in a congregation or other church setting. It may also be adapted as needed for use in a variety of settings, e.g., hospital, nursing home, or other health care facility.

When unction is administered in the context of the Sunday Eucharist or a regular weekday Eucharist, the portion of this service entitled "Laying on of Hands and Anointing" is used. It is recommended that this take place immediately before the exchange of the Peace.

Gather in the Name of God

The service may begin as appointed for a celebration of the Holy Eucharist, or with the Penitential Order, or with the following greeting

Minister	The grace of our Lord Jesus Christ, and the love of God, and the communion of the Holy Spirit, be with you all.
People	And also with you.
Minister	Let us pray.

After a period of silence, the Minister then says one of the following Collects, or some other appropriate Collect

Loving God, the comfort of all who sorrow, the strength of all who suffer: accept our prayers, and to those who seek healing [especially N. and N., and all whom we name in our hearts], grant the power of your grace, that the weak may be strengthened, sickness turned to health, the dying made whole, and sorrow turned into joy; through Jesus Christ our Savior. *Amen.*

116. The Most Rev. Frank T. Griswold, *Enriching Our Worship 2*, Preface, 5.

or this

God our healer, whose mercy is like a refining fire: by the loving-kindness of Jesus, heal us and those for whom we pray; that being renewed by you, we may witness your wholeness to our broken world; through Jesus Christ, in the power of the Spirit. *Amen.*

or this

Gracious God, we commend to your loving care all who suffer, especially those who come [here] seeking your healing grace [for themselves or others]. Give them patience and hope in their distress; strengthen and uphold them in mind and body; and grant, by your intervention, that all your people may be made whole according to your desire, through Jesus Christ, in the power of the Holy Spirit. *Amen.*

Proclaim and Respond to the Word

One or two Lessons are read before the Gospel.
Between the Lessons, and before the Gospel, a Psalm, hymn, or anthem may be sung or said.

The readings may be selected from the following list, or from "A Public Service of Healing" in The Book of Occasional Services, or from the Proper of the Day.

From the Old Testament

Job 7:1–4 (human beings have a hard service on earth)
Isaiah 35 (eyes shall be opened . . . ears unstopped . . . the lame shall leap)
Isaiah 38:1–5 (the healing of Hezekiah); see also 2 Kings 20:1–7
Isaiah 49:14–16 (I will not forget you)
Isaiah 53:4–6 (By his bruises we are healed)
Ezekiel 36:26–28 (a new heart and a new spirit)
Ezekiel 37:12–14 (I am going to open your graves)

Psalms 13; 23; 30; 71; 86:1–7; 103:1–5; 126; 145:14–22; 147:1–7

From the New Testament

Acts 3:1–10 (in the name of Jesus Christ...stand up and walk)
2 Corinthians 1:3–5 (God comforts us)
James 5:14–16 (is anyone among you sick?)
1 Peter 2:21–24 (by his wounds you have been healed)
1 John 5:13–15 (if we ask anything according to his will, he hears us)

The Gospel

Matthew 5:2–10 (Beatitudes); see also Luke 6:20–23
Matthew 8:5–10, 13 (healing centurion's servant); see also
    Luke 7:1–10
Matthew 8:14–17 (healing Peter's mother-in-law); see also
Mark 1:29–34; Luke 4:38–41
Matthew 9:2–8 (your sins are forgiven); see also Mark 2:1–12;
    Luke 5:17–26
Matthew 11:28–30 (come to me all who are weary)
Mark 6:7, 12–13 (the disciples anointed many who were sick)
Mark 14:32–36 (not what I want, but what you want)
Luke 4:22–28 (do here also in your hometown the things you did
    at Capernaum)
Luke 8:41–56 (healing Jairus's daughter and woman with a
    hemorrhage); see also Matthew 9:18–26; Mark 5:21–43
Luke 13:10–13 (healing of woman crippled for eighteen years)
John 5:2–9 (take up your bed and walk)
John 6:47–51 (I am the Bread of Life)
John 21:18–19 (when you are old . . .)

Response to the Word

A homily or other form of response, such as song, talk, dance, instrumental, other art forms, silence, may follow the Gospel.

Pray for the World and the Church, particularly for God's healing grace

One of the following litanies may be used.

A Litany for Healing

The Deacon or other leader introduces the Litany with these or similar words

Let us name before God those for whom we offer our prayers.

The people offer names either silently or aloud.

The Leader continues with these or similar words (any of the indicated petitions may be omitted)

Let us offer our prayers for God's healing, saying, "Hear and have mercy"

(*or* "Answer our prayer" *or* "Have mercy").

Holy God, source of health and salvation,

Here and after each petition, the people respond

Hear and have mercy
    or
Answer our prayer
    or
Have mercy.

Holy and Mighty, wellspring of abundant life,

Holy Immortal One, protector of the faithful,

Holy Trinity, the source of all wholeness,

Blessed Jesus, your Holy Name is medicine for healing and a promise of eternal life,

Jesus, descendant of David, you healed all who came to you in faith,

Jesus, child of Mary, you embraced the world with your love,

Jesus, divine physician, you sent your disciples to preach the Gospel and heal in your name,

Jesus our true mother, you feed us the milk of your compassion,

Jesus, Son of God, you take away our sin and make us whole,

Jesus, eternal Christ, your promised Spirit renews our hearts and minds,

Grant your grace to heal those who are sick, we pray to you, O God,

Give courage and faith to all who are disabled through injury or illness, we pray to you, O God,

Comfort, relieve, and heal all sick children, we pray to you, O God,

Give courage to all who await surgery, we pray to you, O God,

Support and encourage those who live with chronic illness, we pray to you, O God,

Strengthen those who endure continual pain, and give them hope, we pray to you, O God,

Grant the refreshment of peaceful sleep to all who suffer, we pray to you, O God,

Befriend all who are anxious, lonely, despondent, or afraid, we pray to you, O God,

Restore those with mental illness to clarity of mind and hopefulness of heart, we pray to you, O God,

Give rest to the weary, and hold the dying in your loving arms, we pray to you, O God,

Help us to prepare for death with confident expectation and hope of Easter joy, we pray to you, O God,

Give your wisdom and compassion to health care workers, that they may minister to the sick and dying with knowledge, skill, and kindness, we pray to you, O God,

Uphold those who keep watch with the sick, we pray to you, O God,

Guide those who search for the causes and cures of sickness and disease, we pray to you, O God,

Jesus, Lamb of God,

Jesus, bearer of our sins,

Jesus, redeemer of the world,

If the Lord's Prayer is not to be used elsewhere, it follows here.

The following Collect may be added

Compassionate God: You so loved the world that you sent us Jesus to bear our infirmities and afflictions. Through acts of healing, he revealed you as the true source of health and salvation. For the sake of your Christ who suffered and died for us, conquered death, and now reigns with you in glory, hear the cry of your people. Have mercy on us, make us whole, and bring us at last into the fullness of your eternal life. *Amen.*

A Litany of Healing

The Celebrant introduces the Litany with this bidding

Let us name before God those for whom we offer our prayers.

The People audibly name those for whom they are interceding.

A Person appointed then leads the Litany

Healing Touch and Saving Word

God the Father, your will for all people is health and salvation;
We praise you and thank you, O Lord.

God the Son, you came that we might have life, and might have it
more abundantly;
We praise you and thank you, O Lord.

God the Holy Spirit, you make our bodies the temple of
your presence;
We praise you and thank you, O Lord.

Holy Trinity, one God, in you we live and move and have
our being;
We praise you and thank you, O Lord.

Lord, grant your healing grace to all who are sick, injured,
or disabled, that they may be made whole;
Hear us, O Lord of life.

Grant to all who seek your guidance, and to all who are lonely,
anxious, or despondent, a knowledge of your will and an awareness
of your presence;
Hear us, O Lord of life.

Mend broken relationships, and restore those in emotional
distress to soundness of mind and serenity of spirit;
Hear us, O Lord of life.

Bless physicians, nurses, and all others who minister to the suffering,
granting them wisdom and skill, sympathy and patience;
Hear us, O Lord of life.

Grant to the dying peace and a holy death, and uphold by the
grace and consolation of your Holy Spirit those who are bereaved;
Hear us, O Lord of life.

Restore to wholeness whatever is broken by human sin, in our
lives, in our nation, and in the world;

Hear us, O Lord of life.

You are the Lord who does wonders:
You have declared your power among the peoples.

With you, O Lord, is the well of life:
And in your light we see light.

Hear us, O Lord of life:
Heal us, and make us whole.

Let us pray.

A period of silence follows.

The Celebrant concludes the Prayers with one of the following or some other suitable Collect

Almighty God, giver of life and health: Send your blessing on all who are sick, and upon those who minister to them, that all weakness may be vanquished by the triumph of the risen Christ; who lives and reigns for ever and ever. *Amen.*

or this

Heavenly Father, you have promised to hear what we ask in the Name of your Son: Accept and fulfill our petitions, we pray, not as we ask in our ignorance, nor as we deserve in our sinfulness, but as you know and love us in your Son Jesus Christ our Lord. *Amen.*

or this

O Lord our God, accept the fervent prayers of your people; in the multitude of your mercies look with compassion upon us and all who turn to you for help; for you are gracious, O lover of souls, and to you we give glory, Father, Son, and Holy Spirit, now and for ever. *Amen.*

Healing Touch and Saving Word

Confession of Sin

A Confession of Sin may follow, if it has not been said at the beginning of the service.

The Deacon or Celebrant says

Let us confess our sins to God.

Silence may be kept.

Minister and People

God of all mercy,
we confess that we have sinned against you,
opposing your will in our lives.
We have denied your goodness in each other,
    in ourselves,
      and in the world you have created.
We repent of the evil that enslaves us,
    the evil we have done,
      and the evil done on our behalf.
Forgive, restore, and strengthen us
through our Savior Jesus Christ,
that we may abide in your love
and serve only your will. Amen.

The Bishop when present, or the Priest, stands and says

Almighty God have mercy on you, forgive you all your sins
through the grace of Jesus Christ, strengthen you in all goodness,
and by the power of the Holy Spirit keep you in eternal life. *Amen.*

or this

The Deacon or Celebrant says

Let us confess our sins against God and our neighbor.

Silence may be kept.

Minister and People

Most merciful God,
we confess that we have sinned against you
in thought, word, and deed,
by what we have done,
and by what we have left undone.
We have not loved you with our whole heart,
we have not loved our neighbors as ourselves.
We are truly sorry and we humbly repent.
For the sake of your Son Jesus Christ,
have mercy on us and forgive us;
that we may delight in your will,
and walk in your ways,
to the glory of your name. Amen.

The Bishop when present, or the Priest, stands and says

Almighty God have mercy on you, forgive you all your sins
through our Lord Jesus Christ, strengthen you in all goodness,
and by the power of the Holy Spirit keep you in eternal life.
Amen.

Confession of Need

*Instead of or in addition to the Confession of Sin, the following confession of
need may be used.*

The minister introduces the prayer with these or similar words

Let us confess our need for God's healing grace.

Silence

Minister and People

Compassionate God,
we confess our weaknesses and our need for your
    strengthening touch.

Healing Touch and Saving Word

We confess that some illnesses stem from our own fault,
while others are beyond our control.
We turn to you, source of life,
and ask in the name of our Savior Jesus Christ
for the gifts of true healing and life in you. *Amen.*

Minister

May the God of love visit you in your times of trial and weakness, and raise you to newness of life, through Jesus Christ, in the
power of the Holy Spirit. *Amen.*

Laying on of Hands and Anointing

If oil for the anointing of the sick is to be blessed, the priest or bishop says

Blessed are you, O God, source of life and health. In Jesus you
became flesh and came to know the depth of human suffering.
You sent the disciples to heal those who were sick. Sanctify this
oil that all who are anointed with it may be healed, strengthened,
and renewed, by the power of your Holy Spirit. *Amen.*

or this prayer of blessing

O Lord, holy Father, giver of health and salvation: Send your
Holy Spirit to sanctify this oil; that, as your holy apostles anointed
many that were sick and healed them, so may those who in
faith and repentance receive this holy unction be made whole;
through Jesus Christ our Lord, who lives and reigns with you and
the Holy Spirit, one God, for ever and ever. *Amen.*

*The minister may introduce the laying on of hands [and anointing] with
these or similar words*

Holy Scripture teaches us that Jesus healed many who were sick
as a sign of the reign of God come near, and sent the disciples to
continue this work of healing through prayer in his name, that
the afflicted might be raised up and their sins forgiven, bringing

them to eternal salvation. By laying hands upon the sick [and anointing them], the disciples witnessed to the marvelous power and presence of God. Pray that as we follow their example, we may experience Christ's unfailing love.

or this

The ministry of Jesus invites us to new life in God and with each other. In the laying on of hands [and anointing] we proclaim the Good News that God desires us to be healthy and one in the body of Christ. You are invited to offer yourself, whatever your sickness of spirit, mind, or body, and ask for healing and wholeness in the Name of the holy and undivided Trinity.

The minister may invite each person to be anointed to give her or his name and any particular request for prayer. The minister then lays hands upon the sick person [and anoints the person], prays silently, then prays aloud using one of the following forms or similar words

N., I lay my hands upon you [and anoint you]. Receive Christ's gift of healing [especially for __]. May the power of the Savior who suffered for you wash over you, that you may be raised up in peace and inward strength. *Amen.*

or this

N., I [anoint you and] lay my hands upon you in the name of God the holy and undivided Trinity. May Christ be present with you to comfort you, to guard and protect you, and to keep you in everlasting life. *Amen.*

or this

N., I lay my hands upon you [and anoint you] in the name of the Father, and of the Son, and of the Holy Spirit, praying that our Savior Jesus Christ will sustain you, drive away sickness of body and mind and spirit, and give you that victory of life and peace which will enable you to serve and rejoice in God both now and evermore. *Amen.*

or this

N., I lay my hands upon you [and anoint you] in the name of our Savior Jesus Christ, praying you will be strengthened and filled with God's grace, that you may know the healing power of the Spirit. *Amen.*

The minister may add, in these or similar words

As you are outwardly anointed with this holy oil, so may our loving God give you the inward anointing of the Holy Spirit. Of God's bounty, may your suffering be relieved, and your spirit, mind, and body restored to grace and peace. May all of us in the frailty of our flesh know God's healing and resurrecting power. *Amen.*

If communion is not to follow, the Lord's Prayer is said.

The Laying on of Hands [and Anointing] may conclude with one or more of the following Collects

May the God who goes before you through desert places by night and by day be your companion and guide; may your journey be with the saints; may the Holy Spirit be your strength, and Christ your clothing of light, in whose name we pray. *Amen.*

or this

May God who is a strong tower to all, to whom all things in heaven and on earth bow and obey, be now and evermore your defense, and help you to know that the name given to us for health and salvation is the Name of our Redeemer, Jesus Christ. *Amen.*

or this

Generous God, we give you thanks for your beloved Jesus Christ, in whom you have shared the beauty and pain of human life. Look with compassion upon all for whom we pray, and strengthen us to be your instruments of healing in the world, by the power of the Holy Spirit. *Amen.*

or this

Thank you, Holy One of Blessing, for the good work of healing already begun in your servant[s] *N.* Grant that *she/he/they* may wait upon you with an expectant heart and rise up in joy at your call; in Christ's name we pray. *Amen.*

The following may be added

God of all mercy: help us who minister with the sick and dying to remember that though we may appear healthy, we, too, suffer from the universal human condition in a fallen world. Flesh withers, and we must all die to the life we know. Therefore, O God our help, teach us to be aware of our own infirmities, the better to make others understand they are not alone in their illness. Restore us all in the love of the holy and undivided Trinity which is our true health and salvation. *Amen.*

Exchange the Peace

Here or elsewhere in the service, all present may greet one another in the name of Christ.

If the Eucharist is not to be celebrated, the service may conclude with the Exchange of the Peace or with a [Blessing and] Dismissal.

Participate in the Sacrament of Christ's Body and Blood

The service continues with the Offertory (BCP p. 361). Texts from Enriching Our Worship 1 *(pp. 57–71) may be used for the eucharistic prayer, fraction anthem, postcommunion prayer, and the Blessing. The following may be used for the postcommunion prayer, which is especially appropriate when Communion has been received in one kind.*

Faithful God
in the wonder of your wisdom and love
you fed your people in the wilderness with the bread of angels,

and you sent Jesus to be the bread of life.
We thank you for feeding us with this bread.
May it strengthen us
that by the power of the Holy Spirit
we may embody your desire
and be renewed for your service
through Jesus Christ our Savior. Amen.

Or the postcommunion prayer on p. 399 of the Book of Common Prayer may be used.

If a Blessing is desired before the Dismissal, the following may be used

May the God of peace sanctify you entirely, and may your spirit
and soul and body be kept sound and blameless at the coming of
our Lord Jesus Christ. *Amen.*
1 Thessalonians 5:23

or this

May the One who creates and restores everything that is,
the One who is Mary's child and child of God,
the One who is the Holy Spirit,
May this Holy One bring you compassion and peace,
and bless your lives with joy. *Amen.*

or this

May the God of hope fill us with every joy in believing.
May the peace of Christ abound in our hearts.
May we be enriched by the gifts of the Holy Spirit, now and for
ever. *Amen.*

Hymns Appropriate for Ministry with the Sick

The Hymnal 1982

S 190–197	The Song of Zechariah *Benedictus Dominus Deus* (Canticle 4)
S 196–200	The Song of Simeon *Nunc dimittis* (Canticle 5)

S217	The Second Song of Isaiah *Quaerite Dominum* (Canticle 10)
287	For all the saints, who from their labors rest
333	Now the silence
334	Lord, dismiss us with thy blessing
335	I am the bread of life
383, 384	Fairest Lord Jesus
439	What wondrous love is this
453	As Jacob with travel was weary one day
469, 470	There's a wideness in God's mercy
482	Lord of all hopefulness, Lord of all joy
487	Come, my Way, my Truth, my Life
490	I want to walk as a child of the light
517	How lovely is thy dwelling-place (Psalm 84—Brother James' Air)
552, 553	Fight the good fight with all thy might
560	Remember your servants, Lord
593	Lord, make us servants of your peace
602	Jesu, Jesu, fill us with your love
645, 646	The King of love my shepherd is
662	Abide with me: fast falls the eventide
663	The Lord my God my shepherd is
676	There is a balm in Gilead
682	O God, our help in ages past
683, 684	O for a closer walk with God
707	Take my life, and let it be
711	Seek ye first the kingdom of God
712	Dona nobis pacem
714	Shalom, my friends

Wonder, Love, and Praise

727, st. 1	As panting deer desire the waterbrooks
740	Wade in the water
749	The tree of life my soul has seen
753, 754	When from bondage we are summoned
755	The steadfast love of the Lord never ceases

756	Lead me, guide me, along the way
764	Taste and see
765	O blessed spring
770	O God of gentle strength
772	O Christ, the healer, we come
773	Heal me, hands of Jesus
774	From miles around the sick ones came
775	Give thanks for life
776	No saint on earth lives life to self alone
787	We are marching in the light of God
800	Precious Lord, take my hand
801	God be with you till we meet again
804	Steal away
805	I want Jesus to walk with me
810	You who dwell in the shelter of the Lord (Eagle's wings)
812	I, the Lord of sea and sky
813	Way, way, way
820	The eyes of all wait upon you
826	Stay with me
827	O Lord hear my pray'r
881, 882	The First Song of Isaiah *Ecce, Deus* (Canticle 9)

Lift Every Voice and Sing II

4	Better be ready
7	I want to be ready
8	Deep river
9	On Jordan's stormy banks I stand
10	Oh! What a beautiful city
13	My Lord, what a morning
14	Soon and very soon
16	You are near
18	Swing low, sweet chariot
72	Just a closer walk with thee
80	Jesus, Savior, pilot me
88	My faith looks up to thee
89	My Jesus, I love thee
91	Give me Jesus

Lutheran Book of Worship

Voices United (United Church of Canada)

♦ ♦ ♦ ♦

Introduction to A Public Service of Healing [2000]

As the introductory rubrics state, this is a liturgy that can easily be adapted for either congregational or institutional use. One of the valuable additions of A Public Service of Healing [2000] is the helpful introductory material by members of the Expansive Language Committee. "A Note About the Process" (pp. 9–11) informs the reader that the 72nd General Convention "directed the Standing Commission on Liturgy and Music to 'develop supplemental liturgical materials for the Pastoral Offices of *The Book of Common Prayer* and to present those materials to the 73rd General Convention' (Resolution D086),"[117] a task assigned to the Expansive Language Committee, chaired by Phoebe Pettingell. The primary purpose of these materials was "to provide texts using inclusive and expansive language, that is, language which expands the images used to speak of and to, God, and language in which all worshippers find themselves, and their religious experience of God as revealed in Christ, more completely reflected."[118] In drafting these rites,

> . . . the committee drew upon a wide range of sources: Scripture, contemporary prayerbooks of other churches of the Anglican Communion, including Canada, New Zealand, Australia, Ireland, and South Africa; traditional materials from Orthodox and medieval western sources; and hymnody of different American cultures. Rather than borrowing directly from these sources, in most cases the committee has adapted material in order to craft prayers that will resonate with contemporary English-speaking Americans, including those who are not familiar with traditional liturgical language. A number of prayers from the 1979 Book of Common Prayer have been included; a few of these have been revised in order to update the language. [119]

"Praying with the Sick" (pp. 13–17), by Pettingell, provides helpful guidelines on the topic of pastoral visitation and the nature of prayer for healing. Much of this, Pettingell notes, is adapted from Norman Autton's *A Manual of Prayers and Readings for the Sick.*[120] The Introduction to A Public Service of Healing [2000] (pp. 21–26) opens with a very succinct (six-paragraph) description of the theology underlying the church's ministry of healing and in particular, the sacramental rite of unction, which is especially appropriate "at times of illness, a particular procedure, or at a time of great distress."

117. Ibid., 9.

118. Ibid.

119. Ibid., 2.

120. Autton, *A Manual of Prayers and Readings for the Sick.*

In addition to the more familiar General Confession, A Public Service of Healing (2000) offers a new form for the Confession of Sin[121] in more contemporary and distinctly non-juridical language that clearly addresses the nature of sin in a manner designed to create a greater awareness in the penitent of both its personal and corporate dimensions. It is important as we seek to move away from the older understanding of illness as the visitation of God for sin, to continue to acknowledge the holistic nature of the church's understanding of healing, and the wholeness and health that derive from our re-integration with God and with God's body.

A Public Service of Healing (2000) contains, as well, a Confession of Need:

Minister and people

Compassionate God,
we confess our weaknesses and our need
for your strengthening touch.
We confess that some illnesses stem from our own fault,
while others are beyond our control.
We turn to you, source of life,
and ask in the name of our Savior Jesus Christ
for the gifts of true healing and life in you. *Amen.*

This is followed by a blessing:

Minister

May the God of love visit you in your times of trial and weakness, and raise you to newness of life, through Jesus Christ, in the power of the Holy Spirit. *Amen.*[122]

This Confession of Need is a curious addition at first glance, accustomed as we are to the more poetic language of the Ministration to the Sick. While there is no question of its theological soundness, the language seems somewhat clinical and detached in comparison—more like a theological statement of fact than a confession. However, as the architects of A Public Service of Healing [2000] point out, it has the potential to serve as a powerful pastoral tool for individuals who struggle not only with life-altering

121. *Enriching Our Worship 2*, 35.
122. *Enriching Our Worship 2*, 36–37.

illness, but with the guilt and the sort of questions that often accompany such sickness situations: *Why me? What did I do wrong? Why is this happening to me?* Certainly, says physician and author Larry Dossey,

> . . . disease can be a reflection of the psyche. For example, people who experience a tremendous degree of psychological stress at work and have no control over the demands of their job have a higher incidence of heart attacks. Also, it is known that individuals who are burdened with a sense of stress and anxiety and who are cynical and angry toward life in general—the so-called Type A personality—are more likely to die younger of heart disease.

> But examples such as these do not mean that *all* diseases are correlated with psychological problems or spiritual failure. Many great saints and mystics died from dreadful diseases, sometimes at a young age . . . If "being spiritual" immunized one against illness, the saints and mystics should have been healthy and long-lived. The fact that they often were not shows that one can attain great spiritual heights and get very sick.[123]

As Ruth Meyers explains, the Confession of Need is intended not to replace, but to serve as an alternative or addition to the Confession of Sin, acknowledging the fact that we may come to healing both aware of our sinfulness and of our need for healing. Both the Confession of Sin and the Confession of Need, Meyers notes, are approaches to, or immediate preparation for, receiving healing.[124] The Confession of Need, according to Jennifer Phillips, "can serve as an addendum to the regular general confession—sometimes people with illness are particularly burdened with the belief (true or not) that they have caused or contributed to their illness . . . plus admitting weakness or need that becomes inescapable in sickness comes very hard to some people and needs a bit of assistance. Its placement allows the penitent/person seeking healing to get everything out on the table before God in order to be ready and open for healing and forgiveness and God's help (as well as help from the community)."[125]

While I recognize its pastoral value, the Confession of Need leaves me with mixed feelings. There is no question about the importance of being able to come to terms with one's feelings of regret, anger, shame, helplessness,

123. Dossey, *Prayer Is Good Medicine*, 158–59.

124. Ruth Meyers, e-mail to author, 18th May 2006.

125. Jennifer Phillips, e-mail to the author, 17 May 2006.

human frailty and weakness and to "lay them out on the table before God," as Phillips says, in order to enable us to better open ourselves to God's healing. Perhaps it is the phrase "We confess that some illnesses stem from our own fault, while others are beyond our control" that seems out of place. It may be that a slight rewording or re-arranging is in order. The Confession of Need could be preceded by a prayer or a preface by the presider acknowledging these difficult fears and concerns. Then, in the Confession of Need, the sick would be invited to acknowledge these before God, much in the manner of the Instruction that follows the Opening Prayer of Mary Frances Duffy's Ritual of Healing for Families of the Terminally Ill:

> **Presider** The pain and disruption you may nobly try to deny; yet it is there. It may bring you anger, or lead you to bargain with God and with life "if only things could be different." Or it may make you very, very sad.
>
> Yet, however you feel at this moment, the healing power of Christ seeks to touch your hearts. He seeks to lead you to accept and embrace this life with all its mystery, and to discover his love for you in the midst of this sadness and grief.
>
> May we spend a few moments in quiet reflection before our God, and allow ourselves to experience honestly and with reverence the feelings which are uniquely our own. Let us express ourselves to God in truth, without fear or shame.[126]

The Litany of Healing begins, as does the Litany in *The Book of Occasional Services*, with an invitation to worshippers to name, either silently or aloud, those for whom they wish to pray—something that is lacking in the Ministration to the Sick. This affords participants a much welcome 'transitional space' of the type previously noted.

A welcome feature of this new Litany of Healing is the fact that while the 1991 Litany of Healing employs several different responses throughout to the various petitions—"We praise you and thank you," "Hear us, Lord of life," and so on—the Litany in A Public Service of Healing [2000] provides for three possible responses to the petitions—"Hear and have mercy," "Answer our prayer," or "Have mercy"—only *one* of which is employed throughout the Litany, making it easier to use when printed liturgies are not available or are impractical.

---

126. Mary Frances Duffy's "A Ritual of Healing for Families of the Terminally Ill." In *Alternative Futures for Worship*, 7:116.

Another noteworthy feature of A Public Service of Healing [2000] is found in the Collect following the laying on of hands [and anointing], which reads: "May God who is a strong tower to all, to whom all things in heaven and on earth bow and obey, be now and evermore your defense, and help you to know that *the name given to us* [emphasis mine] for health and salvation is the name of our Redeemer, Jesus Christ." Earlier rites for healing in *The Book of Common Prayer* and *The Book of Occasional Services* follow, more or less, Cranmer's wording found in the original 1549 Visitation and Communion of the Sick:

> The almighty Lord, who is a moste strong tower to all them that put their trust in hym, to whom all thynges in heaven, in earth, and under earth, doe bowe and obey: be now and ever more thy defence, and make thee knowe and fele, that *there is no name geven to man*, in whom and through whom thou mayest receyue helth and salvacion, but *only* the name of our Lorde Jesus Christe. Amen. [italics added]

Similarly, the Collect in the 1979 Ministration to the Sick concludes: "make you know and feel that the *only* Name under heaven given for health and salvation is the Name of our Lord Jesus Christ." This very slight alteration in wording in A Public Service of Healing [2000] would appear to signal a subtle but nevertheless significant theological shift. According to Phillips, this change in wording reflects a desire to be more inclusive:

> bearing in mind that healing occasions may include family members or friends of several religions, and also the variety of theological understandings among Episcopalians of John's Gospel's words about Jesus being the (only) Way and Truth, and the only name . . . For example, there is plenty of mainstream belief and good scholarly exegesis (e.g., of Romans) among Christians today that Jews observant of the covenant with Israel and Torah do not have to convert to enter God's salvation. Quite a few clergy stopped using [the earlier form of] this prayer a long while back, finding it especially unuseful [sic] in healing rituals, but we felt there was much of value in it.[127]

In regard to the prayer for anointing, it is worth noting that A Public Service of Healing (2000) provides *four* possible forms, perhaps in order to accommodate different kinds and degrees of sickness-situations:

127. Jennifer Phillips, e-mail to the author, 17 May 2006.

N., I lay hands upon you [and anoint you]. Receive Christ's gift of healing [especially for ___]. May the power of the Savior who suffered for you wash over you, that you may be raised up in peace and inward strength. *Amen.*

or this

N., I [anoint you and] lay my hands upon you in the name of God the holy and undivided Trinity. May Christ be present with you to comfort you, to guard and protect you, and keep you in everlasting life. *Amen.*

or this

N., I lay my hands upon you [and anoint you] in the name of the Father, and of the Son, and of the Holy Spirit, praying that our Savior Jesus Christ will sustain you, drive away sickness of body and mind and spirit, and give you that victory of life and peace which will enable you to serve and rejoice in God both now and evermore. *Amen.*

or this

N., I lay my hands upon you [and anoint you] in the name of our Savior Jesus Christ, praying you will be strengthened and filled with God's grace, that you may know the healing power of the Spirit. *Amen.*

Different forms, different circumstances. The wording of the first two forms, for instance, suggests that they were created to address the situation of individuals for whom the prospect of physical recovery may be impracticable or unrealistic, for whom healing may take the form of, to use Gusmer's words, "the ultimate healing transformation"[128] by way of the Resurrection of the Dead. The wording of the third prayer—"praying that our Savior Jesus Christ will sustain you, drive away sickness of body and mind and spirit, and give you that victory of life and peace which will enable you to serve and rejoice in God both now and evermore"—expresses a clearer hope of recovery from illness. The objective of the fourth prayer is somewhat more ambiguous: "praying you will be strengthened and filled with God's grace, that you may know the healing power of the Spirit." Healing may take many forms, and one could conceivably use this prayer for the healing of addiction, or for 'spiritual malaise,' for those living with serious,

128. Gusmer, *And You Visited Me,* 166.

life altering illness, as well as for those struggling with the frailty and infirmity associated with old age.

Looking Back, Looking Forward

The development of our Anglican sacramental liturgies of healing, from the first Visitation Office of 1549 to the 1979 Ministration to the Sick and the more recent Public Service of Healing rites, reflects an evolving theology of health and healing, a shift of focus from last rites to gospel medicine for the faithful whose lives have been disrupted by sickness or suffering. At this point it would be helpful to consider the different sacramental/liturgical perspectives expressed by the Old School model (represented by the earlier Visitation rites) and the New School model (represented by The Ministration to the Sick, and A Public Service of Healing [1991] and [2000]).

Comparing Anglican Old School / New School Models

THE MODELS AND GRACE

The Old School model of sacramental theology regards the grace of the sacrament as something administered almost in the manner of spiritual 'medicine.' The sacramental ministration is a "means whereby God is moved to change something. . . "[129] In contrast, the New School model expresses a theology in which God's grace is given to us freely before we even think to ask for it.[130] "God's presence, which is 'always already' guaranteed, seeks concrete ways of inserting itself in particular human situations."[131]

THE MODELS AND CHURCH

From the perspective of the Old School model, the Church in the person of the minister brings the sacraments to the sick and 'dispenses' the sacraments. The New School model, on the other hand, places the emphasis on the underlying sacramentality of the Church itself. To this way of thinking,

---

129. Vorgrimler, *Sacramental Theology*, 87.

130. This is particularly well-expressed in both versions of *A Litany for Healing in Enriching Our Worship 2*.

131. Vorgrimler, *Sacramental Theology*, 87.

it is the assembly of the faithful—clergy and laity together—which celebrates the sacraments.

THE MODELS AND LITURGICAL CELEBRATION

The Old School model regards liturgical celebrations as quasi-private rituals and the responsibility of the ordained. The congregation is relegated to the role of recipient. In contrast, the New School model understands sacraments to be liturgical actions which are "not private actions, but the celebrations of the church."[132] Our sacramental liturgies are the shared action of the Church in assembly.

THE MODELS AND THE SCOPE OF SACRAMENTAL EFFECTS

In the light of the Old School model, unction is administered only when one is in danger of dying. Contrast this with the New School model's renewed understanding of the sacramental rite of unction as not only for the healing of body, mind and spirit, but for the 'retooling' of Christians – strengthening and renewal of one's baptismal status. "The sacrament is particularly appropriate at times of illness, a turning point in an illness, a particular procedure, or at a time of great distress."[133]

THE MODELS AND THE RELATION OF WORD AND SACRAMENT

The Old School model is characterized by word-heavy liturgies in which the role of the symbol is treated as subordinate to the proclamation of the Word. There is an emphasis on theological soundness, but with little or no real appreciation for the power of symbols to not merely express and signify God's grace, but to effectively communicate it to the believer. Compare this to the New School model, central to which is an appreciation for the relationship between word and sacrament and the complex proclamatory and symbolic function of both word and ritual in the sacramental event.

132. *SC* I, 26

133. Introduction, *Enriching Our Worship* 2, 21.

Gift From God Or Grace-Filled Encounter?

There is an important theological shift that deserves our attention in regard to our current sacramental rites of healing. One cannot help but be struck, upon examining the earlier Visitation Offices, by the prevailing sense of God's grace as spiritual medicine for the healing of physical illness and the remission of sins, rather than a privileged means by which "God's presence," as Vorgrimler says, "which is 'always already' guaranteed, seeks concrete ways of inserting itself in particular human situations."[134] While Article XXV of the Articles of Religion assures us that the sacraments are "effectual signs of grace, and God's good will towards us . . . ," the grace of the sacrament as expressed in the Visitation Offices ends up sounding more like a gift *from* God, rather than a gift *of* God, or as Vorgrimler would say, like a "means whereby God is moved to change something. . ."[135]

The grace of the sacrament, to this way of thinking, is something that is sought in order to remedy an unfortunate situation, to enable the sick person to endure God's visitation with patience, or to assure him of God's forgiveness of his sins. Little, if any, regard is given to the sacramental grace not merely in terms of strength and comfort, but also in terms of spiritual renewal and of vocation. It is easy to forget that the laying on of hands is not just a healing gesture, but an ancient gesture of ordaining and commissioning. As Empereur notes: "Laying on of hands, because it is a commissioning in the Spirit, is concerned more with the restoration of the significance of life through invitation back into community, than it is with the restoration of one's former health and social role that the person had prior to illness. Imposition of hands with its multivalent meanings becomes an appropriate symbol of the vocational aspect of the sick and elderly because rather than treating them as dependents and recipients of the community's benefactions, it deals with them as adults, not as healthy or productive (according to the present culture's values) adults, but as peers who make a contribution to the community in terms of meaning."[136]

While our current liturgies of healing still leave a great deal to be desired in this respect, one is left with the impression that this is something that will be more fully addressed in future revisions. One encouraging note

---

134. Vorgrimler, *Sacramental Theology*, 87.

135. Ibid.

136. Empereur, *Prophetic Anointing*, 196.

in this respect is found in the conclusion of the postcommunion prayer at the end of A Public Service of Healing (2000):

> We thank you for feeding us with this bread.
> May it strengthen us
> that by the power of the Holy Spirit
> we may embody your desire
> and be renewed for your service
> through Jesus Christ our Savior. Amen.[137]

Beseeching Language

A weakness shared (to various degrees) by the Ministration to the Sick and A Public Service of Healing [1991] is the apparent lack of confidence in the efficacy of this sacramental ministration communicated by the unfortunate wording of the prayer for healing. Consider this prayer from The Ministration to the Sick:

> N., I lay my hands upon you in the Name of the Father, and of the Son, and of the Holy Spirit, *beseeching* [emphasis mine] our Lord Jesus Christ to sustain you with his presence, to drive away all sickness of body and spirit, and to give you that victory of life and peace which will enable you to serve him both now and evermore. *Amen.*[138]

Beseeching? The very term seems to imply that we are uncertain of our Lord's willingness to do all that that the church seeks on the part of the sick and the suffering. It seems particularly inappropriate for a prayer of sacramental ministration. As A. G. Martimort points out: "A distinction can be made among the prayers of the celebrant between those that express his personal devotion, and are thus in a sense private prayers, and those in which he truly acts as president of the assembly and exercises his mediatorial role . . . A further point to be made is that some of the words spoken by the priest are not prayers but actions: indicative formulas, blessings, exorcisms."[139]

The effect of this implicit ambiguity on the individual being anointed must surely be a negative one. Consider, in contrast, the indicative formula

137. *Enriching Our Worship 2*, 56.

138. *The Book of Common Prayer*, 456.

139. Martimort, "The Dialogue between God and His People," in *The Church at Prayer*, 1:156.

used in the prayer of Absolution in the rite of the Reconciliation of a Penitent: "Our Lord Jesus Christ, who offered himself to be sacrificed for us to the Father, and who conferred power upon his church to forgive sins, *absolve you* through my ministry by the grace of the Holy Spirit, and *restore you* to the perfect peace of the Church [emphasis mine]."[140]

One long-time critic of 'beseeching' language is Newbert:

> I have for some time felt that one of the weaknesses of both *The Book of Common Prayer* and *The Book of Occasional Services* is the use of the subjunctive mode rather than the imperative or a "performative" or "efficatory" mode. Blessings, traditionally, are always in the imperative mode—why not the words of sacrament of healing . . . "The Blessing of God Almighty, the Father, the Son and the Holy Spirit be upon you . . ." or "The Lord be with you" (which is as much of a blessing as the former) . . . Contrast that to "I lay my hands upon you . . . beseeching our Lord Jesus Christ to sustain you . . ." Why should the language of the sacrament of healing be in the subjunctive mode and supplicatory in nature while the language of a blessing is clearly in the imperative . . . "The Lord be in your heart and upon your lips that you may truly and humbly confess your sins . . ." [The *Book of Common Prayer*] p. 447 "Our Lord Jesus Christ who has left power to his Church to absolve all sins . . . I absolve you . . ." [These] are in the imperative mode or understood to be "performative" language. Perhaps the words in healing should be something like "The Lord Jesus Christ *heal* you by the mighty power of his presence . . ."[141]

The prayers for anointing in A Public Service of Healing [2000] in contrast, strike a more confident tone: "*Receive* Christ's gift of healing. . . ", "*May* Christ be present with you to comfort you, to guard and protect you, and keep you in everlasting life," "*praying* that our Savior Jesus Christ will sustain you, drive away sickness of body and mind and spirit, and give you that victory of life and peace," "*praying* you will be strengthened and filled with God's grace."

---

140. *The Book of Common Prayer*, 451 (italics added).

141. The Rev. Russell Anderson Newbert, e-mail to the author, 10 February 2006.

Who, When, and How

In regard to the laying on of hands and anointing of the sick, as we have noted, the rubrics in A Public Service of Healing [1991] state that "*Lay persons with a gift of healing may join the celebrant in the laying on of hands,*" while the introductory notes for A Public Service of Healing [2000] read: "*Under the direction of the Rector or other member of the clergy in charge of the local congregation, lay persons with a gift of healing may administer or assist in administering the laying on of hands and anointing.*"[142] Again, as previously noted, we are provided with no criteria for determining who such persons are.

The reason for this particular instruction, says Pettingell, arose out of

> evolving experience with healing rites. As late as the 1990's, the people who had large healing services were in the minority—and were often associated with the Order of St. Luke. However, shortly thereafter, it became normative for parishes to have weekly healing services, often in the context of the eucharist. The rites in EOW assume this later venue, as opposed to the prayer meeting where the service is rather informal and lay people with the [gift of healing] are exercising their ministry through the laying on of hands. The theologians of the Expansive Language committee were concerned with things they had seen in the context of eucharists where lay people seemed to be competing with the eucharist itself in their healing ministries. Therefore, it is made clear that in this context, laity should be doing this *under the direction of the celebrant*—as would not be necessary be the case were the healing rites part of a prayer service. We had no desire to deny or control healing gifts among the laity, but only to illustrate that, when part of the healing and reconciling work of the eucharist, such work becomes a liturgical act . . . regardless of special powers, as an act of the Church . . . rather than by a special charism such as a "healer" might have, inside or outside a service.[143]

Subsequent correspondence with Pettingell confirmed that this competition with the Eucharist to which she referred was related to the fact that in many congregations the laying on of hands and prayers for healing were (and still are in many parishes) taking place *after* the Holy Communion, as the faithful were returning to their seats, often at a side chapel or

142. "Ministers of the Rites," *Enriching Our Worship* 2, 25.
143. Phoebe Pettingell, e-mail to the author, 8 December 2006.

another area of the church. The sacramental rite of unction was effectively being made into a private service in the midst of the corporate worship. Another concern of the committee was the lack of theological training on the part of many of the faithful involved in the church's healing ministry, of individuals possessed of an innate compassion for the sick and in many cases a genuine gift for healing, but a lack of understanding concerning the broader dimensions of healing and wholeness, or of the difference between what the church understands, for instance, by *charism* and *sacrament*.

I believe that it would be prudent for each diocese to have some sort of guidelines in place, such as those established by the Anglican diocese of Toronto.[144] This would help to ensure that everyone who represents the church in her ministry of healing is ably equipped for this important work and understands that healing, as we have seen, is a ministry of the whole church, rather than the prerogative of the clergy and a few special gifted individuals, and most importantly, that this healing always points beyond itself to the greater mystery at its heart. Pettingell further comments: "One of the problems, of course, is that most Anglican healing rites haven't been very explicit about what's going on. Early Anglican prayer books obviously wanted to remove the *magic* or superstitious elements, but rather than stating clearly what the church actually believes, they mostly bowdlerized, while assuming that most people understood what healing is. In 'Ministry with the Sick or Dying,' we hoped to make the theology more explicit. I agree that guidelines would help."[145]

That Perfect Peace

In regard to the Confession, it is unfortunate that the two more recent Public Service of Healing liturgies lack rubrics akin to those in the Ministration to the Sick concerning the possibility of making of a "special confession" beforehand. This provision has been relocated to the introductory rubrics for the Ministration at the Time of Death in *Enriching Our Worship 2*. They state that "*A person approaching death may be offered an opportunity for the Reconciliation of a Penitent.*"[146] And yet, are the dying the only ones who

---

144. Appendix B.

145. Phoebe Pettingell, e-mail to the author, 9 December 2006.

146. *Enriching Our Worship 2*, 96.

can benefit from the healing offered through this, the least-used of all our sacramental rites?

I can well appreciate the intention of the architects of these new liturgies in wishing to avoid the former correlation of sin and sickness, and yet, we cannot, in all good conscience, fail to acknowledge the fact that the healing and wholeness we seek—whether we are dying or not—often requires a serious reconsideration and re-appraisal of our lives, especially in regard to those aspects where our relationship with God and with our neighbor has been disrupted by the effects of sin. This may be something that requires more 'soul work' than that for which a General Confession allows. From a practical point of view, however enlightened we like to imagine ourselves in this regard, as Herbert Benson points out, "for a long span of human history, illness and infections were believed to occur when one lost favor with God or gods. This sentiment survives in a different form today. Modern society fosters other cause-and-effect views of disease—that the affliction is the result of a virus, a bacterium, a poison, or bad living—too much alcohol, smoking, eating the wrong foods, exercising too little or too much, or not learning to handle stress. Either consciously or subconsciously, Americans consider it a failure of character when a person succumbs to illness or death."[147]

"The sick person," says Mitchell, "needs an opportunity to deal with the sense of sin and separation which often accompanies sickness."[148] Of the many instruments of healing available through the church, the Reconciliation of a Penitent is one of the most powerful and yet the most often overlooked. The rite of reconciliation takes seriously the individual's sin and one's responsibility for one's own actions, and yet assures us that it is God who seeks us out, sinners that we are, in the desire to restore harmony to that relationship disrupted by sin. The Reconciliation of a Penitent offers the individual in need of healing the opportunity, with the help of the words of "comfort and counsel" offered by the confessor, to sort through the various questions and issues troubling the individual, in order that he or she may at last be restored to that "perfect peace of the Church."[149]

147. Benson, *Timeless Healing*, 111.

148. Mitchell, *Praying Shapes Believing*, 209.

149. *The Book of Common Prayer*, Reconciliation of a Penitent, 448.

In Conclusion

Today, many Episcopalians, even those from parishes where our sacramental rites of healing are celebrated on a regular basis, are quick to request anointing for family members who are gravely ill or near death, yet less likely to request anointing for someone about to undergo surgery, or recovering from a grave illness, or suffering the physical infirmities related to old age. This is, of course, due to the fact that for several centuries the anointing of the sick was for all intents and purposes, synonymous with 'last rites.' And yet, anointing, as Calhoun and Fink note, is a sacrament for living and not just for dying, and when the ministers of the rite take the time to explain this, the old associations and anxieties related with the notion of anointing as 'last rites' give way to a renewed, more positive perspective which "frees people to ask for the strength and renewed faith offered by the anointing."[150]

In addition, it has as much, I suspect, to do with the fact that we are as a church, on the whole, extremely remiss about educating the faithful regarding the meaning and purpose of our sacraments and sacramental rites (aside from baptism and the Eucharist). Catechesis and liturgical reform must go hand in hand. As Empereur remarks, "Protestant and Anglican communions also must deal with the important area of catechesis. Public worship must be an opportunity for teaching about the Christian view of illness in terms of actual experiences of the church dealing with sick people. Catechesis outside of the liturgy will be useless if the liturgy itself confuses. If the rites continue to relate anointing to the dying or do not speak of the whole person being in need of healing, then catechesis at other times, no matter how theologically informed, will be rendered dysfunctional."[151]

While my home office boasts any number of books regarding the Eucharist or Morning Prayer, and quite a few concerning subjects such as the ministry of the laity, and social justice, I can count on one hand the number of volumes dealing solely or in any great theological depth, with the Episcopal Church's sacramental rite of unction. Clearly, there is much work to be done!

Having examined each of our current sacramental rites of healing, and with a greater understanding of the earlier rites that preceded them,

---

150. Calhoun and Fink, "Alternative 1: Ritual of Anointing for the Long-Term, Seriously Ill," 87.

151. Empereur, *Prophetic Anointing*, 116–17.

in the following chapter I propose to consider in greater depth the ecclesial and sacramental theology they convey. What do they express? What are they trying to express? And how well do they do it?

4

The Work of Reviewing and Re-Envisioning Our Liturgical Rites of Healing

Introduction

In the preceding chapters, we examined the historical development of our sacramental rites of healing, and in particular, the evolution of the Episcopal Church's past and present sacramental healing liturgies, from the first Visitation Office up to the 1979 Prayer Book's Ministration to the Sick and our two newest communal liturgies of healing. The task remaining now is to draw upon the resources of Scripture, reason, and tradition in order to reevaluate and reimagine our current rites of healing in a way that allows them more fully to express that greater vision and purpose for which they were created: *to restore us to health and wholeness in the truest sense, to nurture our faith, to enable our growth into the likeness of Christ at each new turning point in our lives, and to engage us in a mutuality of ministry as a ministering/healing community.*

The corporate worship so central to our Anglican faith expresses a theology centered in an ongoing relationship with and growth into Jesus Christ, in whose life and ministry all baptized persons share. Together, through the medium of ritual and music, word and symbol, prayer and gesture, we celebrate what God has *done* for us, what God is *doing* for us, and what we believe God *will do* for us. Our sacramental liturgies are an important means by which the sense of mission and purpose so central to our identity as Christians is not just expressed but reassessed and renewed.

One has only to consider the concluding lines of our Postcommunion prayers, our "marching orders," as it were:

> And we humbly beseech thee, O heavenly Father,
> so to assist us with thy grace,
> that we may continue in that holy fellowship
> and do all such good works as thou hast prepared for us to walk in;
> through Jesus Christ our Lord. [1]

or

> Send us now into the world in peace,
> and grant us strength and courage
> to love and serve you
> with gladness and singleness of heart;
> through Christ our Lord. [2]

Similarly, consider the dismissal given by the deacon or the presider at the conclusion of the Eucharist, which, as Mitchell observes, "asserts the relationship between liturgy and Christian living. It is a call to mission, not simply in the narrow sense of preaching religion, but in the broader sense of witnessing to the power of the risen Christ in daily living—a call to live the baptismal and eucharistic life in the world." [3] This charge bids us—all of us, sick and well, young and old alike—to take up the work for which we were baptized: to love and serve the Lord, to rejoice in the power of the Spirit, and to make our lives a witness to the life-changing, life-affirming power of the risen Christ.

As it did for many (Baby Boomer) Episcopalians of my age group, my introduction to our sacramental rites of healing took place when a loved one fell seriously ill. In my case, that person was my father, who had been rushed to the hospital with seizures. I had left the church as a teenager and only returned to it in my late twenties. I had no personal acquaintance with the rite of unction, but I knew that it was something that the church offered to the seriously ill and the dying. I phoned my parish priest, Fr. Andy, informed him of the situation, and asked if he would stop by the hospital to anoint my father. Fr. Andy was there shortly afterwards, and when I spoke to him later, I expressed to him how thankful I was, and still am, for his heartfelt ministrations.

---

1. *The Book of Common Prayer*, 339.
2. Ibid., 365.
3. Mitchell, *Praying Shapes Believing*, 182.

This was in the early nineteen nineties. It never occurred to me back then that I—or other members of my family—might be there with Fr. Andy to support my father with our prayers or to take part in the laying on of hands. However often I may have joined in with my fellow Episcopalians in proclaiming to the newly baptized "We welcome you into the household of God. Confess the faith of Christ crucified, proclaim his resurrection, and *share with us in his eternal priesthood*,"[4] I had never given much thought to claiming my own role in that same priesthood. Moreover, I had not yet experienced the anointing of the sick within the context of the Eucharist, and like most Episcopalians I knew, I regarded unction as something private. As well, I thought of the church's ministry of healing as something of a one-way street: it did not occur to me that the sick have a ministry of their own to offer, through their prophetic role and by their witness of faith in the face of suffering, sickness, and uncertainty.

What a dramatic difference in so short a time! It is the rare parish nowadays that does not offer a communal rite of healing on a regular basis, even if it is only once or twice a year. Many celebrate it more often, monthly or weekly. This is a welcome development indeed. However, we are still left with the question of how *well* we communicate, through word and symbol, through presence and prayer, the greater corporate and vocational dimension of our sacramental rites of healing. We need to consider most particularly, the fact that, as Mitchell reminds us, unction, like all our sacramental ministrations, is not just concerned with physical and emotional healing, but also "restoration and renewal of the baptismal state. It unites the sick person with Jesus in his suffering and death and thereby also in his resurrection. The anointing of the sick is the sacrament of resurrection and life in Christ. It renews the relationship of the sick person to Christ and to the Church which continues to exercise Christ's healing ministry. Like all true sacramental signs, the anointing is a sign of new life, of the resurrection life in Christ."[5]

If our sacramental rites of healing are to help us to "grow into the full stature of Christ," then they must help us to "do the work [God] has given us to do," at each stage of our life and our faith journey and in the face of ever-changing circumstances. "Christian living," says Stephen Holmgren, "is baptismal living."[6] It begins with "the act of resurrection-faith that comes

4. *The Book of Common Prayer*, Holy Baptism, 308.
5. Mitchell, *Praying Shapes Believing*, 211.
6. Holmgren, *Ethics after Easter*, 3.

to fruit in Christian baptism,"[7] but the implications of the renunciations we make, the affirmations to which we commit ourselves, and the covenant into which we enter are lived out day by day throughout "that long walk from the baptismal font."[8] It is the crucial task of the church to encourage and support the ongoing growth in faith of all the baptized at every stage of this journey. In the words of Robert Brooks:

> So how do we build communities that continually draw out the new meanings of Baptism, the deeper meanings of Baptism? How do we have mystagogia[9] for life?
>
> *What we need is a change of perception, then, about the baptized . . . They are these people who are the new humanity and the new creation; sons and daughters; heirs co-reigning with Christ; royal, priestly, holy, off-spring of the Divine One. Those are the terms we throw about loosely all the time, but if we really think about them, they are pretty substantial . . . So we need a whole change in our perception about those who comprise our community . . . we need to see that it is possible to have mystagogical communities . . . where the very life of the community—the very pattern and rhythm of its existence—draws meaning out of one another at any age, draws out new understandings and new insights into the rich meaning of our baptism.*[10]

In other words, the challenge before us is to discern how—through our worship, through our mutual fellowship, through ongoing catechesis—those who are struggling with the limit-experience of serious illness can continue to draw renewed purpose and meaning from their present circumstances, to be able to say with St. Paul, "So we do not lose heart. Though our outer nature is wasting away, our inner nature is being renewed

---

7. Ibid.

8. Ibid.

9. *Mystagogy/mystagogia*: "From the Greek *mystagogos*, the term refers to a process of initiation into 'mysteries.' It may take place after the Easter Vigil, lasting throughout the Great Fifty Days of the Easter season. It involves the integration of adult neophytes [newly baptized persons] into the life of the church . . . Members of the Christian community continue to help and instruct the new Christians . . . In the broadest sense, Christians live in *mystagogia* for the rest of their lives as they continue to enter into the mystery of Christ's death and resurrection." Armentrout and Slocum, "Mystagogy." In *An Episcopal Dictionary of the Church*, 348.

10. Robert Brooks, "Post-Baptismal Catechesis," in Merriman, *The Baptismal Mystery and the Catechumenate*, 156–57, (italics added).

every day."[11] To this end we might consider our present rites of healing in light of the sort of questions proposed by Regis Duffy: *Do our sacramental liturgies of healing have an evangelization component that allows the sick to ask new questions about their lives and to clarify their intentions? Do the sacraments administered to the sick enable them to do the work of Christ in a way appropriate to their life-stage and situation? Does the pastoral care of the sick permit a wider vision of and a deeper commitment to the gospel and its mission?*[12] To which I might add: *Do our sacramental liturgies of healing envision and make possible a community that acknowledges both the worth and the vocation of well and sick alike, and values the ministry of both?*

Clearly, despite our best intentions and our ever-evolving theology of health and ministry, it is unrealistic to imagine that such a transformation of consciousness simply demands newer and more inclusive, or better choreographed rites. Unless the underlying theology is embodied, not just in the rubrics, but in the very *spirit* of our liturgies, we cannot hope to be transformed by them. This reshaping of consciousness, this reimagining and renewing of identity, cannot be simply an intellectual enterprise, a fact not fully comprehended by some enthusiastic reformers. However well-written our new liturgies may be, unless they engage us body, mind, and spirit, they will not transform us from within.

Sickness, Crisis, and Opportunity

"Because sickness does not allow for clear identification of its causes," says Empereur, "people at this time [the sick, the aged, or the dying] experience themselves as a mystery. There is an obscurity in their self-understanding that is more obvious at the time. The full depths of themselves exceed their powers of understanding."[13] Anyone whose life has been impacted by the reality of long-term or life-threatening illness can readily attest to its effect not just upon our physical health, but upon our very sense of who we are. It is a difficult time of change, of disruption and loss, of limitation, and over-whelming, painful truths (which we would often prefer not to acknowl-edge—perhaps because we do not wish to burden those whom we love, or perhaps because we cling to the belief that if we refuse to think about them, they are not real). Serious illness leaves in its wake a crisis situation that

11. 2 Corinthians 4:16.

12. Duffy, *A Roman Catholic Theology of Pastoral Care*, 95.

13. Empereur, *Prophetic Anointing*, 209.

may be marked not merely by pain and debility, but also by fragmentation, grief, a sense of powerlessness, and, says Jennifer Glen, the "disintegration of our relational world in confrontation with our mortality."[14]

The effects of our physical illness, which strip from us so much of that from which we once derived our identity—our health, our appearance, our livelihood, our independence, our relationships, our financial security, and so on—are certain to take a great toll upon both our physical and spiritual resources. Much as we might like to think otherwise, our lives will never again be quite the same. We may find ourselves slowly and surely drifting apart from the community that we had for so long taken for granted, as our families, friends, and neighbors gradually relegate us to a new and special category, while they in turn struggle with the fear of their own mortality which this sickness-situation forces them to confront.

To draw upon the metaphor of life as a journey, the effect of any serious illness—a diagnosis of cancer, a bout with heart disease, the experience of liver dysfunction or kidney failure—is to take us to new and uncharted territory, through which we would prefer not to have to travel. We are likely to find ourselves in a state of liminality, focused yearningly on the past—on what we had before our life took an unexpected turn, or off somewhere in the future—in fearful anticipation of what may befall us next, or somewhere in-between, anywhere but in the present. It is as if in our life's journey we suddenly found ourselves at a fork in the road, with two unexplored vistas stretching out before us, both equally uncertain, but one marked by hope and purposefulness, and the other by dread and despair. [15]

PAST
↓
PRESENT - NEW SITUATION
↓
PROSPECT FOR
THE FUTURE

    ↙   ↘

COMMUNITY / INTEGRATION   ALIENATION / FRAGMENTATION
↙   ↘
HOPE / MEANING   DREAD / FUTILITY

14. Jennifer Glen, "Rites of Healing: A Reflection in Pastoral Theology." In Fink, *Alternative Futures for Worship* 7: 43.

15. I am indebted to Glen's essay, "Rites of Healing: A Reflection in Pastoral Theology," which so eloquently describes "the experience of illness [as] the disintegration of our relational world in confrontation with our mortality" (43).

Which path will we choose? Which prospect will we embrace? What will give meaning and hope to our new and radically altered situation? There are no guarantees of what is to befall us in either case, but in taking up the first path, like those first disciples on that Emmaus road, in the company of our fellow travelers, our eyes are opened, our hearts begin to burn within, and the meaning of the gospel message reveals itself to us—even in the midst of our sickness situation—as we walk with the Lord. We do not know what we will find along the way, and the journey may indeed be a difficult one, but we know that at every step of our journey Christ is walking with us. This journey, says Glen, this "conversion . . . from question to conviction, from a world shattered by death to a world made whole again in the very teeth of death, is the sacramental manifestation of the Pasch of Christ lived out at the heart of human history. Thus in their own lives, perhaps enabled by all who have ministered to them, [the sick] themselves stand witness before the rest of the Church, and indeed before all of fragile humanity to whom the Church is in mission, to the eschatological healing toward which all works of cure and reconciliation are directed."[16]

Glen observes, "If the experience of sickness is interpreted as the disintegration of our relational world in confrontation with our mortality, then healing must be interpreted as the reintegration of that world within some bearable perspective on the future."[17] One of the means the church provides to reintegrate us to wholeness and harmony, within and without, is our sacramental liturgies of healing. The Catechism in the *Book of Common Prayer* tells us that the Unction of the Sick is "the rite of anointing the sick with oil, or the laying on of hands, by which God's grace is given for the healing of spirit, mind, and body."[18] This quest for wholeness is not a solitary enterprise, since from the moment of our baptism we are a part of a greater community, a Communion of Saints, whose wholeness derives from the very wholeness of Christ.

In the midst of illness and suffering the sick are comforted and sustained by the real presence of the living Christ in the Eucharist, *the* healing sacrament. The community of the faithful is reintegrated into fellowship with the sick, and into community with that greater body, to share in that perfect wholeness offered by Christ. The sick individual is assured that God is present with them in both sickness and in health, and in the midst of pain

16. Ibid., 48.
17. Ibid., 43.
18. *Catechism*, 861.

and suffering. The entire community is reminded of the common mission of all baptized persons: to reach out to those in need of healing and to bring to them the Good News that through Christ we are given "that victory of life and peace" which will enable us to serve God both now and evermore.

Opportunities for Transformation

> "Each turning point is both a crisis and an opportunity." Ron Grimes[19]

> "I think that any time a person is in pain, there's an opportunity for transformation." Dean Ornish[20]

> "[when] you have cancer and say, "I have cancer," you may begin to think of yourself as the cancer. The identification may then take over so much of your life that if you're not careful to see the cancer as a process that's happening in a larger field, you may lose the opportunity for a certain kind of meaning." Jon Kabat-Zinn[21]

As the above quotation from Kabat-Zinn points out, if we have cancer and say, "I have cancer," there is the likelihood that we will begin to identify our self primarily with our illness, unless we have some means of grounding our self in our true identity, of restoring to our self that harmony of body, mind, and spirit disrupted by illness and suffering. Through our participation in the church's sacramental rites of healing by which we enter into the Paschal Mystery, in which we share with Christ in his death and resurrection, we are reminded that we are more than just our broken bodies, more than our cancer or our arthritis, more than the sum of our faults and failings, more than our fears and misgivings. The healing expressed and realized through the sacramental rite of unction extends far beyond mere restoration to function, or even restoration to function in society, as Michael Wilson points out, but leads us to restoration of purpose of life, in particular, God's purpose for this particular life.[22] We are, after all, children

---

19. Grimes, *Deeply into the Bone*, 6.
20. Moyers, in *Healing and the Mind*, 94.
21. Ibid. Interview with Jon Kabat-Zinn, 122.
22. Wilson, *The Church Is Healing*, 17.

of God, and as Scripture reminds us, it is in God that we live and move and have our being.[23]

Thus grounded in our true identity we are better able to confront our fears, and perhaps even make friends with the body that appears to have let us down. Suddenly we discover that we have a choice: we can identify ourselves with our illness and our limitations, or we can choose to make use of this admittedly difficult situation as an opportunity to stop and take stock, reevaluate, reassess, perhaps even employ our new circumstances as an opportunity for growth. *What is this event, this illness telling me about myself, my life? What aspects of my life must I be willing to let go of, and which do I need to embrace? What inner and outer resources can I draw upon in order to learn to deal with the stresses and challenges of my illness, and perhaps even become more engaged with life?*

Without surrendering to the illness or the hurt we can explore our situation and the possibilities open to us; we can learn to deal in the most effective manner with the options with which we are presented. We are then able to begin to integrate our illness, our pain, our limitations into the framework of our life in ways that we might never have done before, so that they take on new meaning. We may not always be able to alter our physical circumstances, but with God's help we can alter our *response* to them and begin to view our own personal narratives in the framework of the larger ongoing story of the people of God.

By placing our sickness situation within this very special sacramental context, our limit experience may become, with God's help, a rite of passage that moves us from estrangement and fragmentation to reintegration and wholeness. In the midst of uncertainty, our sacramental rites of healing allow us to move forward in a special space and time (the sacred space and time created, or re-created, by the liturgical rite), within special circumstances (in the midst of a caring and supportive community), and in the context of a hopeful vision of the future (in which we will experience fully "that victory of life and peace" that we know now only in part). These rites are more than just sacred rituals to bring us comfort in our pain or to assist us in alleviating our suffering, for at a deeper level they reestablish us as part of a greater whole: they reincorporate us into God's very life. They are not magical ceremonies that seek to manipulate or control the forces of life. Instead they serve to *confine* these seemingly chaotic forces within a horizon of meaning that renders them endurable, even meaningful, much

23. Acts 17:28.

in the manner of the act of God in containing the forces of chaos in the opening chapter of the book of Genesis. This is the power of truly effective rites of healing, whether or not physical cure ensues, that they free us to engage the world fully as human beings and as members of Christ's body, and allow us to continue to be a part of Christ's salvific work, for which we were commissioned at our baptism.

As the 2000 Church of England report, *A Time for Healing*, states, the underlying theology of our sacramental rites of healing is:

- **visionary** . . . because it beckons us towards the future and a glimpse of the kingdom, the hope of creation renewed in perfect health and wholeness.

- **prophetic** . . . because it calls us to reconsider our relationships with God, with each other and the world, and to seek forgiveness and a new start in our lives.

- **dynamic** . . . because Jesus is with us to the end of time: when we pray for his help, he comforts, strengthens and heals us, responding to our deepest needs.[24]

Healing, as we have observed, may take many forms. When we turn to the epistle of James, which is often cited as the *grundschrift*, or foundational text, for the sacramental rite of unction, we find that here the sick person is urged to "call for the elders of the church and have them pray over him, anointing him with oil in the name of the Lord. The prayer of faith will save[25] the sick man, and the Lord will raise him up; and if he has committed sins, he will be forgiven."[26] As Wilson points out, "the word *sozein* in the New Testament is used to mean both 'saved' in a theological context, and 'made whole' in a medical context. The words 'whole' and 'wholeness' are used to describe a state of being towards which we grow, when all shall be one in Christ.[27] It is that fullness of life which we shall realize together when God's purpose is accomplished, and his kingdom proclaimed in all its fullness. Some psychiatrists speak of integration of the person as the process of "wholing." In Christian thought also, *wholeness* suggests something

---

24. *A Time to Heal*, 260, 262, 267.
25. Gr. *sozo*, "To make whole, save."
26. James 5:14–15.
27. Eph. 4:13ff.

(though in a wider sense) towards which we all move both severally and together. It is a dynamic, not a static, concept."[28]

The healing that occurs through the sacramental rite of unction may take place in the context of physical cure. It may bring release from the limitations placed upon us physically or the medical conditions which marginalize us, or it is possible that this reintegration may take place in the presence of, and in spite of, these physical infirmities and barriers. It may entail emotional healing, the healing of relationships or memories, the strengthening of our spirits, the forgiveness of our sins, but certainly, the primary goal of Christian healing is that personal encounter, that personal relationship with Christ, who knows best what we need in order to be restored to perfect wholeness. We would do well to remember, as Morris Maddocks says, that "Christian healing is Jesus Christ . . . it is *he* who comes to meet us at our point of need—a person, not some quick remedy or magical formula or potent medicine. It is Jesus Christ who heals and saves."[29]

The Difficult but Necessary Work of Liturgical Revision

"The word 'health' is so interesting because it comes from a root that means "whole." Part of being a healthy person is being well integrated and at peace, with all of the systems acting together." Candace Pert[30]

It seems to me that the evolution of our Anglican healing rites reveals the swing of the liturgical pendulum from one extreme to another. At one end, we have a liturgical mindset marked by a prevailing private piety, according to which sacraments are (so to speak) by and large for the benefit of the individual to whom they are administered, a matter between the believer and God. This way of thinking produces private baptisms on Saturday afternoons, or Communion to the sick and homebound bereft, says John Richards, of the "central experience of corporate and Christian fellowship."[31] At the other end of the spectrum we have communal rites of healing in which the sick are surrounded by the community, but there is

28. Wilson, *The Church Is Healing*, 18–19.

29. Maddocks, *Twenty Questions about Healing*, 1. Maddocks was for many years the Advisor for the Ministry of Health and Healing to the Archbishops of Canterbury and York, and Director of the Acorn Christian Healing Trust.

30. Moyers, interview with Candace Pert, in Moyers, *Healing and the Mind*, 189.

31. Richards, *But Deliver Us from Evil*, 12.

no place for one-on-one preparation, personal spiritual guidance, or individual words of comfort and counsel, no opportunity to address or engage the individual in the difficult soul work often required by serious sickness situations.

Two steps forward and one step back. Liturgical reform is hard work, and real liturgical renewal requires far more than an updating of our ritual language or a 'rearranging of the furniture,' as the expression goes. It is much more than replacing old phrases with new ones, or ensuring that faithful are afforded a greater opportunity for participation. 'Authentic' liturgy does not merely uplift; it transforms. It strengthens and nurtures us each individually for the purpose of making of us "one body, one spirit in Christ, that we may worthily serve the world in [Christ's] name." In the same way, authentic liturgies of healing are more than simply palliatives for our pain, far more than mere solace and comfort for our suffering, or remedy for our sick and broken bodies.

The section of The Constitution on the Divine Liturgy titled "The Reform of the Sacred Liturgy" reminds us that "both texts and rites should be drawn up *so that they express more clearly the holy things which they signify*; the Christian people, so far as possible, should be enabled to understand them with ease and to take part in them fully, actively, and as befits a community."[32] Taking a leaf from our Roman Catholic brothers and sisters, we might ask ourselves: How well do our Episcopal sacramental rites of healing succeed in this regard? Do they, in fact, clearly *express* the holy things—the divine mystery—at their heart, and into which they invite us—or *should* invite us—to participate? Do they clearly *signify* them in word, symbol and gesture, or are they, instead, well-intentioned, but word-heavy, didactic or moralizing exercises? Are they easily understood by the contemporary worshiper? Do they acknowledge and empower *all* the faithful, as Duffy says, for ministry in ways "appropriate to their situation, gifts, and life-stage"?[33]

Form and content: the challenge of revising our liturgies is to develop new models of prayer that are "true both to the gospel and to the world for which we pray," to quote Mitchell,[34] rites that reflect doctrinal soundness in a manner that resonates not just with our minds, but with our hearts and souls as well. Our healing rites ought to address both our human condition

---

32. *SC* II, 21 (italics added).

33. Duffy, *A Roman Catholic Theology of Pastoral Care*, 89.

34. Mitchell, *Liturgical Change*, 51.

and the fact that we are children of God. They ought to speak to both the personal dimension of our sickness situation and also to our essential interconnectedness, both the private and corporate aspects of every illness. This may involve considerable rethinking on our part, not just about the wording of our rites, not just about the ways in which they are enacted, but with an attention to their many other underlying dynamics as well. In the words of *A Time to Heal*:

> The impact of limitation and illness on the Church's healing ministry is such that Christ's presence and purpose have to be sought within each situation. Christian healing relates not solely or necessarily to the restoration of function, but *also to the restoration of the possibility of fulfilling the purpose for which we were created.* Those with persisting disability and illness may need protection from inappropriate evangelism. Carers [*sic*] have to learn to leave the burdens of the day at the foot of the cross, and understand that caring is a vital expression of the Church's ministry of healing. *It is in caring for one another that a healing community is born.*[35]

Wholeness, Healing and Vocation

As Anglicans, while we are accustomed to thinking about liturgical celebrations in the context of sacraments, we are less likely to envision our own selves in a sacramental light. We need to learn to view both ourselves and one another from that very same, special sacramental perspective. Consider the following: in the context of Holy Communion the passive role customarily assigned to the sick is challenged by the acknowledgment that they, like all of us who share in the life of our risen Savior, still, by virtue of the commission given them at their baptism, share in Christ's ministry of healing and redemption.

"The basic model . . . of the sovereign self," says David Smith, "is the very idea that the holy communion rejects. In it, communicants surrender their sick selves and receive back a renewed and refreshed being. True selfhood is found in the social, communal interaction of the ritual, not in isolation."[36] The Eucharist, and all of our rites of healing, serve to empower the sufferer in a culture that seeks to dis-empower them, and to likewise empower our family and friends, the whole community of faith, to share

---

35. Church of England. House of Bishops. *A Time to Heal*, 127 (italics added).

36. Smith, *Health and Medicine in the Anglican Tradition*, 25.

in this holy work of healing, each in his or her various capacities. The sick person and all those whose lives have likewise been disrupted and altered by the reality of sickness, in fact, are summoned to be sacrament.

If all sacraments are encounters with the risen Christ, then it follows that they are also a call to conversion and ongoing transformation. In that "victory of life and peace" Christ's own sacrificial self-giving elicits from us that commitment by which we, in return, offer ourselves, in fellowship with God and with one another. Like the mother-in-law of Simon Peter, raised from her sickbed by Jesus's healing touch, we are "saved to serve," as the old saying goes. The account of the healing of Simon's mother-in-law found in Mark's gospel,[37] brief as it is, in keeping with Mark's economy of prose, describes in a succinct way this divine cycle of healing, restoration and reaching out in return: "And immediately [Jesus] left the synagogue, and entered the house of Simon and Andrew, with James and John. Now Simon's mother-in-law lay sick with a fever, and immediately they told him of her. And he came and took her by the hand and lifted her up, and the fever left her; and she served them."

Mark tells us that Jesus "lifted her up," and the Greek verb that Mark uses here, *egeiro*, meaning "to lift up" or "to raise up," is the same word that Mark and other New Testament writers will later employ in speaking of God's raising up of Jesus from death in the resurrection. The Savior's healing touch not only raises Simon's mother-in-law from her sickbed but restores her to her rightful place of honor as the matriarch of this little domestic community, her home. Note that her immediate response is to care for others in return—to tend to this little microcosm of the church, in fact—in the way she knows best: she gets up and feeds them. The King James Version tells us "she ministered unto them." This is what resurrection life looks like. Having been ministered to, she now takes her place as fellow minister. True ministry arises as the response of grateful hearts and leads us to desire to lift up others as we ourselves have been lifted up.

"The anointed," says Gelpi, "pray for healing: for the ultimate healing that comes with risen glory, for a deepening of their conversion to Christ which the rites of initiation originally sealed . . . One cannot pray such a prayer publicly and officially without renewing ritually one's Christian covenant of initiation."[38] It seems to me that our current rites of healing struggle—not always successfully—with the tension of attempting to

37. Mark 1:29–31.
38. Gelpi, *Committed Worship*, 2:196.

restore the focus on *healing* without losing sight of the fact that unction is also a sacrament of *vocation*. We are, happily, beginning to appreciate the fact that the primary aim of this sacrament is the restoration both of our physical and spiritual integrity, and that the healing it conveys through God's grace may indeed take the form of physical or emotional cure, or of enabling those who continue to live with serious illness and debility to find meaning in their suffering through sharing in Christ's own suffering.

We must not allow ourselves to lose sight of the fact that the oil with which we are anointed is also for "the inward anointing of the Holy Spirit,"[39] like the chrism of our baptismal anointing. In Susan Wood's words: "Anointing is about the restoration to baptismal integrity of the whole body, which will be definitely achieved when all is restored in Christ."[40] As Empereur notes, "In baptism the person was commissioned to offer praise in the assembly and to fulfill the mission given to the Church by Christ. It becomes the purpose of anointing to help the sick persons to continue to function as people baptized."[41]

Reflections on Sickness and Disability

The familiar account of Jesus's healing of the man blind from birth in the ninth chapter of John's gospel[42] highlights several important points relevant to any examination of the church's liturgies of healing. Particularly worth noting is the initial reaction of the man's community to this miraculous event: "The neighbors and those who had seen him before as a beggar, said, 'Is not this the man who used to sit and beg?' Some said, 'It is he'; others said, 'No, but it is like him.' He said, 'I am the man.'"[43] One assumes that this man, formerly blind, had been a part of this community all or most of his life. Nonetheless, however long he may have lived among them, once he is cured of his blindness, no one is quite sure of who he is! *"I think it's him." "No, I think you're wrong, though it does rather resemble him."* Is it, one wonders, simply because his neighbors so closely associate this man with his disability, or is it, rather, because of the inner change wrought as a result of this miraculous healing? He may have been cured of his physical

---

39. *The Book of Common Prayer*, 456.

40. Susan K. Wood, "The Paschal Mystery," in *Recovering the Riches of Anointing*, 19.

41. Empereur, *Prophetic Anointing*, 150.

42. John 9:1–41.

43. John 9:8.

impairment,[44] but the blindness of his neighbors and of the Pharisees, who inquire into the particulars of this miraculous healing should make us consider well whether we inadvertently fall into the same error.

This leads us to an important question: do our liturgical rites of healing unconsciously or unintentionally relate to the members of our community who live with sickness or disability as *persons with disabilities* or as *persons*? As the *subjects* of our ministrations or as *fellow ministers*? As bodies in need of physical healing or as fellow sinners in need of redemption and that incomparable wholeness which Christ offers us all? All of us, John Chryssavgis reminds us, "with and without a disability, are invited by God to a full life of faith and ministry, including worship, leadership, study, and service."[45] We should therefore ask of ourselves, he goes on to say, whether or not we make it possible in our parish communities for individuals with disabilities to participate fully in the life and worship of the church. What message, for instance, do we unconsciously communicate to the sick and disabled when we unwittingly segregate them from the rest of the community through physical barriers that make many areas of the church building inaccessible to them?

Worse yet, he asks, do our prejudices or personal inhibitions create an unwelcoming atmosphere, where we either overlook or pretend not to notice this or that person's disability, ignoring the fact that it is one characteristic (among many) of that individual that renders him or her unique? Or else do we, like the neighbors in the account of the man blind from birth, think of the individual *as* their disability? What are we saying when little or no provision is made to allow persons with illnesses or disabilities to share their own particular gifts and talents? What precious opportunities for catechesis do we waste when little or no teaching is provided which might enable the community to understand and fully appreciate the incarnational perspective of both sickness and wholeness so central to the Anglican tradition?

All too often pastors and evangelists are guilty, says Samuel Kabue, of paternalistic and patronizing attitudes, presuming to know what the person with a disability needs, even assuming that "disabled people are the same in

---

44. For the purposes of this study, the term *impairment* refers to "the loss or dysfunction of any anatomical or sensory organ" in respect to "what makes [the individual in question] different from others without having to refer to what he or she is seemingly able to do or not able to do." (Kabue, "The Place of People with Disabilities," 10.)

45. Chryssavgis, *The Body of Christ*, 8.

their social behavior, emotional maturity and sometimes even [beliefs]."[46] As we seek to restore to our new pastoral liturgies this focus on healing so long missing from them, we must beware of the unfortunate tendency to presume that the sick or disabled have no other pressing concerns beyond physical well-being, to the neglect of their very considerable spiritual needs. As Kabue points out:

> the fact that a person does not either see, walk or hear [leads] to the assumption that he is not capable of committing sin. Disability in this case [is] assumed to play . . . not only on one's general health but also his/her emotions. Whereas a weak body, a feeble mind or sensory disability is easily noticeable, this is not so with a weak spirit. Measures are usually attempted to compensate these other physical or sensory disabilities, but the soul which might even be easier to put right is forgotten or ignored altogether. The fact that evangelists and church ministers will [often] only see the physical needs of people with disabilities and will more often offer to pray for such deficiencies and will not even think of praying with the concerned is in itself a form of discrimination or prejudice. It may happen as a result of ignorance, but it is nevertheless wrong. The emphasis on the physical dysfunction has often erroneously made people with disabilities feel that their state of being will cause them remission of sins.[47]

One might also add that this same prevalent fixation on physical dysfunction is akin to the way in which our society tends to regard the elderly, as though at some point one reaches an age at which little or nothing is personally expected any longer of one. My experiences in visiting nursing homes, including the one in which my husband was hospitalized following his earlier surgeries, have drawn for me a picture of a health system in which the elderly, the sick, and disabled are cared for (with varying degrees of proficiency and personal consideration), but not encouraged to continue to *grow* as human beings, or valued in the same way that they were when they were younger and healthier. The activities provided for them are, to a considerable extent, designed to keep them content and occupied—bingo, crafts, movies, and so on—but not to help them to continue to develop spiritually or intellectually. Little is done to encourage the elderly in such situations to consider not just what they have *done* with their lives, but what they would still like to *achieve* in terms of accomplishment or self-fulfillment.

46. Kabue, "The Place of People with Disabilities," 13.
47. Ibid., 12.

Regrettably, it would appear, this unfortunate preconception of old age as a cessation of purposefulness is one that is all too often taken to heart by the elderly themselves. Duffy observes: "It is not uncommon for a confessor to hear an elderly person say, 'Well, Father, at my age what can you really do wrong?'" To which one might reply, says Duffy, "'You can stagnate. You can despair.'" He goes on to say, "The radical temptation of our final years is to lose a sense of purpose and of being 'for the sake of others.'"[48] One might add, the radical temptation of the Christian community is to overlook the fact that as Nyambura Njoroge observes, "People with disabilities are God's people and they too are called to be prepared for works of service."[49]

We have examined the history, the underlying theology, the meaning and purpose of the church's sacramental rites of healing, which, as Smolarski notes, "[provide] us with the structure to celebrate God's life-giving power, a celebration that is experienced during some of our weakest moments,"[50] and which serve to restore us to our baptismal integrity. Now we must consider how well our liturgies of healing are allowed to express through word and symbol, through rite and ceremony, the purpose for which they are created. As Weil notes, "Liturgical renewal is not merely a matter of removing anomalies, for example, minor adjustments such as moving the altar from the wall, or a bit of flexibility for different pastoral situations, or the involvement of lay ministers, or even the revising of rites or the authorization of a new Prayer Book. These are all valuable, but they are surface expressions of the real issue. These external factors are a summons to serious corporate prayer. How do we make that summons live?"[51]

Language That Transforms

"To be true to itself," says Mitchell, "a contemporary prayer must be true both to the gospel and to the world for which we pray. We must speak the truth, but we must speak it in the language of today," which, when all is said and done, "is easier to prescribe than to do."[52] Liturgical reform requires more than a modernization of the language of the church's rites. It calls for something more profound than mere clarity of meaning and theological

48. Duffy, *A Roman Catholic Theology of Pastoral Care*, 114.
49. Njoroge, "Not an Option," 7–9.
50. Smolarski, *Sacred Mysteries*, 99.
51. Weil, *Sacraments and Liturgy*, 93.
52. Mitchell, *Liturgical Change*, 51.

correctness. Like poetic language, liturgical speech serves a purpose that goes far beyond merely conveying information. The use of rhyme and rhythm, repetition, metaphor, simile, the employment of special religious vocabulary that might seem odd or out of place in everyday discourse: all these fulfill a special function in our worship.

"It would be . . . difficult to devise experiments to learn how the syntactical and conceptual ambiguities of 'dialectical' or poetic language slow and concentrate the reader's attention," notes Catherine Madsen, who goes on to say,

> But I suspect it will be found—by objective means as it is already found in experience—that when language slows us down, even by saying something disturbing, it is in some way also calming. It gives us something besides its content: even by puzzling and humiliating us, it gives us essential work to do. Language that can be read fast and understood easily—language that speaks to the eye and reason—keeps us on the surface; if it disturbs us the only compensation it offers is a convenient categorical term for the disturbance. Language made for the mouth and the ear goes all the way to the bone . . . Objective and subjective knowledge may eventually support each other in showing that . . . the form of our language is as crucial as the content.[53]

Prayers with "soul," in other words, demonstrate a sensitivity to the character and purpose of liturgical language. Writing prayers for contemporary use, Mitchell observes, is not easy: "We have need of theologians who are poets and of poets who are theologians. Both appear to be in short supply."[54] For instance, he says, we may discover, that however moving or thought-provoking the words and images employed in a particular liturgy may be, they do not, in fact, correspond to either our experience or our understanding of God and the world, or that they no longer speak to the contemporary worshiper.

Semper reformanda.[55] Ongoing liturgical reform is necessary, but as Carol Doran notes, such reform should, ideally, take place "constantly, but almost imperceptibly—the way children and plants grow,"[56] drawing upon tradition and yet enriching it with the shared experience of the faithful,

53. Madsen, "The Common Word," 234–45.

54. Mitchell, *Liturgical Change*, 51.

55. "Forever reforming."

56. Carol Doran, "You Shall Have a Song: Music in Liturgical Renewal," in Marshall and Northrup, *Leaps and Boundaries*, 46.

mindful of the power and meaning of the symbols and words we employ, and yet sensitive to other possible means of expression by which to 're-harmonize' our understanding of who God is and the part that God plays in our lives. Ideally, these new texts should inspire and challenge us with their freshness. At the same time, preferably, they should not distract us with their novelty; in brief, the words should not draw attention to *themselves*, but to the truth—the mystery—which they express and into which they draw us.

The language of our liturgies must be true to doctrine and in accord with the Word of God. Its vocabulary must, the members of the Lutheran Hymnal Project committee observe, reflect "not just the language that [we] sing and know from ages past, but also a language of worship which is common to the church today . . . to utilize a catholic[57] vocabulary that proclaims the Gospel of Jesus Christ in the best that our English language offers today."[58] This means that we cannot, for instance, simply jettison traditional language in the name of inclusiveness or even expansiveness if, in doing so, we strip our liturgies of their emotive and symbolic power. We cannot merely replace old imagery with new if such alterations, as Barry Bates notes, do not maintain "the integrity of the divine narrative."[59]

In regard to the language of our rites of healing, the task of this study is not so much to describe the role of inclusive and expansive language in general, or to discuss the tasks of metaphor and simile, or the value of contemporary versus traditional language—although it must, of course, touch on these. Many scholarly studies, such as James Griffiss' *Naming the Mystery*,[60] or, *How Shall We Pray*,[61] edited by Ruth Meyers, have already treated these important topics in a most comprehensive manner. My intention is not to duplicate their work. Instead, I am concerned with the question of how effectively the texts of our current liturgies of healing do what they are meant to do: to serve not just to strengthen and sustain us through these difficult life passages we must all at some point confront, but also to give voice to our sickness and limit-situations, and to inspire us to

---

57. Universal, comprehensive.

58. "Language Guidelines and Principles for Translation," 2. Lutheran Hymnal Project, The Lutheran Church Missouri Synod Commission On Worship, Sept. 2003.

59. Bates, "A Riotous Mixture of Phrases," 435–68; quotations from original manuscript, courtesy of the author.

60. Griffiss, *Naming the Mystery*.

61. Myers, *How Shall We Pray?*.

incorporate our sickness situation into a faith journey of ongoing transformation and personal growth.

I am reminded of a Holy Eucharist service I attended at St. Paul's Anglican Church on Bloor Street in Toronto one Sunday morning several years ago. I held in my hand the 1962 Canadian *Book of Common Prayer*, with its very traditional language. As we recited the Apostle's Creed and came to the phrase "*Who for us men and for our salvation.*" I stopped suddenly, jarred by what was to my modern ears strange and exclusive language. While rationally I could understand the use of *men* as a collective term for humankind, for the first time, I truly appreciated the importance of inclusive and expansive language in our worship. At the same time, as I look back at my years in seminary, I recall all too well sitting through some truly dreadful liturgies created by earnest and well-meaning fellow seminarians (and sometimes, even, faculty), in which the language had been ineptly and excruciatingly reworked to make it gender neutral. No doubt the effect the revisers were aiming for was one of *in*clusivity, but what they actually achieved would more properly be termed *ex*clusivity: nearly every male pronoun or reference to the male gender was painstakingly removed and replaced—regardless of context or appropriateness—with some feminine or genderless alternative. The results were often rather discordant and self-consciously politically correct texts, whose meaning, in many cases, had been altered and distorted.

There is a world of difference in creating the sort of liturgies in which the language has been effectively neutered, as Richard Norris would say, and the sorts of liturgies that one might call truly inclusive, in which the language of worship is inspired by a reverence for the Creator whose divine image all God's children bear.[62] Such inclusive language liturgies, says Norris, require of us a policy that "will mix up the elements of noncommittal (to express our sense of God's universal indwelling of the creation), of the inclusive (to express our sense of the superabundance of God's being), and of the disarming (to express our recognition that the God who raised Jesus Christ from the dead is no domesticable idol to be pinned down permanently by any words of ours)."[63] Similarly, the words by which our faith is expressed and driven must be inspired by more than simply the desire to avoid offending anyone, lest we inadvertently strip our prayers of their symbolic and evocative power. Mitchell observes, "Modern prayers often

62. Richard Norris, "Inclusive Language Liturgies," in *How Shall We Pray?*
63. Ibid., 38–39.

avoid saying the wrong things by saying nothing at all. Some are so general as to become nothing but pious platitudes."[64]

One noticeable difference between the Ministration to the Sick and our two new communal liturgies of healing is the *style* of language, which in the latter tends to be noticeably more clear-cut and succinct. Is it easily comprehended by contemporary English-speaking Americans? Undoubtedly, *yes*. Will this language resonate with these same contemporary English-speaking Americans? That remains to be seen. One of the problems with the language of our two newest rites is that it tends, at times, to be disconcertingly didactic. The Litany in A Public Service of Healing (2000) has an unfortunate tendency to sound less like a sacred exchange between God and humankind than a list of instructions directed at God: *Do this for us, God, Do that, God. Here's what we need from you...*

> "Restore to wholeness whatever is broken by human sin, in our lives, in our nation, and in the world ... "

> "Mend broken relationships, and restore those in emotional distress to soundness of mind and serenity of spirit. . . "

This is theologically correct, discursive language. It is clear what is expected as a result of our prayers, namely, healing of every dimension of the human condition. It is *performative* language that is intended to bring about that which it proclaims. It is, however, oft times oddly abrupt, and has a tendency to sound more like a monologue than a holy dialogue into which we enter with God, leaving little opportunity to permit God to speak to us of *new* possibilities, or to allow us to be caught up and challenged by the power of the liturgy. There is little anticipation of something unpredicted or unexpected emerging from this meeting of creature and Creator.

In this respect, Donald Reeves, writing on the subject of the language of contemporary worship, invites the reader to contrast the modern language of the Church of England's new *Alternative Service Book*[65] with the more traditional language of The Church of England's *Book of Common Prayer*. Consider, he says, the latter's Introduction to Morning and Evening Prayer:

> Dearly beloved brethren, the Scripture moveth us in sundry places to acknowledge and confess our manifold sins and wickedness;

64. Mitchell, *Liturgical Change*, 51.
65. Church of England, *The Alternative Service Book 1980*.

and that we should not dissemble nor cloke them before the face of Almighty God our heavenly Father; but confess them with an humble, lowly, penitent, and obedient heart; to the end that we may obtain forgiveness of the same, by his infinite goodness and mercy.

"The use of two words," says Reeves, "where one will do ('acknowledge and confess', 'manifold sins and wickedness', 'dissemble nor cloke'), and the rhythm of the sentences, include and invite the listeners to participate; they are not being bombarded with instructions."[66]

The American author William Stafford, in an essay titled "A Way of Writing," observes: "A writer is not so much someone who has something to say as he is someone who has found a process that will bring about new things he would not have thought of if he had not started to say them. That is to say, he does not draw on a reservoir, instead he engages in an activity that brings to him a whole succession of unforeseen stories, poems, essays, plays, laws, philosophies, religions. . ."[67] This poetic sensibility, this willingness to see literary creation as an open-ended process to which we bring our own thoughts and intentions, and through which we find ourselves unexpectedly engaged by new and unforeseen ideas and developments, is something we would do well to keep in mind when we seek to draft new liturgies. Rather than simply laying our agendas (however sound they might be) out before God, we would do well to avail ourselves of the power of poetry, metaphor, symbol, simile, meter, rhythm and cadence, all the riches of our English language and our Christian tradition, in order for us to be mutually engaged by God, so that somehow through this process God might have the opportunity to bring about those 'new things' heralded by the prophet Isaiah.[68]

An outspoken critic of our most recent rites of healing, Barry Bates suggests that the language they tend to employ actually diminishes the religious meaning that can possibly be conveyed because it conforms more to cultural expectations about clarity, but fails, with its technically clear language and "excessively cerebral" theology, to address the ambivalence, the incomprehensibility, the mystery of sickness and suffering. He asks: "And can a claim for the comprehensive nature of *EOW2* be asserted? Can any Anglican prayer book at this time that includes *only* contemporary rites be

66. Reeves. *For God's Sake*, 76–77.
67. Stafford, "A Way of Writing."
68. Isa 43:19.

considered comprehensive? Can one that minimizes traditional language and formulas?"[69]

The text of A Public Service of Healing (2000) reflects the concern of the Standing Committee to employ more "inclusive and expansive language." As Pettingell states, the task of the Committee was "to consider 'forms of worship reflective of our multicultural, multiethnic, multilingual and multigenerational Church while providing rites and structures that ensure the unity of Common Prayer'(C021s)."[70] To its credit, the language does indeed employ a notably wider range of divine images than those found in the Ministration to the Sick or in the Public Service of Healing (1991), a fact that proves beneficial to those who have difficulty with the predominantly masculine, less-inclusive imagery often common to our worship. Consider:

> "Holy and mighty, wellspring of abundant life,"

> "Holy Immortal One, protector of the faithful,"

> "Holy Trinity, source of all wholeness . . ."

These and similar variations on our more traditional God-language are praiseworthy examples of the efforts of the Standing Commission to draw upon the greater depth and breadth of our religious tradition. However, we must be cautious, Griffiss warns us, about attempting to "flee to an unknown and nameless God" or to create liturgies that reflect our desire to "worship a God who is simply the kind of God we want the Holy One to be—a God made in our own image."[71] While our newer inclusive and expansive liturgical language seeks to acknowledge and celebrate our human diversity and uniqueness, it can also prove disconcerting to the more traditional-minded worshiper. Take, for example, the following phrase, one of the optional petitions, from A Public Service of Healing (2000): "Jesus

69. Bates, "A Riotous Mixture of Phrases."

70. Episcopal Church. Standing Commission on Liturgy and Music, *Enriching Our Worship 2*, "A Note About the Process," 9. C021s means that this was a resolution from "Committee #14, Prayer Book and Liturgy" (as it then was—it is now Committee #13, Music, Prayer Book. and Liturgy). The letter *C* indicates that the report comes from the committees. The number 021 is the number in the Blue Book for the particular convention that authorized *Enriching Our Worship*, and *s* means that there was a substitute accepted at General Convention for the original resolution. The Report to the Episcopal Church's General Convention is commonly referred to as the Blue Book. The Blue Book includes reports and proposed legislation from the Committees.

71. Griffiss, *Naming the Mystery*, 178.

our true mother [who feeds us with] the milk of your compassion."[72] Or similarly, consider this excerpt from a Postcommunion prayer in *Enriching Our Worship 2*: "we thank you for Jesus, our Savior, our true Mother."[73] I recall how startled I felt the first time I read these words, in as much as they appear to refute the undeniable fact of the historical Jesus's gender.

In the same way, self-consciously gender-free language may also be a source of discomfort for many worshipers, since to be human is to be either male or female. The challenge such revisions present, says Larry Ellis, writing on the use of expansive and inclusive language in contemporary hymns and choral music, is that "it is fundamental to recognize that, absent clear, unambiguous biblical guidance, defining God to be either feminine or masculine would seem to be taking away God's sovereignty to be and do what He wills. This should never be done lightly." He adds, "The deliberate choice by composers of language that cannot be used to exclude others would do a great service to strengthen our worship experiences and draw those who do feel minimized into a closer fellowship with God. That is what we are all about. I would hope that writers and composers would retain the theology of scripture. Don't proclaim that God has feminine gender and don't mandate that God be male either." [74] Clearly, when we undertake the important task of creating new, more inclusive and expansive texts for our sacramental liturgies, we must take care that in doing so we are true to the original meaning of the Scripture, and sensitive about employing what Ellis calls "gender restrictive" forms. Whereas the aim of the Standing Commission to reimagine the language of our healing liturgies in a more expansive and inclusive manner is a commendable one, one must be cautious about employing conspicuously innovative metaphors that draw attention to themselves and away from the prayer that they embody.

We must consider well, Stanley Fish says, whether the language of our liturgies is designed to be "satisfying," that is to say, to mirror our own opinions and desires, to assure us that "what [we have] always thought about the world is true and that [our] ways of thinking are sufficient," or whether

72. The Notes found at the end of *Enriching Our Worship 2* observe that the phrase "Jesus our true mother" derives from St. Anselm's Prayer 10 to St. Paul and appear as well in other patristic texts and in the writings of St. Bernard of Clairvaux and Julian of Norwich. (148–49).

73. "A Litany for the Discontinuing Treatment: Form 2," in *Enriching Our Worship 2*, 125.

74. Ellis, "When, Why and How Do We Change the Words of Choral Music, Hymns and Liturgy."

they instead require of us what Fish describes as "a searching and rigorous scrutiny of everything [we] believe in and live by."[75] Do they proclaim the truth as we *wish* to perceive it, in other words, or do they invite us to engage the truth for ourselves, even if "this discovery is . . . made at the expense not only of [our] opinions and values, but of [our] self-esteem."[76]

Transforming Symbols

In *Opening the Prayer Book,* Jeffrey Lee describes a conversation he had one Sunday morning with a parishioner who approached him in respect to the disposable printed order of service the parish was now using for worship. *Why were they no longer using the Prayer Book?,* the parishioner wanted to know, adding, "I miss it." Lee explained to her that they were, in fact, still using the *Book of Common Prayer.* "What my parishioner thought . . . was that we were celebrating the Eucharist according to some new and slightly alien rite. Because we were not physically holding those red prayer books, somehow we were not using *The Book of Common Prayer.* We printed in the booklets only those texts that members of the congregation would need to say together, so the texts the priest, deacon, or reader said were not printed. They had to be heard, rather than read along with as they were spoken." *Of course,* replied the parishioner afterwards, apparently reassured: "I recognize it's the same thing now. I just never thought of it without the book in front of me before."[77]

"*I miss it.*" It occurred to me, when I read the above excerpt, that this particular parishioner was touching upon something important that she was unable to adequately communicate. My guess is that while the words of the liturgy were familiar to her, her discomfiture arose from the fact that the disposable service leaflet did not possess for her the same sign value as the familiar and dearly loved *Book of Common Prayer.* Yes, it is true that service leaflets contain the necessary texts taken straight out of the familiar red (or blue or black) Prayer Book, but it seemed to me that what had not been taken into consideration was the importance for this parishioner of holding

---

75. Fish, *Self-Consuming Artifacts*; quoted in Madsen, "The Common Word: Recovering Liturgical Speech."

76. Ibid.

77. Lee, *Opening the Prayer Book,* 125–26.

in her own hands what for her was not simply a collection of prayers and rites, but a powerful and comforting *symbol* of her faith.[78]

In the same way, we often fail to appreciate the importance of the role that sign and symbol serve in our sacramental rites, a fact that becomes all the more apparent when we contrast the lack of forethought frequently given in our rites of healing to the loving attention that generally characterizes our eucharistic celebrations. Even in the most humble of surroundings—the annual parish picnic, or a simple weekday morning Eucharist around the table in the parish hall—we Anglicans pride ourselves on the attention we give to our eucharistic liturgies. Our more formal worship settings are distinguished by beautifully arrayed altars, complete with fair linens, candles, beautiful and costly eucharistic vessels, hangings, and so on. There is special music, carefully choreographed ceremony, and sometimes, incense or holy water. Everything indicates to the worshipper that something wonderful, something very holy is taking place, and such preparation in turn invites one's reverent participation.

Consider, on the contrary, the lack of attention frequently given to the preparations for the sacramental rite of unction that might be scheduled to take place in the course of that very same service. One is likely to find a small oil stock—invisible to just about anyone beyond the first pew—plunked down on a communion rail or placed on the corner of the altar. Following the laying on of hands, the faithful who present themselves for healing are likely to receive a miserly anointing of oil on the forehead, which, disconcertingly, in many instances is often immediately wiped off with a cotton ball! Even more disheartening is the fact that this often takes place in the absence of the assembled congregation—after or between services—rendering the sick and suffering all but invisible to the greater community, robbing the assembly of the presence and powerful witness offered by the sick who choose to make of their sickness situation a testimony, a prophetic call to the church.

In reimagining the symbols central to our sacramental rites of healing, it seems obvious to include the sick themselves, and those who care for them. Lambourne suggests different ways in which "a bold Eucharist" might provide a wealth of powerful and transforming symbolism by which the sick may be further re-integrated into the community:

78. It occurred to me also that she might have been having difficulty hearing those parts of the liturgy that were not printed in the bulletin.

We can only throw out a few suggestions. Let the sick of the parish and those near and dear to them, bring the wine to the priest at the Lord's table, that the community in them, and they in Christ, may offer all the pain of mind, body, and soul of the parish. Let the district nurse, the WVS[79] member, the doctor, or anyone known to minister to the same sick people, carry the water, that cup of cold water which symbolizes the Real Presence of Christ at deeds of mercy. Let these represent the response of the community to their pain. Let the Sunday School teachers, the prayer leaders, the visitors of the Word of God carry the bread. Let them all receive the elements grouped together around the altar that the local congregation may see their sickness-situation made by the work of Christ their salvation situation.[80]

The Oil of Gladness

"thou anointest my head with oil, my cup overflows. . ."[81]

Such eloquent symbols of God's own gracious self-giving as the church's holy oils deserve to be applied more generously, and the anointed allowed to experience the sensation of the oil of anointing on their foreheads, to reflect on what it means, and to open themselves up to God's healing grace. Norman Autton, writing on the Roman Catholic rite for the Anointing of the Sick observes: "This symbolic act will be carried out slowly, reverently and with dignity, for it will remind the sick person of the passion of Christ, and the definite feel of the holy oil marked in the form of a cross will inspire confidence and strength."[82]

As the 2000 document *Built of Living Stones,* issued by the United States Bishops' Committee on the Liturgy, notes:

> Just as Christ invited those who heard him to share his personal union with the Father through material signs, so Christ leads the Church through these same signs in the liturgy from the visible to the invisible.[83] As a result, effective liturgical signs have a teaching

79. The Women's Voluntary Service.

80. Lambourne, *Community, Church and Healing,* 130.

81. Psalm 23.

82. Norman Autton, "Anointing Administered in Hospital," in Dudley and Rowell, ed., *The Oil of Gladness,* 159.

83. Cf. SC, no. 59; *Catechism of the Catholic Church,* no. 1075: "Liturgical catechesis

function and encourage full, conscious, and active participation, express and strengthen faith, and lead people to God. Poorly utilized or minimal signs do not enliven the community's faith and can even diminish active participation.[84] It must likewise be kept in mind that the liturgy and its signs and symbols do not exercise merely a teaching function. They also touch and move a person to conversion of heart and not simply to enlightenment of mind.[85]

The wonderful rich symbolism of our sacramental healing rites should be allowed to more fully communicate—and invite our engagement in—the saving mystery they signify. What message are we communicating when the oil of anointing is stored on the back of the shelf somewhere in the sacristy, in a plastic medicine bottle with a typewritten label? We would never think of keeping the reserved host in plastic food storage containers or the consecrated wine in empty soft drink bottles, so why do we give so little thought to the vessels in which the oil of anointing is reserved? "There is no universal practice here," notes Thomas Ryan, "but it seems quite clear that the oils, even in their smallest vessels, are not to be kept permanently in a priest's jacket, in the rectory, or in a safe or cabinet of the less-frequented sacristy." [86]

William Seth Adams, in a chapter in *Shaped by Images* titled "One who Handles and Embodies Symbols," observes: "I am mindful . . . of the weight and authority that symbols claim in our liturgy and how their power to evoke varies depending on one's sensibilities and orientation towards them. There is obviously a necessary level of engagement of the tradition in order for one to grasp whatever may be the most superficial, didactic level of understanding. But even before engagement with the tradition, there is the necessary human capacity or willingness to let the symbols speak for themselves . . . If there needs to be authenticity in the presider's actions and

---

aims to initiate people into the mystery of Christ (It is mystagogy.) by proceeding from the visible to the invisible, from the sign to the thing signified, from the 'sacraments' to the 'mysteries.'"

84. Cf. National Conference of Catholic Bishops' Committee on the Liturgy, *Music in Catholic Worship* (1983), nos. 6–7. *Music in Catholic Worship* was a 1972 statement of the US Bishops' Committee on the Liturgy (BCL). It was a revision of *The Place of Music in Eucharistic Celebrations* (PMEC), a 1967 statement of an advisory board with no bishop members. The document Music in Catholic Worship is available online at http://home.catholicweb.com/npmdayton/files/MUSICinCATHOLICWORSHIP.pdf/.

85. United States Conference of Catholic Bishops, *Built of Living Stones*, §26. This document replaces *Environment and Art in Catholic Worship*.

86. Ryan, *The Sacristy Manual*, 65.

movements, there needs to be authenticity in the things themselves. Real bread, real wine, real oil, real water."[87] No less than the authenticity of these simple things, the manner in which we treat them—the quality of the ritual vessels and containers in which they are stored, the manner in which they are displayed and distributed—speaks just as eloquently to the assembly about their meaning and importance. A dab with a thumb pressed into a tiny oil stock does not begin to evoke the lavish, extravagant biblical depictions of anointing celebrated in such Scripture passages as the account of the woman who anointed Jesus with costly perfume before his death.[88]

I am reminded of a memorable Sunday morning at my former home parish several years ago, when the morning's gospel featured Luke's account of the unnamed woman anointing the feet of Jesus. In his children's sermon, the rector, Fr. Ralph, spoke movingly of this loving, prophetic gesture to the group of youngsters gathered around him on the chancel steps. Then he produced a jar of scented hand cream and invited the children to take it into the congregation and to apply it to the hands of the parishioners. One little boy rose and took the jar from him, wide-eyed, and proceeded to go to this pew and that, solemnly anointing the hands of several members of the congregation, who proceeded to rub it into their skin and sniff it appreciatively. That simple sacramental gesture vividly brought the words of the gospel to life in an immediate and memorable way.

An oil stock may contain the same oil of anointing as a beautifully crafted glass vessel, just as a disposable worship bulletin contains the same text as the well-loved Prayer Book, but there is a world of difference between the symbolic power of each. With this in mind, perhaps we should give more consideration to the way in which the oil of anointing is stored and displayed. For starters, why not make a point of reserving and displaying it in containers more befitting its dignity? For communal rites of healing, oil stocks, needless to say, being small and difficult to see in so large a space, are inappropriate. More to the point, so tiny a vessel—and so miserly a rationing of this precious oil—poses a serious contrast, signwise, to the lavish descriptions of anointing that one finds in the Scriptures. While oil stocks are necessary for making pastoral visitations, they are less suitable for public celebrations of healing. Medicine bottles, moreover, are for medicine—not holy oils. Smolarski suggests that for public celebrations "the oil can be put in a clear glass bowl or vessel. To highlight the

87. Adams, *Shaped by Images*, 41, 42.
88. Matt 26:6–13; Mark 14:3–9; Luke 7:36–50; John 11:1–2.

oil during the celebration and maintain its distinctiveness the oil can be placed on a pedestal or column—something that does not rival or imitate the altar—and be surrounded with candles to make it sparkle."[89] Likewise, Robert Duggan advises that "the oil ought not to remain a mere object of admiration. It must be experienced. That is to say, its application should be generous enough for all to see and experience—until echoes are heard of the gospel scene in which oil was lavished on the Lord as a sign of love. It is not just oil that is the sign of the sacrament, but oil applied to forehead, palms, and wherever else needs healing. A presider's dainty concern with delicate application in most cases does more than anything else to quench the spirit of this rich ritual gesture."[90]

Moreover, says Peter Drilling, "without overwhelming the symbol with verbiage, it can be helpful to alert people to the ancient meaning of olive oil . . . [and] the way in which we . . . display and hold and administer the oil—and the tenderness and care with which we anoint the sick—can communicate how much it is a healing balm in the context of the invocation of the Holy Spirit who confers participation in the dying and rising of Jesus unto the glory of God the Father."[91]

There have been suggestions by some theologians that the oil of anointing should be consecrated by the priest of the parish rather than by the bishop, in the presence of the congregation on an appropriate Sunday or feast day, rather than at the cathedral. However, as Michael Perham has so rightly observed, like the oil itself, the bishop is likewise a symbol: in this case, of the unity of the church. "The gift of healing is given, not to clergymen in their ordination, but to the Church . . . Where oil, blessed by the bishop, is used, the ministry is seen more clearly to be the work of the Church, not of the individual who administers it."[92]

That Healing Touch

A word in respect to the anointing of *hands*: our own Anglican rites of healing make no specific provision for this. While the Ministration to the Sick and A Public Service of Healing (1991) specify that anointing takes place on the forehead, A Public Service of Healing (2000) states: "*The minister*

89. Smolarski, *Sacred Mysteries*, 102.
90. Duggan, *Parish Liturgy*, 85–86.
91. Drilling, "Anointing the Sick," 20.
92. Perham, *Liturgy, Pastoral and Parochial*, 124.

then lays hands upon the sick person [and anoints the person]." It does not specify on what *part* of the body the anointing is to take place.

From time to time in Episcopal churches it is not unknown to see the anointing of the hands of nurses, physicians and healthcare workers at special liturgies on occasions such as the feast day of St. Luke. In drawing up future rites of healing, we might want to consider incorporating the anointing of the hands not just of healthcare workers, but of all the faithful who present themselves for healing. At the parish where I currently serve, I regularly anoint hands as well as foreheads at the monthly healing liturgy, employing the words from the Roman Catholic rite: "May the Lord who frees you from sin save you and raise you up." When I first began doing this, my actions were met with surprise and bewilderment. Parishioners were accustomed to being anointed on the forehead, but why was I anointing their hands as well? I told them that their hands were being anointed to bless them for the Lord's service, in whatever form that might take. I explained that anointing is not just a sacrament of healing, but also, as Empereur points out, "that sacrament that recognizes that there is a special vocation in the Church of the sick and the aged." As Empereur further observes:

> Anointing is the ritualization of that vocation. This sacrament is a celebration of the fact that because of Christianity the sick and old person who is fragmented can be brought back together again. It is an articulation of the truth that by dying to oneself . . . one opens oneself to a far greater wholeness. In turn, the sick and old person who is anointed, as well as the rite itself, speaks to the Church, reminding it that there is a deeper meaning to sickness and old age than what can be explained by the medical and psychological professions. Thus, those anointed minister to the rest of the church who are well and in the fullness of life. They are called to proclaim that sickness and old age need not be a threat to their fellow Christians whose lives need not be characterized by fragmentation . . . The salvational aspect of sickness and old age may be obscure, but it is the liturgy of anointing which can show them for what they are: real events of personal triumph over the present, and representations of growth towards new life.[93]

---

93. Empereur, *Prophetic Anointing*, 141–42.

To Share in the Communion of Christ's Body and Blood

In many parishes, the ministration of Communion to *"those who for reasonable cause cannot be present at a public celebration of the Eucharist"*[94] is carried out in a thoughtful and reverent manner, but for the most part, unwitnessed by the greater community. The eucharistic minister departs after the service, and often the only evidence afterwards of his or her visit is a notation in the parish register. Since it is, in fact, the church itself—the body of Christ—who visits this or that individual in the person of its duly commissioned representatives, and since, as we have observed, the well-being of one of its members affects the well-being of the community as a whole, this seems very odd indeed, when one thinks about it. How much more appropriate it would be if the sending forth of the eucharistic minister were to take place in a context which proclaims and celebrates both this sign of the community's concern for and affirmation of its missing members! Ideally, in the words of Cuenin and Fink:

> Week after week people in the Sunday assembly see women and men sent forth with the Eucharist to those who for a variety of reasons, usually sickness, are unable to attend. It is the visible link between the faith, love and prayer of the assembly and those who are absent. It provides a context for all who are gathered so that, should the occasion of sickness arise, and should a minister of the Eucharist come to them, they will know whence these ministers have come, and remember the love, the faith, the prayer, and the support these ministers bring with them. How much richer this is than the more familiar situation of the minister showing up, as it were, from nowhere, to "bring Communion" with them.[95]

When the eucharistic ministers are sent forth directly from the setting of the community's worship, rather than at some later time, their very ministry, Empeurer notes, "heightens the ecclesial drama of the eucharist"[96] and itself serves as a powerful catechesis for the community. *The Book of Occasional Services* provides such an acknowledgment for the sending-out of the eucharistic ministers, namely, the Distribution of Holy Communion:

94. *The Book of Common Prayer*, "Communion under Special Circumstances," 396.

95. Walter H. Cuenin and Peter E. Fink, "Alternative 4: Liturgy of Healing to Replace the Blessing of Throats for the Feast of St. Blaise," in Lee and Fink, eds., *Alternative Futures for Worship*, 7:144.

96. Empeurer, *Prophetic Anointing*, 224.

3. It is recommended that the person to be ministered to be prayed for specifically in the Prayers of the People by the congregation on that day.

4. The administration of the Sacrament to the persons visited should take place immediately after the service in the church. Following the communion of the people, the lay Eucharistic Ministers come forward and are commended for this ministry with the following or similar words:

> In the name of this congregation, I send you forth bearing these holy gifts, that those to whom you go may share with us in the communion of Christ's body and blood. We who are many are one body, because we all share one bread, one cup.

5. A suitable container in which to carry the two vessels for the bread and wine, corporals and purificators is to be supplied. The container is to be returned immediately to the parish along with any unconsumed elements.

6. The people to whom Holy Communion is to be administered are to be notified in advance and the time of the appointment clearly set.[97]

The Power of Place, the Significance of Ceremony

Truly transformative rituals are difficult—if not impossible—to fabricate out of the blue, despite the plethora of how-to books by self-proclaimed ritual experts lining the shelves of the local library or the nearby bookstore chain. Rituals become engaging and meaningful for us through our ability to relate their words and symbols to our personal experience, when they speak to us through a language of worship informed by understanding, and when their symbolism invites us to open ourselves up to their underlying divine mystery.

The church's sacramental liturgies enable us to move ever forward into the Paschal Mystery through which we share not simply in Christ's suffering and death but in his new life of the resurrection. They equip and sustain us for that journey not simply by virtue of their theological soundness, but by speaking to us in our totality as persons, by communicating

---

97. Episcopal Church, *The Book of Occasional Services*, 325–26.

their truths in ways that connect not just with our minds but also with our senses: through words; through silence; through music, symbols, actions, architecture, atmosphere, and environment. As Aidan Kavanagh reminds us, "Liturgy is a ritual language, embracing far more than words and texts alone. One who would put a liturgy together cannot stop merely by getting straight the things to be said. Things to be done must also be considered, *where they are done*, and how they are to be done."[98]

Where and when we celebrate our sacramental rites of healing says much about how we understand our theology of the ministry of the baptized. To give an example, it is not uncommon in parishes that regularly celebrate sacramental healing to find it positioned not, as the Prayer Book suggests, *preceding* the distribution of Holy Communion and immediately before the exchange of the Peace, but instead, *following* Holy Communion, at special 'healing stations' –often at a side altar—where the faithful, before they return to their seats, can receive special sacramental ministrations by associate clergy, who may be assisted by members of the laity who feel a special calling to the church's healing ministry.

However well-intentioned, this might be a regrettable arrangement for several reasons. First, locating the sacramental Ministration to the Sick immediately *after* Communion may unwittingly imply that unction serves to make up for something that the Eucharist lacks or for which the Eucharist alone is insufficient. Celebrating sacramental healing *after* the Eucharist also overlooks the fact that it is through the Eucharist that together we offer to God "our selves, our souls and bodies,"[99] and through which, in the words of Lambourne, the sickness situation of those who have received the laying on of hands and anointing is itself made an offertory "that it may be received back as a means of grace and healing."[100] In contrast, positioning the sacramental rite of healing immediately *before* Communion helps, as Richards would say, to point those who struggle with sickness and disability "to the future and a renewed dedication and service."[101]

Moreover, relegating healing to side altars following Communion may give the impression that the church's healing ministry is the prerogative of a few special individuals—the ordained, or those with a special gift, or *charism*—rather than a ministry in which every baptized person has

98. Kavanagh, *Elements of Rite*, 58 (italics added).

99. *The Book of Common Prayer*, Holy Eucharist, Rite I, 336.

100. Lambourne, *Community, Church and Healing*, 130.

101. Richards, *But Deliver Us from Evil*, 15.

a part to play, and to which each brings his or her own special gifts. As the 1964 *Report of the Joint Commission on the Ministry of Healing to the General Convention of the Episcopal Church* reminds us, the ministers of the church's ministry of healing may take the form of "the surgeon, the social worker, the priest . . . the mother who comforts the sick or hurt child, the neighbor who takes over household chores when illness strikes the [home], the person who prays for the afflicted (or troubled) one he may see in a crowded subway train."[102] Those who share in the church's ministry of healing offer their love and support in many different ways—by lifting up the sick in prayer; by bringing the faithful Holy Communion when health and circumstances prevent them from joining the larger community at the Lord's Table; by reminding them with a phone call, a card or note, or perhaps a pot of home made soup, that they matter and are cared about. As important as the church's sacramental ministrations are for the sick, no less important is the sacramental community of caring to which the sick are reintegrated.

Finally, consigning sacramental healing to a "prayer station" at a side altar may serve to reinforce the notion that sacramental healing is entirely a private affair, something totally between the believer and God, when in fact, as Morris Maddocks points out, "The purpose of all . . . healing is the uniting of the . . . sufferer with Christ in his Body, the Church. Healing has a personal and a corporate dimension. True wholeness is enjoyed by those who are integrated into a worshipping community. Everyone who receives Christian healing needs the love, the prayer, and the ongoing support of the Christian community . . . You can't go it alone and be healed in isolation, neither can you remain aloof and decline to play your essential part in Christ's healing community. Every member needs to be equipped, built up, to be part of the healed and healing Body."[103]

In regard to setting, it is regrettable that none of our current rites of healing contain advisory rubrics such as the notes in *Pastoral Care of the Sick* which specifically recommend that when preparing for Communion with the faithful "who are deprived of their rightful and accustomed place in the eucharistic community"[104]—in the home, the hospital, or institution—"those who are with the sick should be asked to prepare a table cov-

---

102. Episcopal Church, *Report of the Joint Commission on the Ministry of Healing*, 8.

103. Maddocks, *The Christian Healing Ministry*, 130–31.

104. Catholic Church and the National Conference of Catholic Bishops, *Pastoral Care of the Sick*, 73.

ered with a linen cloth upon which the blessed sacrament will be placed. Lighted candles are prepared and, where it is customary, a vessel of holy water. Care should be taken to make the occasion special and joyful."[105] The worship of the church, says Gusmer, "should be a sensuous, evocative, moving, humanly attractive religious experience. In other words, it should be good ritual involving the total person: body, mind, heart, imagination, memory, emotions, and feelings. Attention needs to be directed to the liturgical environment."[106]

Again, to quote Gusmer, "More than words themselves, the nonverbal features of ritual worship strike deeply into the unconscious mind and leave a lasting impression."[107] If, for instance, what should be a communal celebration of healing in the setting of the community's worship is, in fact, more or less a one-man show in which the congregation is essentially relegated to the role of observers or recipients, this unwittingly communicates a model of church in which the sacraments are *dispensed* by the clergy rather than *celebrated* by the assembly of the faithful.

To give another example, music can provide a unifying and uplifting component of a communal healing liturgy. Used correctly, it has the power to evoke a prayerful atmosphere, to inspire or stir the hearts of the participants. However, music is all too often used as filler, with a disregard for the value of silence in helping us to focus our attention, or in allowing us to be more fully aware of the importance of what is taking place. Similarly, communal singing often helps to unite worshipers, and the use, in many healing liturgies, of professional musicians and choirs can serve to rouse and motivate the congregation. Unfortunately, as Smolarski notes, such provisions are often allowed to reduce the assembly to the role of audience, or to overpower the congregation when choir directors are permitted to "make choices that seem to value musical performance over [music's] 'servant' role in the liturgy."[108]

In regard to the importance of place in our rituals of healing, Bates notes that "while the practice of public services of healing seems a laudable one, it hardly seems practical or pastorally sensitive to suggest that the Ministration to the Sick should *normally* take place in a church building, as the rubrics of *EOW2* do. This is indeed odd . . . in that it is insensitive to the

---

105. Ibid., 74.

106. Gusmer, *And You Visited Me*, 187.

107. Ibid., 187.

108. Smolarski, *Sacred Mysteries*, 84.

needs of many sick parishioners." He adds: "Are we supposed to transport them in ambulances so that these rites can take place on hallowed ground? Surely, this rubrical suggestion either conflates the ongoing need for spiritual healing in a congregation with the specific needs for someone in crisis or else [what] it proposes risks confusing the miracle of God's healing for magic offered only at God's altar."[109] Cuenin and Fink, on the other hand, suggest that "Even if seriously ill persons are bedridden, it is well worth the effort of transporting them in bed to a chapel or a large room so that they can join others in similar conditions who seek the Lord's healing. Once they are gathered together, arranging in a circle individual sick persons next to one another and with their families and caregivers close by will provide an atmosphere of physical and emotional intimacy. This gives all the participants permission to remain attuned to one another before, during, and after the liturgical celebration."[110]

Certainly, one must exercise a pastoral sensitivity in regard to the individuals who will be participating. The state of health and the physical demands placed upon the individual worshippers, time and circumstances: all these must be taken into consideration, as well as the physical environment in which worship will take place. Indeed, it is not always possible to transport a seriously ill (or dying) individual to the chapel or the church building, but even a bedside rite of healing, with a little forethought and preparation, can become, in the words of the *Pastoral Care of the Sick*, a "symbol of unity between the community and its sick members."[111] While circumstances may not allow for a full celebration of the Eucharist, a thoughtful use of the form for Communion under Special Circumstances[112] in the *Book of Common Prayer* still makes it possible for what would otherwise be a private celebration to express its essential corporate nature.

It is my experience that sometimes smaller, more intimate celebrations—say, during a weekday-morning Eucharist, or in smaller 'house church' type settings—help to foster a special sense of community and may be a little less overwhelming for those who are seriously ill or notably weakened by age or infirmity. In these smaller groups, participants may feel

109. Bates, "A Riotous Mixture of Phrases."

110. Cuenin and Fink, "Alternative 4: Liturgy of Healing to Replace the Blessing of Throats for the Feast of St. Blaise," in Lee and Fink, eds., *Alternative Futures for Worship* 7:88.

111. Catholic Church and the National Conference of Catholic Bishops, *Pastoral Care of the Sick*, 73.

112. *The Book of Common Prayer*, 396–99.

less inhibited about voicing their prayer concerns and about participating fully and prayerfully. I have noticed, for instance, that in the course of my local parish's midweek Eucharist, the members of this smaller assembly are much more likely to take part in the laying on of hands in a most heartfelt manner, and to offer personal testimony to the power of God's healing grace. It is a moving experience to witness this small circle of love and prayer ministering to one another.

My husband, who suffers from numerous serious health problems, finds these healing services a powerful source of comfort and renewal. In the smaller, more personal space of the Children's Chapel where these services take place, he can move about comfortably in his wheelchair and even serve as acolyte or eucharistic minister. He is less self-conscious about his handicaps, and more at ease in the midst of this smaller congregation. As Kew and White observe in *Toward 2015: A Church Odyssey*, "Christians the world over have shown that there is a need for the intimacy of the cell group as well as magnificent celebrational services and assemblies; when combined, these nurture the faith in extraordinary ways."[113] As Duggan notes, "Each parish will have to decide how best to express this ownership of the rite [of healing], but it seems essential to make special provisions for the active participation of the community in ways that are noticeable and striking."[114]

Serious Soul Work

As the report *Faithful Living, Faithful Dying* observes, "Forming ourselves to live with the hope and sufferings of daily existence and with the shadow of death that hangs over them requires hard work."[115] With the advent of serious sickness there is important soul work to do, as the architects of our previous rites of healing understood all too well. In addition to the many practical considerations that begin to consume one's time and energy, such as medical appointments and procedures, special diets and medications, or dealing with insurance companies, there are other certain hard truths to be faced. These challenge us to undertake the task of incorporating this difficult situation into the context of our faith, and to attempt somehow

113. Kew and White, *Toward 2015*, 70.

114. Duggan, *Parish Liturgy*, 84.

115. Cohen et al., *Faithful Living, Faithful Dying*, 73–74.

to extract meaning and purpose from the most daunting and seemingly chaotic situations.

The tone of our earlier Visitation Offices, in keeping with the medieval theology out of which they emerged, was not entirely hopeful. While they did not actually rule out any hope of recovery, they were clearly created for the primary purpose of preparing the sick person for death. Therefore they clearly acknowledged our human frailty: they did not shy away from the reality of death or of sin, and they devoted great attention to the importance of the amendment of life. Their response, as we have observed, to the reality of serious illness was to regard that situation as an opportunity for self-examination and repentance.

If there is a weakness to our two most recent public services of healings, it may be, ironically, their upbeat and sometimes therapeutic tone.[116] True, one must take into consideration the communal nature of these liturgies, but it is to be hoped that parishes that celebrate these public rites of healing will also make provision (separately or perhaps in smaller groups such as I have described) for those individuals who feel the need of serious soul work outside the hospital or bedside environment. As valuable and as necessary as our newest communal rites of healing undeniably are, there is still much to be said for the Ministration to the Sick, which more easily allows for pastoral care and counsel in a more personal and intimate setting.

In our haste to restore a sense of hope and optimism to our sacramental healing liturgies, we should not allow ourselves to lose sight of the fact that what we need when we are seriously ill, or when advancing age or infirmity threaten to unravel the fabric of our lives, is not simply a palliative for our pain, but a way to maintain a sense of meaning and purpose. We require spiritual resources that allow us to prevail in the face of sickness and suffering, that call us into engagement with life rather than flight from it, even when the prospect of physical cure appears to be limited or even nonexistent. We need a safe place in which to communicate, "with or without words," the feelings that we are so often unable to express which can, if left unchecked, form a sort of internal spiritual roadblock. Our rites of healing should help us to face passages in our lives that we would rather avoid, so that we can continue, even in the face of these formidable challenges, to journey on in faith, with purpose and dignity, wresting meaning and

116. Although, these difficult realities are actually well addressed in the section of *Enriching Our Worship 2* following A Public Service of Healing, titled "Prayers for Use by a Sick Person." (71–79).

hope even from these difficult circumstances. Without downplaying our illness and pain, or the dangers and complications encompassed thereby, they should, as Stoutzenberger observes, celebrate "the mysterious truth that—as in Jesus' own death—suffering, sickness, and even death can be part of the healing journey toward resurrected life and wholeness."[117]

The tenor of our most recent healing rites is comforting and reassuring, but we have much work to do if we are to truly create, out of the assembly of healed and healers, a ministering community. As Lambourne reminds us, "it is not the sick person alone, but the root group with sickness within it which needs to be renewed as a healing community."[118] Time and experience will reveal how well our newest healing liturgies contribute to the 'retooling' of Christians whose lives and expectations have been disrupted by serious illness.

The Healing Power of Forgiveness

> "Receive me again into the arms of your mercy, and restore me to the blessed company of your faithful people . . ."[119]

Fundamental to our previous Visitation rites was an appreciation of the essential interconnectedness of sin and sickness, not necessarily in the sense that all sickness is divine retribution for moral transgression, but with an acknowledgment of the interrelatedness of all creation, and with the understanding of illness (in all its various aspects) as symptomatic of the greater brokenness of a creation in disharmony with its Creator. As Prichard explains, the previous emphasis on preparation for death so prominent in our Visitation Offices was based "on an assumption of universality," which is to say, "upon the assumption that we are all sinners, that we will all suffer from illness and accident, and that we will all die. The point of the pastoral care is not to point to a one-on-one relationship between some sequence of acts and the current illness, but upon the general condition of all sinful people. People today often miss that distinction, and as a result many clergy flee from any serious conversion talk with the dying about sin and repentance."[120] It was, notes Prichard, considered to be "appropriate to talk

---

117. Stoutzenberger, *Celebrating Sacraments*, 159.

118. Lambourne, *Community, Church and Healing*, 131.

119. *The Book of Common Prayer*, The Reconciliation of a Penitent, Form One, 450.

120. Prichard, "Sickness, Healing, and Forgiveness."

about sin and repentance to a person who is seriously ill." He adds: "I regard our hesitance to do so [today] as a major impoverishment of our pastoral care. I would hold that it is appropriate to suggest that a dying person lay down petty disputes, to reach out to others, and to make amends. Often that can best be heard by the dying person if couched in terms of the pastoral needs of those who will survive: 'You have an important role here for your family. This is a time to bless and encourage your children, to end disputes, and to provide a model of faith to them. You have their attention in a way that has seldom been the case in your life.'"[121]

Richards observes: "It is no accident that . . . the Order for the Visitation of the Sick in the 1662 Prayer Book instructs the person to make a 'special confession of his sins.' A general confession is frequently made in public services but such an act does not usually help to bring the penitent to a re-appraisal of the direction his life is taking, but merely to a greater awareness of his recent sins."[122] Personal confession, Richards notes, provides the opportunity for pastoral care and spiritual direction, and just as importantly, for that personal assurance of Christ's love and forgiveness.

The architects of the earlier Visitation Offices understood well that the crisis situation produced by serious illness naturally rouses one to engage in serious self-reflection, to consider the meaning and direction of one's life, and one's relationship with God and one's neighbor. For instance, while articulating a greater anticipation of physical and spiritual healing, by which "weakness may be banished and . . . strength recalled,"[123] the 1928 rite is still very much grounded in the immediate reality of the sickness-situation of the individual, and in incorporating that very sickness-situation into the occasion of conversion. It calls, in other words, for serious and sometimes difficult spiritual effort on the part of both patient and minister, as God's grace is sought not just for the alleviating of a particular sickness situation, but for the sanctification of it, "that the sense of his weakness may add strength to his faith, and seriousness to his repentance."[124]

One of the most difficult realities of any serious sickness situation is the all-too human tendency to blame oneself for one's illness. *This must be my fault. I am to blame. If only I had stopped smoking/cut down on the fatty foods/taken my vitamins/exercised more/gone to the doctor sooner . . . and*

121. Ibid.
122. Richards, *But Deliver Us from Evil*, 11.
123. 1928 *Book of Common Prayer*, 315.
124. Ibid., 310.

so on. Much of this is due, no doubt, to a desperate need to feel that we are somehow capable of assuming control of every aspect of our lives. *See what happens when we don't*, goes this sort of reasoning. The truth, however, as Wilson observes, is that the "tragic and moral aspects of sin are interwoven in many sickness situations."[125]

With the incredible advances in the fields of endocrinology, genetics, immunology, neurology, psychiatry, and epidemiology, we enjoy a greater insight today into the many and complex causes of illness, and we can appreciate the fact that there is rarely a simple one-to-one equation to explain the occurrence of any serious sickness. Sickness is a reality of life for even the most virtuous. We have only to consider the lives of such pious figures as St. Francis and St. Teresa, as well as many others who, by our way of thinking, should not have gotten sick at all. However, as physician and author Larry Dossey observes, "Physical bodies are obstreperous, stubborn entities that are given to some very bad habits, such as their susceptibility to genetic diseases, proneness to infection, and so on. Bodies have 'minds of their own,' which do not always accurately represent our physiological and spiritual understanding. Our bodies can act up, break down, and get sick without ever consulting us."[126]

In every serious sickness situation there are certain aspects, of course, for which we can and sometimes should claim personal responsibility, such as our wrong choices or unhealthy lifestyles, while at the same time, as Dossey points out, there are other aspects that are far beyond our control. While today we may be less inclined to think of illness as God's "fatherly correction," we may be just as likely to find ourselves prey to the belief that we must be responsible in some way for *everything* that happens to us. *I must have unconsciously willed this illness on myself.* We are sick, so this way of thinking goes, because for some reason we *chose* to be. It's a New Age spin on an old idea, that sickness is a punishment for sin, only this time the sin may be that of negative thinking, or not loving ourselves enough, or not having reconciled some childhood issue . . . the list goes on and on.

At such times we require pastoral direction, those words of "comfort and counsel" that should be fundamental to our rites of healing, to help us sort out the tragic and moral elements so intrinsic to our sickness situation, to distinguish, as Wilson says, between "guilt and calamity,"[127] and

125. Wilson, *The Church Is Healing*, 43.

126. Dossey, *Healing Words*, 17.

127. Wilson, *The Church Is Healing*, 43.

to help us take to stock of our situation in a way that is productive and beneficial. We need assistance in order to undertake that serious soul work that will lead to the reconciliation with God and neighbor so essential to true healing.

The preliminary material in *Enriching Our Worship 2* states: "Since there continues to be a residue of older prayers and hymns suggesting that illness is judgment from God on the individual, care should be taken to avoid materials that convey a guilt-inducing theology which might undermine the sick person's confidence, breed feelings of worthlessness, and even interfere with recovery, rather than inspire a conviction of God's loving and compassionate presence."[128] To which Bates responds: "*EOW2* asserts that both the 1928 and 1979 prayer books 'moved away from an understanding of illness as divine punishment,' and bravo for that. But how can a priest address the need of a sick person who has *not* moved away from this understanding, but, rather, has fallen rather sharply *into* it in the course of an illness? Can we really expect those in crisis to leap from understandable concern about their illness to the praise of God without *any* sort of transition?"[129]

As much as we may not agree with some of their theology, there is much to be said in favor of the willingness of the earlier Visitation Offices to speak to the painful and difficult truths of serious illness situations and to unflinchingly address their inherent spiritual concerns. Take, for instance, the notion that one must somehow be ultimately responsible for one's own illness or the idea that one is perhaps unworthy to receive healing, despite the fact that (as the 1964 *Ministry of Healing* report reminds us) "we are not rewarded according to our merit, 'for [God] maketh his sun to rise on the evil and on the good, and sendeth rain on the just and on the unjust.'"[130] Rather than deny the fact that "many people may feel afflicted by illness—commonly questioning what they have done wrong to deserve it," says Bates, "it may be that the Visitation Offices, [such as the 1928 rite] were better equipped to meet the sick where they are, and through prayers and psalm groupings, which shifted gradually from affliction to praise,

128. "Praying with the Sick," in *Enriching Our Worship 2*, 14.

129. Bates, "A Riotous Mixture of Phrases."

130. Matt 5:45. Episcopal Church, *Report of the Joint Commission on the Ministry of Healing*, 21–22.

to help to *move* them into a place of thanksgiving, evoking the idea of discernment-commitment.[131]

"Examine your lives and conduct by the rule of God's commandments," reads the Exhortation preceding the Decalogue in the Rite I eucharistic liturgy,

> that you may perceive wherein you have offended in what you have done or left undone, whether in thought, word, or deed. And acknowledge your sins before Almighty God, with full purpose of amendment of life, being ready to make restitution for all injuries and wrongs done by you to others; also being ready to forgive those who have offended you, in order that you yourselves may be forgiven.[132]

Sin, "the seeking of our own will instead of the will of God, thus distorting our relationship with God, with other people, and with all creation,"[133] is something the Anglican tradition takes very seriously. Accordingly, the 1979 Prayer Book, not content with simply making provision for a general confession, drafted two new and separate rites for the Reconciliation of a Penitent directly preceding the Ministration to the Sick. With, Stuhlman notes, its "theology of reconciliation as a second baptism and also a strong emphasis on its corporate dimensions,"[134] with its provision for personal words of "comfort and counsel," and its emphasis on "the need for ongoing conversion,"[135] the Reconciliation of a Penitent offers an important opportunity for the serious soul work so essential to creating a ministering and sacramental community whose mission it is to serve God in Christ's healing and redeeming work.

Neither the preface nor the introduction to A Public Service of Healing (2000) make any mention of the vital role of the Church's sacramental rite of reconciliation in her healing ministry. Our two newest liturgies of healing in particular seem to exhibit an unease with naming and addressing the reality of sin other than in a general, all-encompassing sense. One must wonder if this stems from what Harmon Smith refers to as "modern

131. Bates, "A Riotous Mixture of Phrases."

132. *The Book of Common Prayer*, An Exhortation, 316.

133. *Catechism*, 848.

134. Stuhlman, *Occasions of Grace*, 143.

135. Ibid., 143.

psychological barriers, to say nothing of methodological difficulties in the matter of naming sin."[136]

As Christopher Lasch, in *The Culture of Narcissism,* observes: "The contemporary climate is therapeutic, not religious. People today hunger not for personal salvation . . . but for the feeling, the momentary illusion, of personal well-being, health and psychic security."[137] The comforting and re-assuring images and language in our two newest healing rites are a welcome feature, but we need also to be mindful of the fact that the sacrament of unction is not merely a therapeutic ritual, or simply a source of solace and encouragement, but like every sacrament, an invitation to grasp the hand of the Divine Healer and to be raised up into the Resurrection life.

The Consequence of Catechesis

> Pastors of souls must . . . realize that, when the liturgy is celebrated, something more is required than the mere observation of the laws governing valid and licit celebration; it is their duty also to ensure that the faithful take part fully aware of what they are doing, ac-tively engaged in the rite, and enriched by its effects.[138]

The invitation to receive healing is given, the faithful present them-selves, reverently bowing their heads for the laying on of hands and anoint-ing, surrounded, one would hope, by the assembly of the faithful, perhaps reaching out to rest their hands on this or that individual's shoulder or back, lifting them in prayer. How much real understanding, however, does the congregation, on the whole, possess about the meaning of this impor-tant sacramental rite? How well have they been *prepared* for what is to take place? Moreover, how well equipped are the faithful who carry Com-munion to those who cannot be present, or even those who (with special permission, if they are not ordained) bring to the sick the oil of anointing?

Likewise, I suspect that such private piety that for so long character-ized our liturgical mindset has not yet been successfully shaken off. On the whole, I believe that we do a better job of educating the faithful about the importance of healing for body, mind and spirit than we do of proclaiming the social significance of our rites of healing. A glance at the choice of many of the hymns frequently selected for special healing services, which often

136. Smith, *Where Two or Three Are Gathered,* 89.
137. Lasch, *The Culture of Narcissism,* 33.
138. *SC,* I, 11

fall into the category of what a clergy colleague refers to as "me and my Jesus," speak volumes about the need for a greater awareness of the *corporate* aspect of our healing sacraments.

It stands to reason that we cannot expect mindful participation without understanding. And yet, in many cases the service of healing celebrated on a regular basis in the local parish is simply inserted into the service with little or no effort given to preparing the soil of the hearts and minds of the faithful, by way of the sermon, say. This seems surprising, when one thinks about it, since the Ministry of the Word would appear to be a logical place to begin such catechesis, by employing the lessons drawn from the day's scripture, or drawing upon the themes of the prayers and collects, in order to emphasize the importance of faith and hope, and of God's power to heal and restore. In this way the faithful should be prepared to participate more fully through an understanding of what sacraments are, and how they enable us, even in the midst of sickness and debility, even in the face of suffering, to find a 'gospel comfort' that includes new meaning for our lives, as Duffy would say. It would make sense to regularly include a lesson or message about our sacramental rites of healing in the Sunday bulletin or in the parish newsletter. How much more advantageous it is to be able to learn about the meaning of sickness and old age, notes Empereur, when one is well, rather than waiting until one is suddenly stricken with serious illness![139]

Kathleen Hughes observes, "sacraments come at crossroads moments of the human journey. They are the faith community's intervention and blessing at times of birth and coming of age, of vocation, of rupture and reconciliation, of sickness and debilitation and death. These are the critical passages of human life, each of them a new invitation to join ourselves to Christ, a new call to conversion as turning to God or moving more deeply into the life of God."[140] In teaching the faithful about the purpose of the sacraments in their lives, says Duffy, we enrich the church's care of the sick with "an evangelization component that allows them to ask new questions about their lives and to clarify their intentions."[141]

"The best catechesis for any sacrament," says Gusmer, "is a well-done liturgical celebration: the participation of all the available ministers, the verbal and nonverbal symbols with all their inherent power speaking for

139. Empereur, *Prophetic Anointing*, 214.

140. Hughes, *Saying Amen*, 180.

141. Duffy, *A Roman Catholic Theology of Pastoral Care*, 95.

themselves."[142] As we have seen, authentic sacramental liturgy requires more than simply the correct form and matter, and goes far beyond concerns of validity and liciety. To simply launch into the rite of unction, as is often done (*"and this being the first Sunday of the month, you will now be invited to come up for anointing and the laying on of hands"*) with little or no real opportunity for the assembly to prepare their hearts and minds for what is about to take place, overlooks the fact that at some level every sacramental rite is, in the words of Schanz, a "genuine human event"[143] that seeks to invite our participation by engaging our senses, our imagination, our memory, our understanding. One thought presents itself: Forward Movement[144] publishes a small booklet titled *The Eucharist with notes: Rite II*.[145] On the right hand page one finds the service for Holy Eucharist, Rite II, while the left hand side contains easy-to-understand notes regarding the service itself. Perhaps it might be helpful to print healing liturgies in attractive, easy-to-read, self-contained booklets with corresponding notes.

Summing Up

Authentic liturgy requires more than aesthetically pleasing worship spaces, beautifully crafted rites, or painstaking orchestration, however important these elements undoubtedly are. Our response to our liturgies says much about how we understand ourselves as church and how we perceive our own individual roles and mission. If, for instance, a community is guided by a vision of mutual ministry, and understands itself as a priestly and prophetic community, then a style of liturgy marked by a private piety, and in which the laity—if they participate at all—are consigned to the role of helpers, will prove unsatisfying and unengaging.

Have we been successful in creating new sacramental rites in which "God speaks to his people and Christ is still proclaiming his gospel. And the people reply by song and prayer"?[146] Are we generating liturgies in which meaning arises out of our acknowledgement of God's presence in

142. Gusmer, *And You Visited Me*, 184.

143. Schanz, *Introduction to the Sacraments*, 77.

144. An official nonprofit agency of the Episcopal Church that publishes devotional aids, books, and tracts. The Chair of Forward Movement is the Presiding Bishop.

145. Hardebeck, *The Eucharist with Notes*. Adapted from a booklet prepared by St. Mark's Church, Glen Ellyn, Illinois.

146. *SC*, I, 33.

our lives, individually and as a community, by our offering of ourselves and our opening ourselves to the experience of God's grace? Or are we, instead, fashioning therapeutic ritual celebrations that give voice and form to our own deepest aspirations and hopes, but which are incapable of challenging us, transforming us, and which leave us with little more than that with which we started? I will address these and similar questions in the final chapter.

5

Conclusions

From Catechism Definition to a
Refreshed Understanding of Sacraments

THE VARIOUS STAGES AND cycles of our lives, and the important occur-
rences, from birth to death (moments critical to salvation)—and in most
particular, sickness and debility—are related and interpreted anew in
the sacraments, through the Paschal framework of the life we share with
Christ, and in which we share with all the members of Christ's Body. What
Anglicans believe is interpreted and embodied in our worship, in the *Book
of Common Prayer* and our other authorized liturgies, through which the
faithful, in turn, are formed through their participation. Accordingly, at
a time when our lives have been disrupted and disordered by illness, as
well as strengthening and comforting us, our liturgies of healing ought to
embody and convey a Christian understanding of the meaning and place
of sickness and suffering in our lives, and the purpose and direction of our
own Christian vocation in the midst of that sickness and suffering.

Review: Chapter One

A sacrament is "an outward and visible sign of inward and spiritual grace,
given by Christ as sure and certain means by which we receive that grace."
In Chapter 1, using the familiar Catechism definition, we attempted to flesh
out that very concise explanation. In so doing we arrived at the understanding that there are fundamentally three levels to every sacrament: First, there
is the outward and perceptible level, or the level of the *sign*, which *signifies*,

or draws attention to something other than itself. Through signs we have access to another, more profound level of meaning capable of conveying the *idea* or *concept* of something. This is the level of the *symbol*. Through their ability to resonate with our thoughts, our senses, our emotions, and our memories, symbols possess a richness and complexity of meaning that goes far beyond what can be expressed by simple signs or discursive language. Finally, there is the inmost level of the sacrament, the divine mystery at its heart, its inner reality. At this level the sacrament not only expresses and signifies its ultimate meaning, but, in giving expression to that deeper reality—grace, God's self-giving—allows it to be actualized and thus effectively *communicates* it to the believer who is properly disposed, or, in the words of the Council of Trent, "places no obstacle in the way." Thus we move by degrees away from the old, mechanical, almost magical understanding of sacraments to a renewed understanding that begins to do justice to that sacred mystery out of which sacraments arise.

As Louis Weil observes, "it is impossible to discuss sacraments apart from liturgical practice."[1] Sacraments are *liturgical actions* of the assembled church, rooted in the Paschal Mystery, and derived from the life and ministry of Christ and the lived experience of the faithful. We must consider them not just from a theological perspective, but from the perspective of sacred ritual as well, in order to truly understand them. As we have observed, when rituals are truly effective, they resonate deeply within us; they are, as Ronald Grimes, observes, etched upon our very marrow. They have the ability to establish us within a particular community or reality. They have the power not only to mark our passage from one state to another, but to transform us through our active and meaningful participation.

While Scripture assures us that we are made in the image of God, we are at the same time very much creatures of flesh and blood, with all the blessings and limitations this implies. It is important that our sacramental liturgies take our creatureliness into consideration. Re-inventing and re-imagining our rites of healing requires not just theological correctness or liturgical savvy, but a sensitivity to such things as the intermingled role and nature of tradition, belief, symbolism, imagination, and memory. At the same time, intrinsic to our human nature is a fundamental openness to the divine, a desire to be able to make sense of our existence in a way that does justice to that physical and spiritual complexity. For this reason, we must be sensitive to the function and power of our symbols, those tangible

---

1. Weil, *Sacraments and Liturgy*, 3.

and perceptible signs by which God's love is proclaimed, manifested, and encountered. Unless our sacramental rites acknowledge these two different and complimentary aspects of our human nature, they may inspire us, but they will not necessarily leave us different people.

Review: Chapter Two

"Bringing together the old and the new," as Tad Guzie says, "is the task of the church in every age."[2] In chapter 2 we examined preconciliar and postconciliar approaches to sacramental theology with the use of two contrasting models, the Old School model (characterized by the prevailing preconciliar sacramental/liturgical mindset dominated by the theology of Scholasticism) and the New School model (which regards sacraments in a more dynamic, relational way, as part of a process that leads the believer to a personal encounter with Christ, and which arise, in part, out of the church's reflection on its lived experience of the Paschal Mystery). To briefly summarize:

1. The Models and Grace

Is the grace of the sacraments an "infused quasi-substance" or an "imputed judicial decree"?[3] Or, rather than some metaphysical reality—something apart from God's self, imparted by God to the world at particular times and places—is the grace of the sacraments something more immediate: *relationship* with God, God's self-giving, God's love? Which theology of grace—the Old School or the New School—are we communicating in the way we celebrate our sacramental rites? This section considered the different ways in which the church has traditionally understood grace, and focused in particular on the gradual loss—and recovery—of the understanding of the grace of the sacraments as God's offer of God's very self, by which, as Hughes notes, we are able "to grow in God's love within our relation to one another in the Church."[4]

2. Guzie, *The Book of Sacramental Basics*, 1.
3. Hughes, "Sacraments and Ordination."
4. Ibid.

2. The Models and Church

This section focused on two very different models of the underlying ecclesiology of the sacraments: one that regards the church as a hierarchical structure (whose ministry is primarily the work of the ordained) and the official dispenser of the sacraments, and the other model, which understands sacraments in light of their essential corporate, ecclesial nature. The former model would give rise to a reductionist approach to sacraments marked by an emphasis on particulars and a theology of worship exemplified by the image of *Christus solus* ("Christ alone, present in the ministry of the priest, and acting on behalf of the people").[5] The latter model would find its expression in a renewed theology of worship that more and more embodies, however imperfectly, the truth that sacraments are *liturgical actions* of the assembled church, a model characterized by the image of *totus Christus* ("Christ in the midst of the church, together with the church that is gathered into union with him").[6] Sacraments, to this way of understanding, are realities to be experienced rather than simply studied, celebrated rather than simply administered, as we attempt to give tangible expression to the essentially inexpressible: the mystery of salvation. In the centuries between the Council of Trent and the Second Vatican Council and following, the way we think of sacraments has undergone a dramatic transition and has been greatly enriched by our gradual recovery of the appreciation of the church's own essential sacramental nature, and by a care for the way in which that sacramental nature is expressed in the church's liturgy.

3. The Models and Liturgical Celebration

The way in which we celebrate our sacramental liturgies proclaims loudly and clearly whether we consider them to be the sole responsibility of the ordained clergy, and private affairs between the believer and God, or the work of all the people of God with both a private and corporate aspect. How, when, and where we celebrate our sacraments—in the shadows or in the midst of the assembly of the faithful, as a highly clericalized one-man show or as an articulation of a mutuality of ministry—speaks volumes about our theology of sacraments and the ministry of the baptized. The care we devote to allowing every aspect of our sacramental liturgies— word, symbol, music, movement, space, setting, and the like—to engage us in body, mind, and spirit—tells us much about the way in which we

5. Fink, *Worship: Praying the Sacraments*, 47-48.
6. Ibid.

understand sacraments. When the majority of attention is given to the trappings of liturgy, and little or none to the role of the baptized in that same liturgy, this reveals a lack of appreciation for the basic sacramentality of the church. On the other hand, when the manner in which our rites are celebrated expresses the understanding that our sacramental liturgies are the shared action of the church in assembly, this is a powerful reminder of the sacramental dimension of *every* aspect of life—regardless of age, health or circumstances—for those believers who share in the life of Christ, the Primordial Sacrament.

4. The Models and the Scope of Sacramental Effects

The title of the Church of England report on the sacraments of Christian initiation, *On the Way*, fittingly expresses a contemporary understanding of sacramental celebrations as part of a transformational journey: "The image of the Way expresses the developing character of the journey into faith. The starting point and natural pace of the individuals involved needs to be respected."[7] This section began with the unfortunate but prevalent misconception of sacramental rites as rituals that take place solely within the time of celebration, and contrasted this with a renewed understanding of sacramental celebrations as the source and climax of a lifelong journey of faith that begins with God's prevenient grace calling us into relationship, and whose meaning unfolds throughout the successive stages of our lives. The significance of this difference is important. According to this renewed perspective, all of our sacramental rites invite us to look *beyond* the immediate horizon of their effects to that broader and more eschatological dimension inseparable to them, and equip us, nourish us, support us and invite us to continue on in our journey of faith at every stage of life and in every circumstance.

5. The Models and the Relation of Word and Sacrament

Among other things, this section laid particular stress on the ways in which, in later centuries, the conflict between the Roman Catholic Church and the reformers would find expression in what has been (falsely) perceived as a word/sacrament dichotomy. In crafting new sacramental liturgies, we must be mindful always of the importance of the relationship of word and sacrament, and the proclamatory or revelatory power of both. We explored the complementary role of both word and symbol in creating

7. Church of England. House of Bishops, *On the Way*, 115.

liturgical celebrations that fully engage our complex bodily and spiritual natures, and, as Cooke would say, lead us to growth in grace, to "the transformation of human persons under the impact of God's loving self-gift in Christ."[8]

Review: Chapter Three

Chapter 3 was an overview of our Anglican sacramental rites of healing, from the 1549 Visitation Office to *Enriching Our Worship 2*'s "A Public Service of Healing," in the context of both their history and underlying theology. Until relatively recently, unction was still synonymous in the minds of many of the faithful with last rites. Once little more than final preparation for death, a "cram session for the Last Judgment," in the words of Prichard,[9] our revised liturgies of healing have restored that hopeful aspect so long wanting.

A cursory examination of our previous rites of healing suggests that one of the aspects where they were most lacking was their underlying ecclesiology, which unwittingly created privatized rituals out of what should have been communal liturgies. This reality is addressed most particularly by our newest liturgies of healing, which have effectively restored the missing corporate dimension with their essentially communal settings.

As we have noted, our current sacramental rites of healing, with their focus on healing rather than on preparation for death, and their greater corporate dimension, are reflective not just of contemporary liturgical renewal movements but of the growing interest on the part of both Anglicans and other Christian faith traditions in the church's ministry of healing. A widespread, heartfelt appreciation for the healing and restorative grace of our sacramental rites is evident in the increasingly regular celebration of sacramental healing in our parishes throughout the Episcopal Church. At the same time, I perceive a lack of awareness regarding the power of our sacramental healing rites as tools of ongoing spiritual growth and renewal, and a similar lack of appreciation for the way in which the healing and blessing imparted by the grace of the sacrament empowers us—at every age, at every stage of life, in our various and ever-changing circumstances—to continue to claim our essential dignity as God's priestly people, sharing in God's work.

8. Cooke, *Sacraments and Sacramentality*, 238.

9. Prichard, "Sickness, Healing, and Forgiveness."

From the first Visitation Offices to *Enriching Our Worship 2*, it appears that we Anglicans have struggled with the question of what to make of our sacramental rites of healing. For instance, in most parishes, while parishioners may not hesitate to request anointing for family members who are gravely ill or near death, they are less likely to request anointing for someone about to undergo surgery, or who may be recovering from a grave illness or struggling with the infirmities accompanying old age. I can only conclude that however far we may have come in recognizing the value of our sacramental rite of unction—for so long misunderstood and often neglected—as a church we have not yet fully begun to plumb its spiritual riches, to embrace its incredible potential for healing and transformation, the Easter hope out of which it springs.

Review: Chapter Four

How can we create truly transforming sacramental liturgies capable of addressing both our pain and suffering, rites which, as the Catechism says, "sustain our present hope and anticipate its future fulfillment"[10] and that at the same time equip the faithful—most especially the sick and those who minister with the sick and the dying—to claim their identity as God's priestly people and partners in mission? Chapter 4 addressed the subject of how we might reevaluate and reimagine our rites of healing in a way that more fully gives expression to their potential to restore us to health and wholeness, to call us to conversion and nurture our faith, and to engage us in a mutuality of ministry as a God-enabled ministering/healing community. The work of creating truly transforming sacramental rites is no easy task. As well as offering healing and comfort for those facing difficult life passages, they must, if they are to do justice to what Fink terms the "paschal movement of faith"[11] that they enact, combine good theology, good liturgy, and good pastoral sensibility.

As we have observed, where, when, and how we celebrate our sacramental liturgies speaks volumes about how we understand the ministry of

---

10. *Catechism*, 861.

11. A phrase coined by Peter Fink, "described theologically in terms of God's approach, [our] response to God, God's response, and the consequence." Sedgwick, *Sacramental Ethics*, 41. As Sedgwick explains, "Worship opens worshipers to acknowledge God's presence and thereby offer themselves and experience God's grace. In the movement worshipers are changed and formed into a community of faith" (ibid., 42).

the baptized. One of the concerns on which we focused in chapter 4 was the question of whether the church's healing ministry is the work of a few special individuals—the ordained, or those with a special "gift" or *charism*—or truly a ministry in which all the faithful have a part to play and a special contribution to make. We also focused on the intricate and essential interconnectedness of sin and sickness, not necessarily in the sense that all sickness is divine chastisement for our moral transgressions, but in as much as sin is symptomatic of the greater brokenness of a creation in disharmony with its Creator. As well we gave special attention to the fact that the cause of any illness is likely to be a complex mixture of components: physical, spiritual, and psychological.

In every serious sickness situation, we noted, there are certain aspects for which we can and sometimes should claim personal responsibility, and just as certainly, other aspects of that illness that lie beyond our control. For this reason we need assistance—*"words of comfort and counsel"*—in order to undertake the serious spiritual discernment that will help us to sort out those tragic and moral aspects, to make sense of our personal situation, and to lead to that reconciliation with God and neighbor so essential to true healing.

Unfortunately, in our eagerness to eliminate all traces of the former notion of illness as punishment for sin, and in our attempts to replace the last-rites character of our former Visitation Offices with a focus on healing and restoration, we are in danger of losing sight of the healing power of the sacramental rite of penitence. Those words of comfort and counsel offered to those troubled with some "weyghtie matter" (in the words of the 1552 Visitation Office) are among the most powerful—and often undervalued—of the church's instruments of healing. The therapeutic value alone of the act of making a special confession merits its thoughtful consideration. The diversion of our emotional and psychological resources which we experience in the course of any serious illness not only impedes our physical and emotional healing but hinders our spiritual healing as well. As the Church of England report *A Time to Heal* notes, "The healing value of the assurance of forgiveness, which is at the heart of the gospel, should not be underestimated. Our culture does not take sin seriously. But separation from God is 'a sickness unto death.' To be released from the power of sin is healing."[12]

One aspect of our liturgies deserving special attention is the role of liturgical language. As Robert Trabold observes, "People have a need to

12. Church of England, *A Time to Heal*, 247.

touch, see and hear signs of the sacred. Liturgical language, however, can be too abstract. We need to have a language that captures both. The language of the sacred must have a certain distance from the here and now in order to communicate a sense of mystery, but its return to the concrete and the here and now is also necessary in order to preach the Christian message."[13] Creating truly effective sacramental rites requires more than simply substituting new language for old, replacing exclusive expressions with more inclusive ones, or balancing popular piety with theological soundness. It calls for a sensitivity to, and an appreciation for, the transformative power of language. Depending upon how thoughtfully it is employed, liturgical language, observes R. Kevin Seasoltz, can function within the gathered community of believers as "superficial signs"—flat and unexciting, unengaging—or in a symbolic manner as "the medium in which God's revelation takes place and through which the community realizes its participation in that revelation."[14] We must take care in our attention to doctrinal soundness not to strip our liturgies of their emotive and symbolic power. Likewise, we must never lose sight of the power of liturgical language, in the same way as signs, symbols, setting and music, to engage the participant in a process that opens him or her up to new and unexpected ideas and developments.

We often fail to appreciate the fact that all our liturgies also possess a nonverbal language, expressed through such things as architecture, setting, movement, and gesture. Consider the following: when we go to great lengths to make the Eucharist an aesthetically pleasing, sensuous, engaging celebration, yet treat our sacramental rites of healing with little forethought and even less preparation, we betray a lack of appreciation both for their transformative power and for the divine mystery being conveyed in that sacred place and time. The wonderful rich symbolism essential to our sacramental liturgies of healing should be more fully communicated in order to invite our engagement in their saving mystery. Do our rites of healing—through signs and symbols, through the elements of organization and direction, through prophetic proclamation and the honest acknowledgment of suffering—effectively convey a vision of mutual ministry, of a community of believers who understand their calling as a priestly and prophetic community? Sometimes, ironically, what is missing from our liturgies is that which speaks loudest of all.

13. Trabold, "Popular Piety and Liturgical Reform," 73.
14. Seasoltz, "The Language of Liturgical Celebrations," 28.

New Life, New Hope

> "*As you are outwardly anointed with this holy oil, so may our heavenly Father grant you the inward anointing of the Holy Spirit . . .*"[15]

The Holy Spirit, notes John Polkinghorne, is truly at work within the unfolding fruitfulness of God's purpose for all creation, "drawing the universe on to purposed levels of fulfillment . . . concealed within the flow of present process."[16] It is that *forward-looking* aspect that we often fail to appreciate, the fact that in our sacramental rites of healing we are given not simply balm for our woundedness or comfort and reassurance in our affliction, but, in the Holy Eucharist, nourishment for the work ahead, and through the anointing of the Holy Spirit, not simply the opportunity to pick up where we have left off, but the grace of a fresh start. What we celebrate in our sacramental liturgies is not just what God has done for us in the past, nor even solely what God is doing for us here and now, but the anticipation of "the coming of Christ in glory, and the completion of God's purpose for the world."[17] Charles Hefling notes that an understanding of sacraments that focuses only on the time of celebration or envisions a narrow sphere of effect misses the fact that sacramental celebrations are not endings but new *beginnings*. Just as the grace of our baptismal anointing is realized gradually over time throughout our lives, just so the grace of our sacramental rites of healing also unfolds throughout the different stages of our lives. A confined notion of sacraments, Hefling says, leaves out "purpose, expectation, intention, commitment: in a word, orientation to the future."[18] He explains:

> the church does not exist only to praise God for creation, or even for the *magnalia Dei*, God's mighty acts in history, after he has done them. It does exist for that. But also, and even more crucially, *the church exists to be the thing that God is doing, and to become the thing God will be doing until the End.*
> . . . As Archbishop Rowan Williams has written—and it is significant that he wrote it in an article on liturgy—the characteristic form of God's doing is the formation of the church, the formation of common life lived in such a way as to manifest not just the inherent goodness of creation but the possibility of new

15. *Book of Common Prayer*, Ministration to the Sick, 456.

16. Polkinghorne, *The Faith of a Physicist*, 152.

17. *Catechism*, 861.

18. Available in print: Hefling, "What Do We Bless, and Why?" Originally presented at the Episcopal Church Foundation Fellows Forum, Philadelphia, 2002.

creation, of healing and justice and forgiveness. *The characteristic form of God's doing is bringing about community that anticipates the kingdom that is coming.*[19]

In other words, the healing and wholeness made possible by God's grace is the act by which God's creative and redeeming love fashions, out of the brokenness and fragmentation of illness, suffering and old age, a community (in anticipation of the coming kingdom proclaimed by Jesus) in which the citizens not only celebrate God's sacraments but *become* sacrament for one another and for the world. While at any moment the focus in our liturgies of healing may be on this individual or that, this sickness situation or that, the healing that occurs, by God's grace, is for the benefit not just of the particular individual but of the *whole* body of Christ. The healing of one member of the body, in this way, helps to renew the body as a whole.

That Victory of Life and Peace

For a long time, we have tended to look at unction—indeed, nearly all of our sacramental rites—in isolation and from a limited perspective in regard to their scope of effect: *"This is holy matrimony. This celebrates the love between this individual man and woman." "This is reconciliation. This reconciles this individual sinner with God." "This is unction. This is for the healing of this particular individual in this particular situation."* But see what happens when we, instead, look at these sacramental rites from a different, more theologically sound, more holistic perspective, namely, that of the paschal mystery: as Wood rightly notes, "When a theology of anointing is linked to a theology of baptism and Eucharist we discover its ecclesial dimension."[20] It is important to be ever mindful of the way unction—like the other sacramental rites—flows out of the sacraments of Christian initiation and formation, namely,

- *Baptism.* By which we are adopted by God as God's children, made members of Christ's body, the church, brought into fellowship with Christ and with all those who are buried with Christ in his death and raised with Christ in his resurrection in order that we might share in Christ's healing and saving work.

19. Ibid (italics added).
20. Wood, "The Paschal Mystery: The Intersection of Ecclesiology and Sacramental Theology in the Care of the Sick," in *Recovering the Riches of Anointing*, 11.

- *Confirmation.* Through which those who are baptized into the life and mission of Christ are, by the Holy Spirit, empowered for service "that they may serve [God] in this life and dwell with [God] in the life to come."[21] As the Vatican II document *Lumen Gentium* proclaims, "The lay apostolate . . . is a participation in the salvific mission of the Church itself. Through their baptism and confirmation, all are commissioned to that apostolate by the Lord Himself."[22]

- *Eucharist.* Through which, as the Postcommunion prayer so eloquently reminds us, we are assured not only of God's favor and goodness towards us, but of the fact that we are "very members incorporate in the mystical body of [God's] Son, the blessed company of all faithful people, and also heirs, through hope, of [God's] everlasting kingdom."[23] Through the Eucharist we are given God's grace in order that "we may continue in that holy fellowship, and do all such good works as [God] hast prepared for us to walk in . . ."[24]

"None of these," say Beguerie and Duchesneau, "can be understood unless we envisage its relationship to the two others. [Confirmation and eucharist] are already present in embryo in baptism, but the fullness of baptism unfolds in the later stages."[25] Likewise, when we envision all of our sacramental rites in relation to these foundational sacraments, we begin to perceive them in their true light: as *vocational* sacraments. In some way, throughout our journey of faith, as our lives unfold, they serve to enable each of us to more perfectly realize that commitment that we undertook at our baptism; and to serve that commitment in ways which, as Duffy would say, renew our sense of purpose and vision.

Consider, for example, the sacramental rite of marriage. Many an overwrought bride-to-be, anxious and stressed in her quest for the perfect wedding, has exclaimed, "It's *my* wedding! This day is all about *me*!" This mistaken (but, sadly, not uncommon) impression betrays a very privatized and clearly inadequate understanding of the meaning of Christian

---

21. *The Book of Common Prayer*, Confirmation, 419.

22. Catholic Church. Pope Paul VI. Dogmatic Constitution on the Church/*Lumen Gentium*, 21 November 1964. Online: http://www.vatican.va/archive/hist_councils/ ii_vatican_council/documents/vat-ii_const_19641121_lumen-gentium_en.html/.

23. *Book of Common Prayer*, Holy Eucharist I, 339.

24. Ibid.

25. Beguerie and Duchesneau, *How to Understand the Sacraments*, 109.

marriage, which, as the Prayer Book's liturgy states, not only blesses the "union of husband and wife, in heart, body, and mind . . . for their mutual joy" but also "signifies to us the mystery of the union between Christ and his Church,"[26] which they are to model in their lives and their love for one another. "Give them such fulfillment of their mutual affection," is the church's prayer for the couple, *"that they may reach out in love and concern for others."*[27]

Similarly, through the sacramental rite of reconciliation, "the word of forgiveness," says Rahner, *"which always builds upon the word that was spoken in baptism"* reconciles the individual sinner both to God and to the Church whom he or she has wounded by his or her transgressions, and thus "accompanies the ever new and ever to be deepened conversion of each person."[28] In the same way, while the sacramental rite of orders, says Fink, invokes God's Holy Spirit upon this or that particular individual, placing them "at the disposal of God's abiding presence," the power "unleashed" in the ministry in which the priest serves "is a fundamental empowering by God for the purpose of activating and illustrating the priesthood that belongs to all."[29] It is, as the Prayer of Consecration in the Prayer Book's ordination liturgy declares, for the purpose of "[equipping] the saints for the work of ministry and the building up of [Christ's] body. "[30]

This is no less true for the sacramental rite of unction, which like all of our sacraments and sacramental rites, arises out of the Paschal Mystery into which we are initiated by water and the Holy Spirit and through which we are empowered for God's service. This and every sacrament helps us to better understand, to renew, to deepen that commitment through our encounter with its true Minister, Christ. As a recent document by the Catholic Bishops' Conferences of England and Wales, Ireland, and Scotland entitled "One Bread, One Body," observes:

> Serious sickness often physically cuts a person off from full participation in the life of the Christian community. It can seem to impair full visible communion with the Church, especially when it gathers for the Eucharist. When we are ill or house-bound, we can feel isolated from God's family, and weakened by the lack of

26. *Book of Common Prayer*, Celebration and Blessing of a Marriage, 423.
27. Ibid., 429 (italics added).
28. Rahner, *Foundations of Christian Faith*, 422 (italics added).
29. Fink, *Worship: Praying the Sacraments*, 131.
30. *Book of Common Prayer*, 533.

visible, tangible involvement. Through the sacrament of anointing, we are kept 'in touch' with the community of the Church in our sickness, and *the bonds of communion are refreshed and strengthened. Through the laying-on of hands and the anointing with oil, the sick are empowered to serve the Lord in a new way, and the Church turns to them for their prayerful assistance and support . . . a desire to receive this sacrament of healing should imply a longing for deeper communion with the Church.*[31]

Where Do We Go from Here?

Today in more and more Episcopal parishes, regularly scheduled weekly or monthly celebrations of the sacramental rite of unction are the norm, and an ever-increasing number of clergy and laity are actively involved in a healing ministry in their home parish or as members of an organization such as the Order of St. Luke.[32] In the past generation or so the Episcopal Church has placed an ever-increasing emphasis on empowering all the faithful to realize and to live out—each according to his or her personal gifts and talents, and with regard to the personal circumstances of each—the calling for which Christians are all baptized: to share in the royal priesthood of Christ as members of that holy fellowship, the church. The fruits of this theological reorientation, as Stuhlman and others have noted, are evident not simply in our present Prayer Book's new Catechism and our most recent liturgies but in the increasing mutuality of ministry evident in our public worship, leadership, and governance. It is a good start, but we have a long way yet to go. While our sacramental rites of healing play a notably more prominent role in the life and worship of the Episcopal Church today, we have, in truth, only barely begun to realize their potential for equipping the worshiping community for ministry and mission.

"Understanding . . . new rites," notes Smolarski, "requires understanding the new principles. Using the new rites requires the ability to apply the new principles. An ongoing challenge is to make sure that the forms

31. Catholic Bishops' Conferences of England & Wales, Ireland and Scotland. "One Bread, One Body." (italics added).

32. The official website for the Order of Saint Luke states, "The International Order of St. Luke the Physician is an ecumenical organization dedicated to the Christian healing ministry. Members meet together in local chapters to study Scripture, especially the biblical stories of the healing miracles, as well as other books on Christian healing. Members also engage in healing prayer, often with the laying-on of hands."

contained in our revised ritual books are given a life and a spirit by those who lead them."³³ For the average seminarian, I wonder, struggling under an already arduous course load, do sacramental studies provide a basis for a deep and rewarding personal spirituality that equips and inspires them for loving and faithful service, or are these courses in sacramental theology regarded as just one more academic requirement to satisfy? Does the preparation in sacramental theology offered by our seminaries and other educational programs reflect a thoughtful, multivalent understanding of sacraments that does justice to a new era of liturgical theology? The answer is critical to both the quality of our pastoral care as well as our liturgical celebrations. Without a deep, informed, and abiding sacramental spirituality we may create aesthetically pleasing celebrations, but will they be life-changing? Will they help the faithful to grow into the full stature of Christ, and assist the church in realizing its true identity as a sacrament of the ecclesial Christ?

I find myself in agreement with the recommendations contained in *A Time to Heal,* which state that "the Church should use suitable opportunities to communicate through preaching and teaching, good example and practice, the theology of the healing ministry to members of the Church and our wider society in order to promote its better understanding particularly amongst those who most need this ministry", that "this theology should be communicated in ways which are accessible to all age groups, all social and cultural backgrounds," and finally, that "the theology of this healing ministry should be given greater prominence in training for ordinands, as part of continuing ministerial education . . . and for licensed lay workers in pastoral care ministry."³⁴

The study of our sacramental rites and their underlying theology should be a regular part of ongoing postbaptismal catechesis. It concerns me greatly that to a surprising degree, our liturgies of healing tend to receive little more than a passing mention in most of the Episcopal Church's contemporary sacramental and liturgical studies, even those that focus on the sacraments in general. To the extent that they do, the emphasis is often on the relevant biblical and historical foundations, as an examination of the rites in isolation, and with only a nod given to them as a means to ongoing spiritual growth. While one hears much discussion regarding such subjects as the popularly perceived dichotomy between natural healing and divine

33. Smolarski, *Sacred Mysteries,* 13.
34. Church of England, *A Time to Heal,* 329–30.

healing, considerably less consideration is given to the ecclesial and vocational implications of our Anglican rites of healing.

Genevieve Glen observes: "Ministry to the sick tends to absorb all the time and energy that a too-limited body of caregivers can provide, leaving no space for study. Yet study and reflection on the part of those who bring the day-to-day experience of pastoral ministry to bear upon their inquiry are truly essential to the work ahead."[35] In many such situations, she notes, "those upon whom the rites were thrust as a pastoral task have not had sufficient leisure to absorb their full significance and even, in some cases, their wide pastoral ramifications."[36] In this respect, Glen says, the Roman Catholic Church's *Pastoral Care of the Sick* proves to be "an extraordinarily rich sourcebook, not only for the celebration of the rites for the sick and dying, but also for their understanding."[37] Hopefully, in the not too distant future we will see an annotated version of the Church Hymnal Corporation's pocket-sized *Ministry to the Sick*,[38] an edition that will provide more guidance in regard to the rites, that goes beyond simply what to do and how to do it, and that will help to inform our actions and our prayers by articulating the underlying theology. In the meanwhile, I am gratified to observe that the introductory notes in *Enriching Our Worship 2* have begun to address the increasing desire on the part of the faithful for instruction that goes beyond advisory rubrics such as "*The Priest then lays hands upon the sick person, and says one of the following . . .*"

Final Observations

Much of what I have said will already be familiar to my fellow Episcopalians. What may be new to many is the perspective I have sought to bear throughout, namely, an understanding of unction as a *vocational* sacrament. As the work of liturgical revision continues, we need to look closely at our sacramental liturgies with a regard for that mutual engagement, that transforming encounter central to them, and ask: Do our liturgies of healing, at every age and at every stage of life, help us to draw purpose and meaning from our present circumstances, and inspire within us renewed commitment to

---

35. Genevieve Glen, "Going Forth in the Spirit." In *Recovering the Riches of Anointing*, 118.

36. Ibid., 119.

37. Ibid.

38. Malania, *Ministry to the Sick*.

our baptismal commission? Do they provide us with "gospel medicine" for the healing of body, mind and spirit, and at the same time, in the words of Sedgwick, enable "the community to share and entrust themselves to each other and thereby [enable] individuals to grow in their ability to embrace and care for those beyond themselves"?[39] Do they challenge us, transform us, call us to conversion, and inspire us, even in the midst of sickness and pain, to place our hope and trust in God?

Every sacrament is a personal encounter with Christ, and, as Michael Wilson reminds us, "To meet one who is Holiness-in-action [should draw one] into the wholing activity of God as a *co-operator*. It is not enough—here on earth in this age—to enjoy God: *to be with God is to work with God*."[40] For those struggling with life-altering illness, placing that illness in an extended sacramental context allows the very sickness-situation that once threatened to rob life of all meaning to take on a different and very special significance, transformed into a new—if challenging—stage of one's lifelong faith journey, a means of witness, even an opportunity for spiritual growth. The grace and heavenly benediction conveyed by the sacraments is not simply to relieve us of the pain and suffering arising out of our sickness situation, but to relieve us of that amnesia, that *dis-ease* imposed upon us by these difficult circumstances which leads us to believe that we are no more than our broken bodies, our infirmity, our sickness, our limitations. Blessing and restoring, "wholing" and commissioning: at the heart of our sacramental liturgies of healing is that sacred encounter with the true Source of all healing, whose grace enables us to maintain a sense of our worth and identity in the face of sickness and debility. It is time for us to wholeheartedly embrace the fact that these bodies, these wonderful and complex creations of flesh and spirit—whether they be frail and broken, or whether, through God's grace, they be strong and healthy—are created (as the old Baltimore Catechism tells us) in order for us *to know God, to love God, to serve God in this world, and be happy forever with God in the next.*[41]

39. Sedgwick, *Sacramental Ethics*, 107.
40. Wilson, *The Church Is Healing*, 32 (italics added).
41. Deck, *The Baltimore Catechism, No. 1, With Explanation*, 3rd ed., 7.

Appendix A

Decalogue and Penitential Order, Rite I & II[1]

The Decalogue: Traditional

God spake these words, and said:
I am the Lord thy God who brought thee out of the land of
Egypt, out of the house of bondage. Thou shalt have none
other gods but me.
Lord have mercy upon us,
and incline our hearts to keep this law.

Thou shalt not make to thyself any graven image, nor the
likeness of any thing that is in heaven above, or in the earth
beneath, or in the water under the earth; thou shalt not bow
down to them, nor worship them.
Lord have mercy upon us,
and incline our hearts to keep this law.

Thou shalt not take the Name of the Lord thy God in vain.
Lord have mercy upon us,
and incline our hearts to keep this law.

Remember that thou keep holy the Sabbath day.
Lord have mercy upon us,
and incline our hearts to keep this law.

---

1. *The Book of Common Prayer*, 317–18

Honor thy father and thy mother.
Lord have mercy upon us,
and incline our hearts to keep this law.

Thou shalt do no murder.
Lord have mercy upon us,
and incline our hearts to keep this law.

Thou shalt not commit adultery.
Lord have mercy upon us,
and incline our hearts to keep this law.

Thou shalt not steal.
Lord have mercy upon us,
and incline our hearts to keep this law.

Thou shalt not bear false witness against thy neighbor.
Lord have mercy upon us,
and incline our hearts to keep this law.

Thou shalt not covet.
Lord have mercy upon us,
and write all these thy laws in our hearts, we beseech thee.

A Penitential Order: Rite One[2]

For use at the beginning of the Liturgy, or as a separate service.

A hymn, psalm, or anthem may be sung.

The People standing, the Celebrant says
                        Blessed be God: Father, Son, and Holy Spirit.
People   And blessed be his kingdom, now and for ever. Amen.

In place of the above, from Easter Day through the Day of Pentecost

2. Ibid., 319–21

Celebrant	Alleluia. Christ is risen.
People	The Lord is risen indeed. Alleluia.

In Lent and on other penitential occasions

Celebrant	Bless the Lord who forgiveth all our sins.
People	His mercy endureth for ever.

When used as a separate service, the Exhortation, page 316, may be read, or a homily preached.

The Decalogue, page 317, may be said, the People kneeling.

The Celebrant may read one of the following sentences

Hear what our Lord Jesus Christ saith:
Thou shalt love the Lord thy God with all thy heart, and with all thy soul, and with all thy mind. This is the first and great commandment. And the second is like unto it: Thou shalt love thy neighbor as thyself. On these two commandments hang all the Law and the Prophets. Matthew 22:37–40
If we say that we have no sin, we deceive ourselves, and the truth is not in us; but if we confess our sins, God is faithful and just to forgive us our sins, and to cleanse us from all unrighteousness. 1 John 1:8,9

Seeing that we have a great high priest, that is passed into the heavens, Jesus the Son of God, let us come boldly unto the throne of grace, that we may obtain mercy, and find grace to help in time of need. Hebrews 4:14,16

The Deacon or Celebrant then says

Let us humbly confess our sins unto Almighty God.

Silence may be kept

Appendix A

Most merciful God, we confess that we have sinned against thee
in thought, word, and deed,
by what we have done,
and by what we have left undone.
We have not loved thee with our whole heart;
we have not loved our neighbors as ourselves.
We are truly sorry and we humbly repent.
For the sake of thy Son Jesus Christ,
have mercy on us and forgive us;
that we may delight in thy will,
and walk in thy ways,
to the glory of thy Name. Amen.

or this

Almighty and most merciful Father,
we have erred and strayed from thy ways like lost sheep,
we have followed too much the devices and desires of our
        own hearts,
we have offended against thy holy laws,
we have left undone those things which we ought to
        have done,
and we have done those things which we ought not to
        have done.
But thou, O Lord, have mercy upon us,
spare thou those who confess their faults,
restore thou those who are penitent,
according to thy promises declared unto mankind
in Christ Jesus our Lord;
and grant, O most merciful Father, for his sake,
that we may hereafter live a godly, righteous, and sober life,
to the glory of thy holy Name. Amen.

The Bishop when present, or the Priest, stands and says

The Almighty and merciful Lord grant you absolution and remission of all your sins, true repentance, amendment of life, and the grace and consolation of his Holy Spirit. Amen.

A deacon or lay person using the preceding form substitutes "us" for "you" and "our" for "your."

When this Order is used at the beginning of the Liturgy, the service continues with the Kyrie eleison, the Trisagion, or the Gloria in excelsis.

When used separately, it concludes with suitable prayers, and the Grace or a blessing.

The Decalogue: Contemporary [3]

Hear the commandments of God to his people:
I am the Lord your God who brought you out of bondage.
You shall have no other gods but me.
Amen. Lord have mercy.

You shall not make for yourself any idol.
Amen. Lord have mercy.

You shall not invoke with malice the Name of the Lord your God.
Amen. Lord have mercy.

Remember the Sabbath Day and keep it holy.
Amen. Lord have mercy.

Honor your father and your mother.
Amen. Lord have mercy.

You shall not commit murder.
Amen. Lord have mercy.

3. Ibid., 350.

You shall not commit adultery.
Amen. Lord have mercy.

You shall not steal.
Amen. Lord have mercy.

You shall not be a false witness.
Amen. Lord have mercy.

You shall not covet anything that belongs to your neighbor.
Amen. Lord have mercy.

A Penitential Order: Rite Two[4]

For use at the beginning of the Liturgy, or as a separate service.

A hymn, psalm, or anthem may be sung.

The people standing, the Celebrant says
>   Blessed be God: Father, Son, and Holy Spirit.
People   And blessed be his kingdom, now and for ever. Amen.

In place of the above, from Easter Day through the Day of Pentecost

Celebrant   Alleluia. Christ is risen.
People   The Lord is risen indeed. Alleluia.

In Lent and on other penitential occasions

Celebrant   Bless the Lord who forgives all our sins.
People   His mercy endures for ever.

When used as a separate service, the Exhortation, page 316, may be read, or a homily preached.

The Decalogue may be said, the people kneeling.

4. Ibid., 351.

The Celebrant may read one of the following sentences

Jesus said, "The first commandment is this: Hear, O Israel: The Lord our God is the only Lord. Love the Lord your God with all your heart, with all your soul, with all your mind, and with all your strength. The second is this: Love your neighbor as yourself. There is no other commandment greater than these." Mark 12:29–31

If we say that we have no sin, we deceive ourselves, and the truth is not in us. But if we confess our sins, God, who is faithful and just, will forgive our sins and cleanse us from all unrighteousness. 1 John 1:8,9

Since we have a great high priest who has passed through the heavens, Jesus, the Son of God, let us with confidence draw near to the throne of grace, that we may receive mercy and find grace to help in time of need. Hebrews 4:14,16

The Deacon or Celebrant then says

Let us confess our sins against God and our neighbor.

Silence may be kept.

Minister and People

Most merciful God,
we confess that we have sinned against you
in thought, word, and deed,
by what we have done,
and by what we have left undone.
We have not loved you with our whole heart;
we have not loved our neighbors as ourselves.
We are truly sorry and we humbly repent.
For the sake of your Son Jesus Christ,
have mercy on us and forgive us;
that we may delight in your will,
and walk in your ways,
to the glory of your Name. Amen.

Appendix A

Almighty God have mercy on you, forgive you all your sins
through our Lord Jesus Christ, strengthen you in all
goodness, and by the power of the Holy Spirit keep you
in eternal life. Amen.

*A deacon or lay person using the preceding form substitutes "us" for "you" and
"our" for "your."*

*When this Order is used at the beginning of the Liturgy, the service continues
with the Gloria in excelsis, the Kyrie eleison, or the Trisagion.*

*When used separately, it concludes with suitable prayers, and the Grace or a
blessing.*

Appendix B

Ministry of Healing[1]

As Christians we are called to be whole in body, mind and spirit. Through Christ, we are enabled to minister to one another. The healing ministry recognizes the role we all have through prayer and sacramental ministry in helping to bring about that wholeness.

1. Every minister of God's word and sacraments needs to be aware of the many ways in which God's healing power may be communicated. In particular, all clergy should be aware of the provisions in the *Book of Common Prayer* and *The Book of Alternative Services* (laying on of hands, anointing, confession and absolution as and when requested) for ministering to the sick. It is important that time be taken for proper preparation and counseling so that both those who are sick and those ministering to the sick are clear about the role of prayer and sacrament in encouraging healing and wholeness. It must be understood that prayer and sacrament are meant to open us to the healing power of God, and are intended to support (rather than replace) accepted medical treatment. It is recommended that parish study groups be established to learn about the role of prayer and sacrament in the ministry of healing. Clergy may wish to contact the Bishop's Committee on Healing for information and resources. The *Book of Common Prayer* and *The Book of Alternative Services* are the church's appointed means of ministering to the sick, and the Eucharist is the fullest sacramental communication of God's grace for wholeness inhumanity.

2. Every Christian is called to minister to the sick, the bereaved and the troubled through intercessory prayer, and to pray as well for those

1. Anglican Church of Canada—Diocese of Toronto. "Liturgical Standards and Resources." Section 3.1. (2010).

who minister to the above. One of the easiest ways to support those who are sick, bereaved, or troubled is to include their names (and the names of those who minister to them) in the prayers of the people. This enables the parish to be more aware of the needs of individuals within the parish and to pray as a community for them.

Lay Anointers

1. The permission of the area bishop is required for laypeople to anoint the sick with consecrated oil. For a layperson to be involved in this ministry, he/she must be licensed by his/her area bishop and must have completed a training program offered by the Bishop's Committee on Healing. The lay anointer will function under the supervision of his/her parish priest.

2. Those who become licensed lay anointers may minister to the sick through prayer and sacramental anointing with oil. They may **not** minister to the sick through sacramental laying on of hands. Sacramental laying on of hands is the placing of both hands on the head of the person being prayed for in the same way you see a bishop laying hands on a candidate for confirmation. It does not refer to touching a person's hand, for instance, during a prayer for healing, (always with the permission of the one being prayed for).

3. Laypersons wishing to be involved in this ministry need to be recommended by their clergy, be acceptable to the congregation, and be communicants in good standing. The role of the lay anointer is classified as High Risk under the diocesan *Responsible Ministry: Screening in Faith* policy. Therefore, laypersons must have completed all screening steps required for high-risk ministry as described under the policy prior to their being recommended by their clergy. This includes a police records check and Sexual Misconduct Policy training.

4. The Bishop must have a preliminary interview with both the newly trained lay anointers and the incumbent if lay anointing is new to the parish or the incumbent. If there is a history of lay anointing within the parish and the incumbent has experience and training, then a meeting with the Bishop will be at his/her discretion.

5. The lay anointers' training program will include the biblical, historical, and theological background of this ministry, as well as pastoral and listening skills and the practice of prayer. **Clergy are required to**

attend the portion of the training weekend that covers supervision, direction, and support of lay anointers each time a candidate from his/her parish takes the training program.

6. Lay anointers are required to attend regular refresher programs, which will be offered at least once a year to provide further education and support. **Clergy may also be required to attend those sessions focusing on supervision, direction, and support of lay anointers.**

7. It will be the incumbent's responsibility to make certain that every lay anointer has completed the necessary requirements for this ministry before presenting the candidate to the bishop for licensing.

8. It is recommended that after having successfully completed their preparation and having been licensed by the bishop, it is recommend lay anointers be commissioned in a public service. This will help the congregation to understand the role of the lay anointer within the context of the parish community. Lay anointers typically function in two ways within a parish. Lay anointers may support the priest in pastoral duties by anointing those in nursing homes or hospitals or at home. They may also join the priest in a public healing service, anointing those who come forward for prayer and anointing with oil. The role each lay anointer takes within the parish community is to be negotiated with the parish priest, and a lay anointer must have the parish priest's permission before anointing anyone.

9. It is recommended that when a parish wishes to include healing in a service, it be included as part of the regular Eucharistic liturgy, typically during the intercessions or following the confession. Although this may lengthen the service a little, it allows the congregation to support the ministry by praying for those who come forward for anointing and is therefore preferable to anointing done privately during the service. It is not recommended that people be anointed when they come forward for communion because it can detract from the Eucharist, which should be the primary focus during this time. The practice of anointing by proxy is not permitted. If a person is not present, then specific prayer for the person's well being may certainly be offered. However, anointing is intended to address the needs of those present at the service.

10. It is strongly recommended that clergy who wish to have lay anointers ministering within their parishes educate their parishioners so that

they understand the ministry of healing within the Christian church and the role of the lay anointer within that ministry

11. Clergy are required to provide supervision, direction, and support for their lay anointers. The frequency and style of supervision will vary according to what the lay anointer is doing and the particular needs of each individual lay anointer. However, supervision sessions should take place at least once a month. It is also strongly recommended that lay anointers have a support group within the parish that can support their ministry with prayer—a group of people with whom they can reflect on issues that may arise from their ministry.

12. Lay anointers are typically licensed for a three-year period. The bishop may revoke a licence at any time if a lay anointer is unable or unwilling to follow the guidelines or attend training and refresher programs. A licence may also be revoked if the incumbent is unable or unwilling to provide the necessary supervision and support. Licences may be renewed providing both lay anointers and their clergy have attended the refresher programs and have been faithful to the guidelines presented here. It is the clergy's responsibility to approach the bishop to have a licence renewed. There are two exceptions to the above: a) when the incumbent leaves the parish the lay anointer's licence ceases; b) when the lay anointer leaves the parish, his/her licence ceases.

13. A new incumbent may approach the area bishop to have the lay anointers relicensed. If a significant amount of time has passed, it is recommended that the layperson attend another training weekend before resuming ministry as a lay anointer If the incumbent is unfamiliar with the role and ministry of the lay anointer he/she should attend the next training weekend so that he/she can provide adequate supervision, direction, and support.

14. Lay anointers who move to a new parish may (on the recommendation of the incumbent) be licensed in the new parish. If it has been some time since the layperson has functioned as a lay anointer or the incumbent is unfamiliar with the role and ministry of the lay anointer, then the procedures recommended in item 12 should be followed.

15. Those having further questions not answered in these guidelines or the training program should seek further clarification from their bishop or from the chair of the Bishop's Committee on Healing.

Licensing of Laity for Anointing with Oil

When a lay person has completed the training program offered by the Bishop's Committee on Healing, he/she may, with the recommendation of the incumbent, apply to the area bishop to be licensed. Both laity and their clergy will meet with the bishop (separately) and will be asked the following or similar questions.

Lay Person

- What experience have you had in the healing ministry?

- How do you feel you have been 'called out' of the congregation for this ministry?

- What was the content of the training you received?

- The healing ministry is an integral part of the ministry of the church, the Body of Christ. Tell me what that means to you.

- Do you have a support group that can help you to reflect on the issues that may arise in your ministry?

- What opportunities are being provided by your incumbent for supervision, direction and support? To whom will you be accountable?

- What plans do you and your incumbent have for commissioning this ministry? With whom have you shared these plans?

Incumbent

- What experiences have you had in the ministry of healing?

- How do you feel 'called' to this ministry?

- What education and training do you have in the ministry of healing?

- The ministry of healing is an integral part of the ministry of the church, the Body of Christ. What does this mean to you?

- Do you have a support group that can help you to reflect on issues that may arise in this ministry?

- What opportunities for supervision, direction, support and accountability have been put in place?

- What education has been/will be given in the parish before this ministry becomes fully active?

Appendix B

- What plans do you have for commissioning this ministry? With whom have you shared these plans?

- How will you continue to grow in your knowledge of the healing ministry? Are you willing to use professional development opportunities and to support your lay anointers by attending training sessions or refresher courses offered by the Bishop's Committee on Healing?

Select Bibliography

Adams, William Seth. *Shaped by Images: One who Presides*. New York: Church Hymnal, 1995.

Anglican/Roman Catholic Joint Preparatory Commission. "ARCIC I Final Report, "Elucidations on Authority in the Church." (Sept 1981) No pages. Online: http://www.pro.urbe.it/home_en.html.

———. "ARCIC II: Salvation and the Church An Agreed Statement." Online: http://www.anglicancommunion.org/ministry/ecumenical/dialogues/catholic/arcic/docs/salvation_and_the_church.cfm/.

Anglican Church of Canada, Diocese of Toronto. "Liturgical Standards and Resources." Section 3.1. (2010). Online: http://www.toronto.anglican.ca/parish-administration/human-resources-for-clergy/liturgical-standards-and-resources/.

Armentrout, Don S., and Robert Boak Slocum, editors. *An Episcopal Dictionary of the Church: A User-Friendly Reference for Episcopalians*. New York: Church Publishing Inc., 2000.

Autton, Norman. *A Manual of Prayers and Readings with the Sick*. London: SPCK, 1970.

Baillie, Donald M. *The Theology of the Sacraments and Other Papers*. New York: Scribner, 1957.

Bates, J. Barrington. "A Riotous Mixture of Phrases: Ian Ramsey's Assertion of the Impropriety of Religious Language, the Need for This in Liturgical Texts, and How One Contemporary Rite Fails to Be Odd Enough." *Sewanee Theological Review* 45 (2002) 435–68.

Bausch, William J. *A New Look at the Sacraments*. Mystic, CT: Twenty-Third Publications, 1998.

Beguerie, Philippe, and Claude Duchesneau. *How to Understand the Sacraments*. New York: Crossroad, 1994.

Benson, Herbert. *Timeless Healing: The Power and Biology of Belief*. New York: Scribner, 1996.

Birmingham, Mary. *Word & Worship Workbook for Year B: For Ministry in Initiation, Preaching, Religious Education, and Formation*. New York: Paulist, 2000.

Bishops' Committee on the Liturgy. *Environment and Art in Catholic Worship*. Washington, DC: National Conference of Catholic Bishops, 1978.

Bliese, Richard H., and Craig Gelder. *The Evangelizing Church: A Lutheran Contribution*. Minneapolis: Augsburg Fortress, 2005.

Bokenkotter, Thomas S. *Dynamic Catholicism: A Historical Catechism*. New York: Image Books, 1992.

Bourke, Vernon J., editor. *The Essential Augustine*. Mentor-Omega Book. New York: New American Library, 1964.

Bouyer, Louis. *Rite and Man: Natural Sacredness and Christian Liturgy*. Notre Dame, IN: University of Notre Dame Press, 1963.

Brill, Earl H. *The Christian Moral Vision*. The Church's Teaching Series 6. New York: Seabury, 1979.

Bronowski, Jacob. *The Ascent of Man*. Boston: Little, Brown, 1973.

Brown, David, and Ann Loades. *Christ: The Sacramental Word*. London: SPCK, 1996.

Callahan, Annice C. "Karl Rahner's Theology of Symbol: Basis for His Theology of the Church and the Sacraments." *Irish Theological Quarterly* 49 (1982) 195–205.

Catholic Bishops' Conferences of England & Wales, Ireland and Scotland. "One Bread, One Body: A Teaching Document on the Eucharist in the Life of the Church, and the Establishment of General Norms on Sacramental Sharing." Dublin: Veritas, 1998. Online: http://www.iec2012.ie/downloads/One_Bread_One_Body.pdf/.

Catholic Church, and United States Catholic Conference. *Catechism of the Catholic Church*. Liguori, MO: Liguori, 1994.

Catholic Church and the National Conference of Catholic Bishops. *Pastoral Care of the Sick: Rites of Anointing and Viaticum*. Rev. ed. New York: Catholic Book Publishing, 1983.

Chryssavgis, John. *The Body of Christ: A Place of Welcome for People with Disabilities*. Minneapolis: Light & Life, 2002.

Church of England. *Alternative Service Book: The Alternative Service Book 1980: Services Authorized for Use in the Church of England in Conjunction with the Book of Common Prayer: Together with the Liturgical Psalter*. Colchester, UK: Clowes, 1980.

Church of England, Archbishops' Commission on Divine Healing. *The Church's Ministry of Healing: Report of the Archbishops' Commission*. Westminster, UK: Church Information Office, 1958.

Church of England, Archbishops' Council. "Initiation Services: Commentary by the Liturgical Commission." Liturgical Commission and the General Synod's Revision Committee on the Initiation Services. Online: http://www.cofe.anglican.org/commonworship/resources/rtf_files/ini_cmnt.rtf/.

Church of England, Doctrine Commission of the General Synod. *The Mystery of Salvation: The Story of God's Gift*. London: Church House Publishing, 1995.

Church of England. House of Bishops. *A Time to Heal: A Report for the House of Bishops on the Healing Ministry*. London: Church House Publishing, 2000.

———. *On the Way: Towards an Integrated Approach to Christian Initiation*. London: Church House Publishing, 1995.

Clarke, W. K. Lowther, and Charles Harris. *Liturgy and Worship: A Companion to the Prayer Books of the Anglican Communion*. London: SPCK, 1932.

Cohen, Cynthia B. et al., editors. *Faithful Living, Faithful Dying: Anglican Reflections on End of Life Care*. Episcopal Church, End of Life Task Force of the Standing Commission on National Concerns. Harrisburg, PA: Morehouse, 2000.

Cooke, Bernard. *Sacraments & Sacramentality*. Mystic, CT: Twenty-Third Publications, 1983.

Cross, F. L., and Elizabeth A. Livingstone, editors. *The Oxford Dictionary of the Christian Church*. 2nd ed. London: Oxford University Press, 1974.

Davies, Michael. *Pope Paul's New Mass*. Dickinson, TX: Angelus, 1980.

Deck, E. M. *The Baltimore Catechism, No. 1, with Explanation*. 3rd ed. Buffalo: Rauch & Stoeckl, 1930.

Denzinger, Heinrich, and A. Schoenmettzer, editors. *Enchiridion symbolorum Definitionum et Declarationum de Rebus Fidei et Morum.* 36th ed. Freiburg: Herder, 1976.

Donovan, Leo J. *A World of Grace: An Introduction to the Themes and Foundations of Karl Rahner's Theology.* New York: Seabury, 1980.

Dossey, Larry. *Healing Words: The Power of Prayer and the Practice of Medicine.* San Francisco: HarperSanFrancisco, 1993.

———. *Prayer Is Good Medicine: How to Reap the Healing Benefits of Prayer.* San Francisco: HarperSanFrancisco, 1996.

———. *Reinventing Medicine: Beyond Mind-Body to a New Era of Healing.* San Francisco: HarperSanFrancisco, 1999.

Drane, John. *Introducing the New Testament.* San Francisco: Harper & Row, 1986.

Drilling, Peter. "Anointing the Sick." *The Priest* 54/11 (November 1998) 10–21.

Driver, Lisa D. Maugans. *Christ at the Center: The Early Christian Era.* Louisville: Westminster John Knox, 2009.

Dudley, Martin, and Geoffrey Rowell, editors. *The Oil of Gladness: Anointing in the Christian Tradition.* London: SPCK, 1993.

Duffy, Regis. *A Roman Catholic Theology of Pastoral Care.* Theology and Pastoral Care. Philadelphia: Fortress, 1983.

Durant, Will. *The Story of Civilization.* Vol. 4, *The Age of Faith.* New York: Simon & Schuster, 1950.

Duggan, Robert D. *Parish Liturgy: A Handbook for Renewal.* Kansas City, MO: Sheed & Ward, 1996.

Eliade, Mircea. *The Sacred and the Profane: The Nature of Religion.* Translated by Willard R. Trask. New York: Harcourt, Brace & World, 1959.

Ellis, Larry D. "When, Why and How Do We Change the Words of Choral Music, Hymns and Liturgy to Use Inclusive and Expansive Language?" *Worship and Church Music.* Online: http://www.worshipandchurchmusic.com/inclusive_expansive_language. htm/.

Empereur, James L. *Prophetic Anointing: God's Call to the Sick, the Elderly, and the Dying.* Message of the Sacraments 7. Wilmington, DE: Glazier, 1982.

Episcopal Church. *The Book of Common Prayer and Administration of the Sacraments and Other Rites and Ceremonies of the Church: Together with the Psalter or Psalms of David According to the use of The Episcopal Church.* New York: Church Hymnal Corp., 1979.

Episcopal Church. General Board of Examining Chaplains. Background Material from General Ordination Exam 2006: "Set. 2. Liturgy and Church Music."

Episcopal Church, Joint Commission on the Ministry of Healing. *Report of the Joint Commission on the Ministry of Healing: to the General Convention of the Episcopal Church, St. Louis, Mo., 1964, with resolutions adopted.* San Diego: [Distributed by] SHARING, 1964.

Episcopal Church. Standing Commission on Liturgy and Music. *Enriching Our Worship 2: Ministry with the Sick or Dying: Burial of a Child: Supplemental Liturgical Materials.* New York: Church Publishing, 2000.

Episcopal Church. Standing Liturgical Commission. *The Book of Occasional Services: Conforming to General Convention 1991.* New York: Church Hymnal Corp., 1991.

———. Standing Liturgical Commission. *The Order for the Ministration of the Sick.* Prayer Book Studies 3. New York: Church Pension Fund, 1951.

――――. *Pastoral Offices.* Prayer Book Studies 24. New York: Church Hymnal Corporation, 1970.

Episcopal Diocese of Newark Total Ministry Task Force, Mary Barrett, and Hattie Stone, Co-Chairs. "Report of the Task Force on Total Ministry to the 126th Convention of the Episcopal Diocese of Newark. Report of the Task Force on Total Ministry to the 126th Convention of theEpiscopal Diocese of Newark, January 28 & 29, 2000. Online: http://www.dioceseofnewark.org/totalmin.html/.

Episcopal Diocese of Olympia, Diocesan Executive Council. "Diocesan Policy on Alcoholism and Substance Abuse Adopted by Diocesan Council, May 25, 1989." Online: http://www.ctepiscopal.org/images/customer-files//PolicyAlcoholDrugAbuse.pdf.

Faulconer, James F., editor. *Transcendence in Philosophy and Religion.* Indiana Series in the Philosophy of Religion. Bloomington: Indiana University Press, 2003.

Fink, Peter E. *The New Dictionary of Sacramental Worship.* Collegeville, MN: Liturgical, 1990.

――――. *Praying the Sacraments.* Washington DC: Pastoral Press, 1991.

Fish, Stanley. *Self-Consuming Artifacts: The Experience of SEventeenth-Century Literature.* Berkeley: University of California Press, 1972.

Foley, Edward. *From Age to Age: How Christians Have Celebrated the Eucharist.* Chicago: Liturgy Training Press, 1991.

Freedman, David Noel, editor. *The Anchor Bible Dictionary.* 6 vols. New York: Doubleday, 1992.

Hardebeck, George. *The Eucharist with Notes: Rite II.* Cincinnati: Forward Movement Publications, 1992.

Gamber, Klaus. *The Reform of the Roman Liturgy: Its Problems and Background.* San Juan Capistrano, CA: Una Voce Press, 1993.

Gelpi, Donald L. *Committed Worship: A Sacramental Theology for Converting Christians.* 2 vols. Collegeville, MN: Liturgical, 1993.

Gleason, Robert W. *Grace.* New York: Sheed & Ward, 1962.

Glenn, Genevieve, editor. *Recovering the Riches of Anointing: A Study of the Sacrament of the Sick.* Collegeville, MN: Liturgical, 2002.

Gould, David H. "Eucharistic Practice and the Risk of Infection." *Anglican Church of Canada.* The General Synod of the Anglican Church of Canada. Online: http://www.anglican.ca/faith/ministry/euc-practice-infection/.

Griffiss, James E., editor. *Anglican Theology and Pastoral Care.* Anglican Study Series. Wilton, CT: Morehouse-Barlow, 1985.

――――. *The Anglican Vision.* New Church's Teaching Series 1. Cambridge, MA: Cowley, 1997.

――――. *Naming the Mystery: How Our Words Shape Prayer and Belief.* Cambridge, MA: Cowley, 1990.

Grimes, Ronald. *Deeply into the Bone: Re-inventing Rites of Passage.* Life Passages. Berkeley: University of California Press, 2000.

Griswold, Frank T. "From Canterbury: Glimpses of the Eternal Design." *Episcopal Life* 9/8 (Sept. 1988) sec. Presiding Bishop's Column: 32. *Episcopal Life Online.* Online: http://www.episcopalchurch.org/presiding-bishop/postings/angspir.html. (site discontinued).

――――. "Praying as We Believe—and Living as We Pray." *Episcopal Life* 11/4 (Apr. 2000) sec. Presiding Bishop's Column: 28. *Episcopal Life Online.* Online: http://www.

episcopalchurch.org/presiding-bishop/downloads/el-4000_EpisLifePraying.   (site discontinued).

Gusmer, Charles. *And You Visited Me: Sacramental Ministry to the Sick and Dying.* Studies in the Reformed Rites of the Catholic Church 6. New York: Pueblo, 1989.

————. *The Ministry of Healing in the Church of England: An Ecumenical-Liturgical Study.* London: Alcuin Club, 1974.

Guzie, Tad. *The Book of Sacramental Basics.* New York: Paulist, 1981.

————. *Jesus and the Eucharist* New York: Paulist, 1974.

Haigh, Christopher, editor. *The Cambridge Historical Encyclopedia of Great Britain and Ireland.* Cambridge: Cambridge University Press, 1985.

Harper, Howard V. *The Episcopalian's Dictionary: Church Beliefs, Terms, Customs, and Traditions Explained in Layman's Language.* New York: Seabury, 1974.

Hatchett, Marion. *Commentary on the American Prayer Book.* San Francisco: HarperSan-Francisco, 1995.

————. *A Manual of Ceremonial for the New Prayer Book.* Sewanee, TN: St. Luke's Journal of Theology, 1977.

————. *Sanctifying Life, Time, and Space: An Introduction to Liturgical Study.* New York: Seabury, 1976.

Hefling, Charles. "What Do We Bless, and Why?" *Anglican Theological Review* 85 (Winter 2003) 87–96. Online: http://www.findarticles.com/p/articles/mi_qa3818/is_200301/ai_n9231334. (site discontinued)

Hefling, Charles C., and Cynthia L. Shattuck. *The Oxford Guide to the Book of Common Prayer: A Worldwide Survey.* New York: Oxford University Press, 2006.

Hellwig, Monika. "New Understanding of the Sacraments." *Commonweal* 150 (1978) 375–80.

Henri de Labac: An Online Archive. Unsigned review of *Surnaturel: A Controversy at the Heart of the Twentieth-Century Thomistic Thought* (Faith and Reason: Studies in Catholic Theology and Philosophy), by Henri de Labac. Online: http://henridelubaconline.blogspot.com/2009/12/books-about-henri-de-lubac.html/.

Holmes, David L. *A Brief History of the Episcopal Church.* Valley Forge, PA: Trinity, 1993.

Holmgren, Stephen. *Ethics after Easter.* The Church's New Teaching Series 9. Cambridge, MA: Cowley, 2000.

Horvath, Tibor. *Thinking about Faith: Speculative Theology.* Vol. 1, *Love.* Montréal: McGill-Queen's University Press, 2006.

Hughes, Kathleen. *Saying Amen: A Mystagogy of the Sacrament.* Chicago: Liturgy Training Publications, 1999.

Hughes, Robert D., III. "Retrieving and Reconstructing 'Justification by Grace through Faith": Some Disturbing Questions ." *Sewanee Theological Review* , January 1, 2001. Online: http://www.Sewanee.edu/theology/Facultyfolder/hughes/justification.html. (site discontinued)

————. "Sacraments and Ordination." Course material for Senior Ecclesiology, School of Theology, University of the South, Sewanee, Tennessee, Fall 2001. Online: http://www.Sewanee.edu/theology/Facultyfolder/hughes/ecclhandout2.html. (site discontinued).

Irwin, Kevin W. "Recent Sacramental Theology: A Review Discussion." *The Thomist* (October 1983) 593–608. Online: http://www.thomist.org/journal/1983/Oct/1983%20Oct%20A%20Irwin%20web.htm.

Jones, David. *Epoch and Artist.* London: Faber & Faber, 1959.

Jones, W. T. *A History of Western Philosophy.* Vol. 2, *The Medieval Mind.* 2nd ed. New York: Harcourt Brace Jovanovich, 1969.

Kabue, Samuel. "The Place of People with Disabilities in the Mission and Calling of the Church." *Ministerial Formation* (Jan 2001) 10–15. Online: www.wcc-coe.org/wcc/what/education/mf92.pdf/.

Kavanagh, Aidan. *Elements of Rite: A Handbook of Liturgical Style.* New York: Pueblo, 1982.

Kelsey, Morton. *Psychology, Medicine & Christian Healing: A Revised and Expanded Edition of Healing and Christianity.* New York: Harper & Row, 1988.

Kew, Richard, and Roger White. *Toward 2015: A Church Odyssey.* Cambridge, MA: Cowley, 1997.

Lambourne, R. A. *Community, Church and Healing: A Study of Some of the Corporate Aspects of the Church's Ministry to the Sick.* London: Darton, Longman & Todd, 1963.

Langer, Susanne K. *Philosophy in a New Key: A Study in the Symbolism of Reason, Rite, and Art.* 3rd ed. Cambridge: Harvard University Press, 1957.

Larson-Miller, Lizette. *The Sacrament of Anointing of the Sick.* Lex Orandi Series. Collegeville, MN: Liturgical, 2005.

Lasch, Christopher. *The Culture of Narcissism: American Life in an Age of Diminishing Expectations.* New York: Norton, 1979.

Lebon, Jean. *How to Understand the Liturgy.* New York: Crossroad, 1988.

Lee, Bernard J., general editor, and Peter E. Fink, editor. *Alternative Futures for Worship.* Vol. 4, *Reconciliation.* Collegeville, MN: Liturgical, 1987.

———. *Alternative Futures for Worship.* Vol. 7, *Anointing of the Sick.* Collegeville, MN: Liturgical, 1987.

Lee, Jeffrey D. *Opening the Prayer Book.* The New Church's Teaching Series 7. Cambridge, MA: Cowley, 1999.

Leijssen, Lambert. *With the Silent Glimmer of God's Spirit: A Postmodern Look at the Sacraments.* New York: Paulist, 2006.

Leuenberger, Samuel. *Archbishop Cranmer's Immortal Bequest. The Book of Common Prayer of the Church of England: An Evangelistic Liturgy.* Grand Rapids: Eerdmans, 1990.

Lohse, Bernhard. *Martin Luther: An Introduction to His Life and Work.* Translated by Robert C. Schultz. Philadelphia: Fortress, 1986.

Lutheran Hymnal Project. Lutheran Church Missouri Synod Commission On Worship, "Language Guidelines and Principles for Translation." September 1999. Online: http://www.lutheransonline.com/lo/378/FSLO-1332170378-111378.pdf/.

Mackenzie, Ross, general editor. *Education for Ministry, Year One.* Sewanee, TN: University of the South, 1990.

———, general editor. *Education for Ministry, Year Three.* Sewanee, TN: University of the South, 1991.

Macquarrie, John. *A Guide to the Sacraments.* New York: Continuum, 1997.

Maddocks, Morris. *The Christian Healing Ministry.* London, SPCK, 1981.

———. *Twenty Questions about Healing.* London, SPCK, 1988.

Madsen, Catherine. "The Common Word: Recovering Liturgical Speech." *Cross Currents* 52 (2002) 234–45.

Malania, Leo, compiler. *Ministry to the Sick: According to the Use of the Episcopal Church as Set Forth in the Book of Common Prayer.* New York: Church Hymnal Corp., 1977.

Marshall, Paul V., and Lesley A. Northrup, editors. *Leaps and Boundaries: The Prayer Book in the 21st Century.* Harrisburg, PA: Morehouse, 1997.

Martimort, A. G. et al. *The Church at Prayer: An Introduction to the Liturgy.* Translated by Matthew J. O'Connell. 4 vols. Collegeville, MN: Liturgical, 1987.

Martos, Joseph. *Doors to the Sacred: A Historical Introduction to Sacraments in the Catholic Church.* Liguori, MO: Liguori/Triumph, 2001.

McBrien, Richard P. *Catholicism.* Study edition. Oak Grove, MN: Winston, 1981.

McGrath, Alister. *Historical Theology: An Introduction to the History of Christian Thought.* Oxford: Blackwell, 1998.

———. *Christian Theology: An Introduction.* 3rd ed. Chichester: Wiley-Blackwell, 2011.

———. *The Christian Theology Reader.* Oxford: Blackwell, 1995.

———. *Studies in Doctrine.* Grand Rapids: Zondervan, 1997.

McManners, John, editor. *The Oxford Illustrated History of Christianity.* Oxford: Oxford University Press, 1990.

Merriman, Michael W., editor. *The Baptismal Mystery and the Catechumenate.* New York: Church Hymnal Corp., 1990.

Meyers, Ruth A., editor. *How Shall We Pray? Expanding Our Language about God.* Liturgical Studies 2. New York: Church Hymnal Corp., 1994.

Mitchell, Leonel L. *Liturgical Change, How Much Do We Need?* With Study Guide. NY: Seabury, 1975.

———. *Pastoral and Occasional Liturgies: A Ceremonial Guide.* Cambridge, MA: Cowley, 1998.

———. *Praying Shapes Believing: A Theological Commentary on The Book of Common Prayer.* Harrisburg, PA: Morehouse, 1985.

Mitchell, Nathan. "The Spirituality of Christian Worship." *Spirituality Today* 34/1 (1982) 5–17.

Moyers, Bill D. et al. *Healing and the Mind.* New York: Doubleday, 1993.

Murray, Michael H. *The Thought of Teilhard de Chardin: An Introduction.* New York: Seabury, 1966.

Mursell, Gordon, general editor. *The Story of Christian Spirituality: Two Thousand Years, from East to West.* Minneapolis: Fortress, 2001.

Njoroge, Nyambura J. "Not an Option: Ministry with and for People with Disabilities." *Ministerial Formation* 92 (2001) 7–9. Online: www.wcc-coe.org/wcc/what/education/mf92.pdf/.

Norris, Richard A. *Understanding the Faith of the Church.* The Church's Teaching Series 4. New York: Seabury, 1979.

The Order of St. Luke the Physician. Official website. Online: http://www.orderofstluke.org/.

Osborne, Kenan B. *Sacramental Theology: A General Introduction.* New York: Paulist, 1988.

Palmer, Paul F., editor. *Sacraments and Forgiveness: Sources of Christian Theology II.* Westminster, MD: Newman, 1959.

Paul VI, Pope. *Constitution on the Sacred Liturgy/Sacrosanctum Concilium,* 4 December 1963. Online: http://www.vatican.va/archive/hist_councils/ii_vatican_council/documents/vat-ii_const_19631204_sacrosanctum-concilium_en.html/.

———. *Lumen Gentium,* 21 November 1964. Online: http://www.vatican.va/archive/hist_councils/ii_vatican_council/documents/vat-ii_const_19641121_lumen-gentium_en.html/.

Pius X, Pope. *Vehementer Nos* (11/02/1906). Online: http://www.vatican.va/holy_father/pius_x/encyclicals/documents/hf_p-x_enc_11021906_vehementer-nos_en.html/.

Perham, Michael. *Liturgy, Pastoral and Parochial*. London: SPCK, 1984.

———. *Lively Sacrifice: The Eucharist in the Church of England Today*. London, SPCK, 1992.

Polkinghorne, John. *The Faith of a Physicist: Reflections of a Bottom-Up Thinker*. Minneapolis: Fortress, 1996.

———. *Science and Providence: God's Interaction with the World*. Boston: Shambhala, 1989.

Price, Charles P., and Louis Weil. *Liturgy for Living*. Rev. ed. Harrisburg, PA: Morehouse, 2000.

Prichard, Robert W. "Lecture 1B "Sickness, Healing, and Forgiveness." Virginia Theological seminary. Course lecture for LTG 6, Introduction to Anglican Worship. Spring 2005. Online: http://old.vts.edu/classes/lma5/LTG6_05/Case_1_hands/Lecture1b_Sickness.htm/. (site discontinued).

Radner, Ephraim, and George R. Sumner. *The Rule of Faith: Scripture, Canon, and Creed in a Critical Age*. Harrisburg, PA: Morehouse, 1998.

Rahner, Karl. *Foundations of Christian Faith: An Introduction to the Idea of Christianity*. New York: Seabury, 1978

———. *Theological Investigations*. Vol. 2, *Man in the Church*. Translated by Karl Kruger. Baltimore: Helicon, 1963.

Reader's Digest Editorial Staff. *After Jesus: the Triumph of Christianity*. Pleasantville, NY: Reader's Digest Association, 1992.

Reeves, Donald. *For God's Sake*. London: Collins, 1988.

Richard, Lucien et al. *Vatican II, The Unfinished Agenda: A Look to the Future*. New York: Paulist, 1987.

Richards, John. *But Deliver Us from Evil: An Introduction to the Demonic Dimension in Pastoral Care*. New York: Seabury, 1974.

Richstatter, Thomas. "General and Introductory Materials: Part 3 Theological Issues Chapter d31 Sacrament." Online: http://www.tomrichstatter.org/dDocuments/d31sacra.htm#Michael%20Himes/.

Roguet, A. M. *Christ Acts through the Sacraments*. Collegeville, MN: Liturgical, 1961.

Rowthorn, Anne. *The Liberation of the Laity: In Search of an Accountable Church*. Harrisburg: Morehouse, 1986.

Ryan, Thomas G. *The Sacristy Manual*. 2nd ed. Chicago, IL: Liturgy Training Publications, 2011.

Schnitker, Thaddaeus A. *The Church's Worship: The 1979 American Book of Common Prayer in a Historical Perspective*. European University Studies. Series 23, Theology. Frankfurt: Lang, 1989.

Seasoltz, R. Kevin. "The Language of Liturgical Celebrations." *Journal of the Liturgical Conference* 4/4 (Spring 1985) 27–34.

Sheed, Frank J. *Theology for Beginners*. London: Continuum, 1958.

Sedgwick, Timothy. *Sacramental Ethics: Paschal Identity and the Christian Life*. Philadelphia: Fortress, 1987.

Shanz, John P. *Introduction to the Sacraments*. New York: Pueblo, 1983.

———. *The Sacraments of Life and Worship*.Contemporary College Theology Series. Ecclesial Theology Section. Milwaukee: Bruce, 1966.

Skelley, Michael. *The Liturgy of the World: Karl Rahner's Theology of Worship.* Collegeville, MN: Liturgical, 1991.

Smith, David H. *Health and Medicine in the Anglican Tradition: Conscience, Community, and Compromise.* Health/Medicine in the Faith Traditions. New York: Crossroad, 1986.

Smith, Harmon L. *Where Two or Three Are Gathered: Liturgy and the Moral Life.* Cleveland: Pilgrim, 1995.

Smolarski, Dennis C. *Sacred Mysteries: Sacramental Principles and Liturgical Practice.* New York: Paulist, 1994.

The Society of Archbishop Justus. The Book of Common Prayer Online. "The 1549 Book of Common Prayer: Visitation of the Sick." Online: http://justus.anglican.org/resources/bcp/1549/Visitation_Sick_1549.htm/.

Stafford, William. "A Way of Writing." University of Arkansas at Little Rock. Online: http://ualr.edu/rmburns/RB/staffort.html/.

Staudt, Kathleen Henderson. "The Text as Material and Sign: Poetry and Incarnation in William Blake, Arthur Rimbaud, and David Jones." *Modern Language Studies* 14/3 (Summer 1984) 13–30.

Stoutzenberger, Joseph. *Celebrating Sacraments.* Winona, MN: St. Mary's, 1984.

Stuhlman, Byron David. *Occasions of Grace: An Historical and Theological study of the Pastoral Offices and Episcopal Services in the Book of Common Prayer.* New York: Church Hymnal Corp., 1995.

———. *Prayer Book Rubrics Expanded.* New York: Church Hymnal Corp., 1987.

Sykes, Stephen and John E. Booty, editors. *The Study of Anglicanism.* London: SPCK, 1988.

Talley, Thomas. "Healing: Sacrament or Charism?" *Worship* 46 (1972) 518–527.

Tavard, George. Course lecture for TRT 3566F: "Spirituality and Symbolism." Regis College, Toronto, March 15, 1999.

Taylor, Barbara Brown. *The Preaching Life.* Cambridge, MA: Cowley, 1993.

Temple, William. *Nature, Man and God: Being the Gifford Lectures Delivered in the University of Glasgow in the Academical Years 1932–1933 and 1933–1934.* London: Macmillan, 1949.

Thomas Aquinas, Saint. *Summa Theologica.* Translated by the Fathers of the English Dominican Province. 1948. 5 vols. Westminster, MD: Christian Classics, 1981.

Thomas, Keith. *Religion and the Decline of Magic.* New York: Scribner, 1971.

Thomas, Owen C. *Introduction to Theology.* Rev. ed. Harrisburg, PA: Morehouse, 1983.

Trabold, Robert. "Popular Piety and Liturgical Reform." *Journal of the Liturgical Conference* 4/4 (Spring 1985) 71–76.

United States Conference of Catholic Bishops. *Built of Living Stones: Art, Architecture, and Worship.* Publication United States Catholic Conferece. Washington, DC: USCCB Publications, 2000.

Vaillancourt, Raymond. *Toward a Renewal of Sacramental Theology.* Translated by Matthew J. Connell. Collegeville, MN: Liturgical, 1979.

Vorgrimler, Herbert. *Sacramental Theology.* Translated by Linda M. Maloney. Collegeville, MN: Liturgical, 1992.

Wagner, Clare. "Current Trends: Can We Be a Sacramental Church?" *Spirituality Today* (Sept 1985) 160–69. Online: http://www.spiritualitytoday.org/spir2day/853727wagner.html/.

Wainwright, Geoffrey. "Renewing Worship: The Recovery of Classical Patterns." *Theology Today* 48 (1991) 45–56. *Theology Today*. Online: http://theologytoday.ptsem.edu/apr1991/v48–1-symposium6.htm/.

Wallace, James. *Preaching to the Hungers of the Heart: The Homily on the Feasts and within the Rites.* Collegeville, MN: Liturgical, 2002.

Weil, Louis. *Sacraments and Liturgy: The Outward Signs; A Study in Liturgical Mentality.* Faith and the Future. Oxford: Blackwell, 1983.

———. *A Theology of Worship.* New Church's Teaching Series 12. Cambridge, MA: Cowley, 2002.

Wilson, Michael. *The Church Is Healing.* London: SCM, 1966.

———. editor. *Explorations in Health and Salvation: A Selection of Papers by Bob Lambourne.* Birmingham, England: University of Birmingham. Institute for the Study of Worship and Religious Architecture, 1983.

Worgul, George S., Jr. *From Magic to Metaphor: A Validation of the Christian Sacraments.* New York: Paulist, 1980.

33942762R00155

Made in the USA
San Bernardino, CA
14 May 2016